KEY MARCO'S

BURIED

TREASURE

Ripley P. Bullen Monographs in Anthropology and History Number 8

The Florida Museum of Natural History

"Frank Hamilton Cushing in Bow Tie," by Thomas Eakins. This photograph was probably taken just prior to the expedition, but its exact date is uncertain. Reproduced with permission of the Hirshhorn Museum and Sculpture Garden, Smithsonian Institution, gift of Joseph H. Hirshhorn, 1966 (HMSG 83.89).

KEY MARCO'S

BURIED

TREASURE

Archaeology and

Adventure in

the Nineteenth Century

MARION SPJUT GILLILAND

University of Florida Press / The Florida Museum of Natural History / Gainesville

Ripley P. Bullen Monographs in Anthropology and History   *Jerald T. Milanich, general editor*

Number 1. *Tacachale: Essays on the Indians of Florida and Southeastern Georgia during the Historic Period*, edited by Jerald T. Milanich and Samuel Proctor (1978).

Number 2. *Aboriginal Subsistence Technology on the Southeastern Coastal Plain during the Late Prehistoric Period*, by Lewis H. Larson (1980).

Number 3. *Cemochechobee: Archaeology of a Mississippian Ceremonial Center on the Chattahoochee River*, by Frank T. Schnell, Vernon J. Knight, Jr., and Gail S. Schnell (1981).

Number 4. *Fort Center: An Archaeological Site in the Lake Okeechobee Basin*, by William H. Sears, with contributions by Elsie O'R. Sears and Karl T. Steinen (1982).

Number 5. *Perspectives on Gulf Coast Prehistory*, edited by Dave D. Davis (1984).

Number 6. *Archaeology of Aboriginal Culture Change in the Interior Southeast: Depopulation during the Early Historic Period*, by Marvin T. Smith (1987).

Number 7. *Apalachee: The Land between the Rivers*, by John H. Hann (1988).

Number 8. *Key Marco's Buried Treasure: Archaeology and Adventure in the Nineteenth Century*, by Marion Spjut Gilliland (1988).

UNIVERSITY PRESSES OF FLORIDA is the central agency for scholarly publishing of the State of Florida's university system, producing books selected for publication by the faculty editorial committees of Florida's nine public universities: Florida A&M University (Tallahassee), Florida Atlantic University (Boca Raton), Florida International University (Miami), Florida State University (Tallahassee), University of Central Florida (Orlando), University of Florida (Gainesville), University of North Florida (Jacksonville), University of South Florida (Tampa), University of West Florida (Pensacola).

Orders for books published by all member presses should be addressed to University Presses of Florida, 15 NW 15th Street, Gainesville, FL 32603.

Library of Congress Cataloging-in-Publication Data

Gilliland, Marion Spjut, 1918–
Key Marco's buried treasure : archaeology and adventure in the nineteenth century / Marion Spjut Gilliland.
p.   cm. — (Ripley P. Bullen monographs in anthropology and history ; no. 8)
Bibliography: p.
Includes index.
ISBN 0-8130-0884-0 (alk. paper)
1. Marco Region (Fla.)—Antiquities.   2. Marco Island (Fla. : Island)—Antiquities.   3. Archaeology—Florida—Marco Island (Island)—History—19th century.   4. Excavations (Archaeology)—Florida–Marco Island (Island)   5. Cushing, Frank Hamilton, 1857–1900.   6. Florida—Antiquities.   I. Title.   II. Series.
F319.M39G55   1988
975.9'44—dc19   88–17165

CONTENTS

ILLUSTRATIONS

Frontispiece. "Frank Hamilton Cushing in Bow Tie" by Thomas Eakins, date unknown.

Map. South Florida, showing sites and locations visited by Cushing, xii

Illustrations follow page 52

Incidental drawings in the text are by Wells Sawyer.

FOREWORD

The Florida Museum Associates are pleased to join the Florida Museum of Natural History in the publication of Marion Spjut Gilliland's new book, *Key Marco's Buried Treasure: Archaeology and Adventure in the Nineteenth Century*. The author, an archaeologist and scholar who published an earlier book on Key Marco, is a past president of the associates (1973–1975) and one of the organization's charter members.

The Pepper-Hearst Expedition to Key Marco in 1895–1896 is one of the most famous archaeological endeavors in the United States, as well as one of the most infamous. Led by the controversial Frank Hamilton Cushing, the expedition's crew excavated a number of unique, finely crafted artifacts, all preserved in the coastal muck at the north end of Marco Island: painted wooden masks, carved figurines, fishing nets, hafted tools and many other objects fashioned by aboriginal peoples. The extraordinary collections made a stir in the professional community as well as in the popular press of the day. Many of those arti-facts are now housed at the Florida Museum of Natural History where they are a part of research and exhibit collections.

But the expedition was not without its detractors. Several individuals cried fraud and fake, casting a pall over Cushing's efforts that has lasted until Marion Gilliland's recent investigations. Using firsthand documents, letters, and diaries—many previously unknown—she has been able to peel back the layers and bring the expedition back to life.

South Florida in 1895 was only sparsely settled, and the southwest coast was largely unpopulated and unknown. The observations of Cushing and other members of the expedition paint a marvelous picture of the region at that time. Many other scholars followed Cushing there over the next decades, including botanist John Kunkel Small and anthropologist Aleš Hrdlička.

Today, led by William Marquardt, archaeologists from the Florida Museum of Natural History are once again organizing expeditions to Southwest Florida to resume study of the aboriginal societies that have inhabited the region. Many local residents, scientists, and students have joined to support and participate in this new Southwest Florida Project, and various museum programs are under way to make the public aware of the area's unique natural history.

The Florida Museum Associates are excited to be a part of these activities. It is especially gratifying that one of our members has made such an important contribution to these en-

deavors and that the associates can help in the publication of her book.

Roy Hunt
President
The Florida Museum Associates

Peter Bennett
Director
The Florida Museum of Natural History

ACKNOWLEDGMENTS

Much important information in this narrative has been pieced together from letters, family records, writings, and newspaper clippings whose time or place sometimes can no longer be identified. Much information comes also from Cushing's letters and other writings, never published, and from two diaries of individuals on the scene. The participants in this adventure are allowed to tell as much of the story as possible in their own words, in every case more graphic and revealing of the time and place in which they lived than any reconstruction could be. The diaries are quoted verbatim with spelling, grammar, and syntax (or lack thereof) as faithfully reproduced as some of the handwriting and condition of documents will allow.

I also carried out research at the National Anthropological Archives of the Smithsonian Institution and in the Southwest Museum in Pasadena, California. My appreciation is tendered the staff of Herman J. Viola at the National Anthropological Archives and Ruth M. Christiansen of the Southwest Museum for their considerable help.

To Helen Sawyer Farnsworth, daughter of Wells Sawyer, I am deeply indebted for the privilege of free access to and use of her father's papers in her possession and for her generous hospitality. I am indebted to the late Margaret Parrish Clarke, granddaughter of W.D. Collier, for allowing me to peruse, copy, and publish material from her family records, including her grandmother's diary. Without the materials and the cooperation from these sources this work would not have been possible.

I am indebted to Jerald Milanich of the Florida Museum of Natural History for his encouragement and helpful suggestions and to the Florida Museum Associates and the University of Florida's Office of Academic Affairs for their financial contributions to the publication of this book.

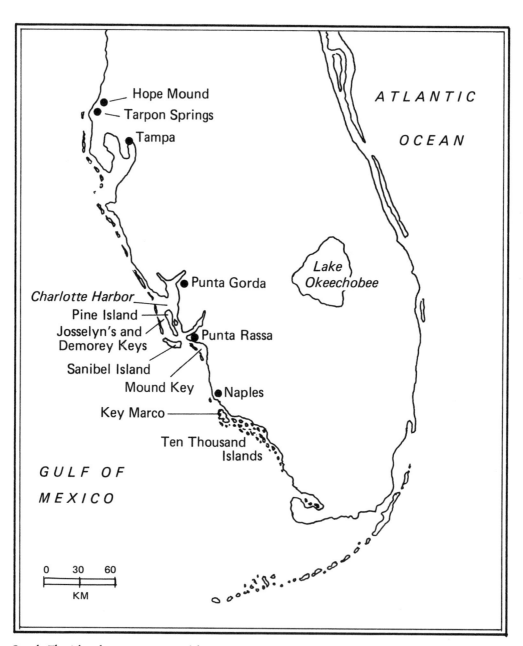

South Florida, showing sites and locations visited by Cushing.

1

OF

TIME

AND

PLACE

AS I WRITE this I look out across Payne's Prairie in north-central Florida where I can see traffic moving north and south across the prairie on the four lanes of Interstate 75 and, in the distance, the lighter traffic on the four lanes of U.S. 441. Had I sat in this same spot in 1895, less than one hundred years ago, I would have been looking at paddle-wheel steamers plying the waters of Alachua Lake carrying produce and passengers to the wagons waiting to transfer them to the railroad at Gainesville.

The rest of Florida too has changed drastically in those intervening years. This story is of that earlier day, when Florida was frontier and those who came to stay were pioneers. It is written for the history buff, for the lover of the lore of the past, for the tourist or new resident, for the lover of romance and adventure, and certainly for those with a particular interest in the mangrove coast.

It is not meant to be a complete history of Florida, political, social, or economic—not even of a limited area of the state. But since it is a tale of an earlier day, some brief comments are neces-sary to help place events in the context of the time, to help carry the reader back a century to that other Florida, now gone and hard to imagine—to nudge the reader gently into the shadows of the past, not to tell all there is to tell. It is the story of an archaeological expedition, but it is not an archaeological analysis or treatise. It is not a tale of modern techniques of today's ma-ture science but rather history, a story full of the romance of an earlier day.

Though archaeologists should also find this story interesting, it is not written for them. Be-cause it is written primarily for others, archaeolo-gists will find familiar material, but it will be new to nonanthropologists and essential to the back-ground and to the story itself.

Because it is a true story, all of the characters are real. They were all pioneers, some in the de-velopment of their profession, some in the devel-opment of their world. Fortunately for this story, many have left written records, some volumi-nous, some fragmentary, all contemporary with events, all fascinating.

This is the story of the Pepper-Hearst Expedition of 1895–96, named for Dr. William Pepper, president of the Archaeological Department of the Museum of the University of Pennsylvania, one of the sponsors of the expedition, and Mrs. Phebe Hearst, wife of publisher William Randolph Hearst, a financial sponsor. Led by thirty-eight-year-old Frank Hamilton Cushing, it was the first archaeological expedition to Marco Island— an important expedition, and not just in the small scheme of Marco Island. Marco is one of the most important archaeological sites in North America. The collections are unique because of a remarkable coincidence of fine craftsmanship and fortuitous preservation in the coastal muck. Never surpassed in beauty or quality, these materials include sophisticated three-dimensional wooden sculptures, painted face masks, carved bone and shell implements and ornaments, a variety of netting and cordage in a wide range of sizes whose quality is as high as today's, and a complete line of tools for their manufacture. Such is the stuff of an archaeologist's dream.

This book is not an archaeological treatise and does not contain specifics of techniques or analysis of artifacts recovered. For that information the reader is referred to an earlier publication, *The Material Culture of Key Marco, Florida* (Gilliland 1975), which contains a complete inventory of existing materials recovered from that site, 149 illustrations, complete analysis of the artifacts, and a detailed description of tools and technologies. It describes the fragmentary condition of some of the records and the inaccessibility of others at that time. While it includes some of the flavor of the times, it was written primarily as an archaeological reference text.

Since the earlier account was written, other manuscript materials have become available. They fill in some of the gaps in the information and substantiate some earlier conclusions based on available fragmentary materials. They also prove inaccurate some earlier conclusions and statements made over the years and widely accepted as true. These new materials have never before been available for research and are still held in the private collections. Many are contemporary and eyewitness accounts. In some instances I have included more than one version of the same incident to demonstrate that accounts, incidents, and artifacts are authentic, described and recounted when they took place, written by different individuals from different perspectives, for personal rather than public use. Each account lends emphasis and credence to the others, and some lend color as well. Many misconceptions, false conclusions, and controversies about Key Marco have resulted from incomplete information and fragmentary records. I hope to lay some of them to rest.

Dating of the artifacts excavated by Cushing from the muck has also been controversial. Two sets of radiocarbon dates from the site span nearly 2,000 years. And a small collection of pottery from the muck appears to be younger than another collection recovered by Cushing and other archaeologists from the shell middens that surrounded the muck. These lines of evidence are sorted out in the last chapter, and the conclusion is reached that the site and the extraordinary collection of artifacts both resulted from a considerable span of time, from A.D. 750 to 1513.

There was great controversy over one of the recovered painted shells, and some are still skeptical of its authenticity. No such skepticism was expressed, either while Cushing lived or after his death, by any member of the expedition crew or anyone present at the time this shell was found. Quite the contrary: We have statements, one of them notarized, attesting to its genuineness, as well as diaries and accounts documenting its discovery, evidence that today would be considered proof in a court of law. Reason too substantiates its authenticity.

Key Marco is an important site for a variety of reasons: archaeologically, because it was the first significant wetlands site in the Southeast; historically, because it documents one of the most sophisticated cultures of an early date on this continent; artistically, because of the sophisticated and sensitive art forms produced, never yet surpassed, some of which are still in excellent condition; and technologically, because the site produced a complete range of artifacts and the tools for their manufacture, thus enabling us to reconstruct the technologies used on wood, bone, shell, and fiber.

While the central story is essentially one of a single place and a limited time—the last half of the final decade of the nineteenth century—history and biography first take us to other times and places to bring the central characters together in this bit of history. Newly available records shed much light on the backgrounds and personalities of the main participants in the Pepper-Hearst expedition. The men involved had considerable and diverse talents though little in common in their backgrounds.

Three men and an island are central to this story. William David Collier owned the island; Frank Hamilton Cushing led an archaeological expedition to the island; and Wells Moses Sawyer was artist and photographer on that expedition. (Sawyer, the last survivor, died in 1960 at the age of ninety-seven. His long and unusual simultaneous careers as painter and financier will be documented in another volume.) The island, now often referred to as Marco, of course is still there though its transformation is as dramatic as that of Alachua Lake.

By coincidence, the Centennial Exposition held in Philadelphia in 1876 was an important event in the lives of Cushing, Sawyer, and Collier, though, as far as is known, each was unaware of the presence of the others. For Frank Hamilton Cushing the time spent at the exposition as curator of an exhibit from the Smithsonian broadened and deepened his interest in archaeology; for the thirteen-year-old Wells Moses Sawyer the trip to the exposition provided the inspiration for his original career; and for William David Collier the exposition must certainly have helped to intensify his already keen interest in nature. Nearly twenty years later they would come together in this bit of the history of Marco Island.

To Cushing, beset by ill health and problems of finances, jealousy, and controversy (and at times a victim of his own devices), goes the credit for the enthusiasm, persistence, and instinct that enabled him to carry on his research in what must have been at times most unpleasant circumstances. While to some extent he can be faulted for consistently interpreting everything he found in the light of his prior Zuñi Indian experiences in the southwestern United States, in 1895 there

was but a small body of pertinent reported research to fall back on, making his repeated references to the Zuñi more easily excused. Though some of his premises regarding Marco—most notably his theory of key building—have been proven to be in error, his work stands as a major contribution to American archaeology.

Sawyer was not only a consistently keen observer and a faithful reporter, but he was also fair and objective in his approach. His sensitive, perceptive accounts and analyses add stability and balance, and they also help to substantiate many of Cushing's statements that at first seem to be imaginative or farfetched.

Collier, uneducated man that he was, had the vision to understand the value of the almost unrecognizable artifacts of organic materials that he discovered. He was generous enough to allow undisturbed excavation on his property and the retention in the public domain of all recovered artifacts.

One other person must be recognized. Neither scientist nor previous friend of Cushing, just a laborer hired to help with the excavation, George Gause, foreman of the excavation crew at Marco, kept a diary that is extremely valuable. It is written in pencil on a small, lined, pocket-sized note pad, difficult to read and far from having literary value, but it, probably more than any other documentary evidence, lends weight to the authenticity of artifacts and truth to the story. It reflects his enthusiasm and sense of humor, probably kept to tell those at home the details of his unusual adventure. It is quoted in its entirety as the story unfolds.

Even after the turn of the century Florida was still very much a pioneer state, the major cities of today not even showing promise of size or importance. Cedar Key, Fernandina, and Key West were the major commercial ports. Throughout the second half of the nineteenth century Florida's population grew rapidly. From 1840 to 1860 it nearly tripled, from 54,000 to 140,000. By 1870 it had jumped to 188,000 and by 1880 to 270,000. The 1890 census showed 397,000 residents in the state. Many things attracted them.

Citrus had been introduced early in the state. Pedro Menéndez de Avilés in 1579 reported citrus growing abundantly around St. Augustine, and by the time the early Florida settlers arrived two centuries later citrus was scattered all over the state. On the west coast one of the earliest cultivated groves was planted in Pinellas County some time between 1809 and 1820. There were early groves along the St. Johns River, from Civil War days but they were badly damaged by the hard freeze of 1893–94. By the time of that freeze Florida's citrus production had reached its peak of more than five million boxes. The freeze almost destroyed the industry, and it would not reach such a level of production again for another fifteen years, after the industry had moved farther south.

As early as 1850 sugar was being produced and refined in Manatee County and shipped to New Orleans. Lumber and deer, bear, and panther hides were shipped out; wrecking, fishing, turtling, and sponging were growing industries. Cattle were being raised in the southwest Gulf coast area to be shipped to Cuba, Savannah, and Charleston.

Tourism began in the post–Civil War era, and by 1890 the southwest Gulf coast was famous for its tarpon fishing, even bringing surprising numbers of British military officers to the area. Many who could afford to make the trip were drawn to the mild climate in search of improved health, including such notables as General Robert E. Lee, who came in 1870, and Sidney Lanier, who came in 1876. The state was gaining a reputation as a sanitarium because of the many sufferers of tuberculosis who made their way south in search of improvement.

By 1885 cigar manufacturing had begun in Tampa. Phosphate had been discovered in the Peace River area, where mining began in 1888. In the post–Civil War era Key West became the biggest city in the state and a sizable naval base was built there.

Between 1830 and 1860 at least twenty corporations had been chartered by the territorial and state governments to build railroads. However, most railroads were short and did not connect to make an effective transportation network. Both Henry M. Flagler on the east coast and Henry B. Plant on the west coast had been building railroads and hotels to accommodate their rail pas-

sengers. By 1881, Plant finished connecting the lines from Savannah to Jacksonville; by 1884 he had secured the line from Sanford to Kissimmee as well as the undeveloped charter to extend the line to Tampa. In 1883 he began construction of a railroad to link Tampa with lines leading into Jacksonville. By 1891 railroad mileage in the state had increased from 500 to 2,560 miles. The first train did not reach Miami until 1896. Plant also contemplated a line from Ft. Myers to Miami, but it was never built.

By the 1880s the developers had come to Florida. By 1893 when the railroad reached Punta Gorda on the Peace River, it traversed much land bearing the stamp of Hamilton Disston of the Atlantic and Gulf Coast Canal and Okeechobee Land Company of Florida, which also owned the Clyde Steamship Line from New York to Jacksonville. Disston, an early developer, contributes to the story of Key Marco. At one time he owned more of Florida than any other man, an area larger than Rhode Island and Connecticut combined. A member of one of Philadelphia's prominent industrial families—tool makers—he had, during his youth, made frequent fishing trips to Florida and had recognized the potential of the state.

By 1895, Disston was a man under a tremendous financial burden. In 1851, Florida's General Assembly had created the Internal Improvement Board to manage swamp and overflowed lands in the state as well as the federal lands transferred to the state's domain when Florida attained statehood in 1845. A few years later this board recognized the need for a system of railroads and canals to connect various key areas of the state and recommended that state lands be used to assist private capital in achieving these ends. To implement this plan, the General Assembly created in 1855 the Internal Improvement Fund. The governor, state comptroller, treasurer, secretary of agriculture, and registrar of state lands were its trustees, charged with giving financial assistance to the projects to build railroads and canals that met their approval. These companies would receive 200-foot rights-of-way through the state lands and would be granted alternate sections six miles deep along both sides of the rights-of-way. Bonds were authorized, to become a lien on the railroad, for building trestles and bridges, and for the purchase of rails but only after construction of the grade and laying of crossties. These thirty-five-year bonds carrying 7 percent interest were endorsed by the state, to be paid by it through sale of public lands if the railroads failed to pay principal and interest.

Unfortunately they did fail. Before the railroads became profitable the Civil War began and the bonds became the obligation of the Internal Improvement Fund. In the depression of 1873 the lands reverted to the state when the railroads failed. These lands were sold at such low prices that the state was almost a million dollars short of the funds needed to pay off the principal and interest on the bonds. Bondholders became alarmed when lands were sold for such low prices and the commitments for reclamation tied to the sales were not fulfilled. Many of them had not been paid, so, through legal means, they forced the lands to be placed in receivership. Thereafter sales had to be approved by the bondholders. The state was all but bankrupt.

In a desperate effort, Governor Bloxham appealed to Hamilton Disston, offering to sell him four million acres of Florida lands for twenty-five cents an acre in order to realize the necessary million dollars to pay off the bonds. Though Disston too was under obligation to drain and reclaim acreage, he was also granted large tracts already above water and suitable for development. He proceeded both to develop and to reclaim his lands, draining and reclaiming large acreages. He dug several canals allowing settlement of Runnymeade, Ashton, and St. Cloud. He straightened and deepened the Kissimmee River and dug canals making steamboat travel possible from Kissimmee through Lake Okeechobee and out to the Gulf by way of the Caloosahatchee River.

At St. Cloud, Disston persuaded the U.S. government to establish an agricultural experiment station where he directed experiments in the production of rice, many vegetables, potatoes, and such fruits as peaches, grapes, and pineapples. He also raised cattle there. Near Orlando he planned a settlement for 250 families, selling them twenty to eighty acres for $1.25 to $5.00 an acre, requiring the purchasers to have $1,000 for investment in developing their lands. He planted large acreages of sugarcane and erected a sugar mill, bringing in an expert from Louisiana to supervise the operation. Because he had used credit instead of cash, he could not meet his heavy financial obligations, and in April 1896 he died by his own hand, crushed under the burden of his monumental financial failure.

That was Florida in 1895–96 when this story takes place. The characters in the story are real, so it seems most effective to let them tell it for themselves. Fortunately they have left us many records—accounts, diaries, and letters to loved ones and associates, words not meant for public record. Through them the men themselves take form, their graphic descriptions of scenes and events allowing us to live their story with them.

It might be useful to the nonanthropologist reader to make a brief statement about the state of the art of archaeology in 1895. Though humans have always been curious about their origins and past, the science of archaeology was relatively young in Cushing's day, and, in fact, many scientific fields were having a hard time.

Though Darwin's theory of evolution had been published in 1859 (two years after Cushing's birth), the storm over this revolutionary theory was not over in 1895; the Bible was to be believed literally, and nothing could be believed that was not confirmed by documentary evidence. Excavations were still in the nature of treasure hunts. Earth was tossed out by the shovelful and discarded without sifting. Only complete and recognized curios were kept, and most ended up in private collections from which they were often discarded as rubbish when the first owner died. Very few ended up in museums, and those that did were usually exhibited as individual items with no thought given to placing them in any kind of developmental or chronological sequence.

Sir Flinders Petrie (1853–1942), a contemporary of Cushing's, was a pioneer in the recognition of the value of small and often apparently insignificant objects, and he suffered from the ridicule of ignorant curators because of it. In fact, it was so bad that he referred to museums as "the charnel-houses of murdered evidence." Not until the twentieth century would museums employ experts to repair and preserve their collections of "curios."

Augustus Henry Pitt-Rivers (1827–1900), another Cushing contemporary, had done such excellent work that he was sometimes called the father of British archaeology and the prince of excavators. He had set high standards for excavation and publication well in advance of his contemporaries. He was the first to have three-dimensional recording on the site and one of the first to use stratification. He insisted on accurate plans, sections, and models and an adequate staff. He stressed the distribution of similar forms and the value of full publication.

In his early career Pitt-Rivers had concentrated on the evolution of firearms, which led him to consider primitive arts and crafts from a developmental point of view. He classified ethnographical and archaeological materials on an evolutionary basis, not a geographic one, showing their development from primitive forms to the specialized tools of more advanced cultures. Both he and Petrie stressed a sociological rather than an art-historical approach to archaeology.

Auguste Mariette, Gaston Maspero, and James Henry Breasted had all worked in Egypt, and a few years prior to 1895 Petrie had also begun work there. Heinrich Schliemann had dug Troy in 1871, identifying seven of the nine layered cities there, and Mycenae in 1876. Work had been done in Greece too, but all of these efforts were made to substantiate the written word of history or legend. Austin Henry Layard had published descriptions of his finds at Nimrud and Nineveh between 1849 and 1861, these too journeys into the known.

Arthur John Evans had paid his first visit to Knossos in 1894, one year prior to Cushing's first journey to Florida, but because the Cretan revolution broke out in 1896, before he had completed arrangements to excavate there, he would not begin his work until 1899. Harappa, Mohenjo Daro, Ur, even the tomb of Tutankhamen were far in the future.

All of this was of course before the dawn of sophisticated dating techniques. Alexander Cunningham and Pitt-Rivers had made some effort to establish sequences of artifacts, but it was 1948 when Willard F. Libby discovered the carbon 14 process to yield fairly precise dates that lay beyond history. Aleš Hrdlička, W. H. Holmes, C. B. Moore, and J. Walter Fewkes were all Cushing contemporaries whose work was not yet completed.

Since the cast of characters in this story is extensive, an identification list may prove useful to the reader. They are grouped in categories for easy reference.

Pepper-Hearst Expedition

Mrs. Phebe Hearst, wife of William Randolph Hearst, financial sponsor of expedition

Frank Hamilton Cushing, leader of expedition, employee of Bureau of Ethnology, Smithsonian Institution (later renamed Bureau of American Ethnology)

Wells Moses Sawyer, artist and photographer

Irving Sayford, field secretary

Carl F.W. Bergmann, preparer of artifacts, employed by the Bureau of American Ethnology

Emily Magill Cushing, wife of Frank Hamilton Cushing

George Gause, foreman of excavators, from Tarpon Springs

Antonio Gomez, captain of schooner *Silver Spray*

Thomas Brady, mate of *Silver Spray*

Alfred Hudson, sailor on *Silver Spray,* also excavator

Robert Clarke, sailor on *Silver Spray,* also excavator

Frank Barnes, sailor on *Silver Spray,* also excavator

George Hudson, black cook on *Silver Spray*

George Dorsett, black steward on *Silver Spray*

John Calhoun, excavator

Zuñi-Hemenway Expeditions

Frank Hamilton Cushing, leader of expeditions

Charles Garlick, topographical engineer, field manager

Frederick Webb Hodge, field·secretary, personal assistant to Cushing on Hemenway expedition, later originator of accusation of toad fraud

Emily Magill Cushing, wife of Cushing, with him at Zuñi after marriage

Margaret Magill Hodge, sister of Emily Magill Cushing, married Frederick Hodge sometime during this story (date unknown) with Cushings at Zuñi after their marriage, also on Hemenway expedition

Colonel James Stevenson, leader of first expedition to Zuñi

Mathilda Coxe Stevenson, wife of James Stevenson, Zuñi expedition, Cushing's nemesis

Governor, chief of Zuñi

J. Walter Fewkes, prominent anthropologist who completed Hemenway expedition after Cushing's forced retirement from it

Bureau of American Ethnology, U.S. National Museum (now National Museum of Natural History), Smithsonian Institution

Joseph Henry, secretary of Smithsonian Institution

Spencer Baird, assistant secretary of Smithsonian, encouraged Cushing during his early years

S. P. Langley, secretary, Smithsonian Institution

Professor W. J. McGee, Smithsonian anthropologist

William Henry Holmes, Smithsonian anthropologist

Major John Wesley Powell, Smithsonian anthropologist, immediate superior of Cushing

Charles Rau, Belgian scholar at Smithsonian Institution, Cushing's first boss there

James Pilling, chief clerk at the Smithsonian

University of Pennsylvania Museum

Stewart Culin, director of the museum

Henry Mercer, curator of the American section of the Archaeological Department

William Pepper, president of the Archaeological Department, Cushing's personal physician

Robert C. H. Brock, chairman of the executive committee of the Archaeological Department

Samuel T. Bodine, member of the Museum Board of Directors

Developers-Benefactors

Hamilton Disston, from prominent Philadelphia family, president of Atlantic and Gulf Coast Canal and Okeechobee Land Company of Florida, early large-scale developer

Joseph Disston, from same family, with same company, apparently in charge after death of Hamilton Disston

J. M. Kreamer, engineer for Disston's company

Anson P. K. Safford, developer in Tarpon Springs, former governor of Territory of Arizona, active member of Disston syndicate, owner of one of Tarpon Springs sites excavated by Cushing

Leander T. Safford, adopted son of Anson Safford

John K. Cheyney, one of owners of Tarpon Springs hotel

J. K. Leslie, one of owners of Tarpon Springs hotel

Other Friends and Benefactors

Dr. Matthews, from Ft. Wingate, helpful to Cushing during Zuñi days

Adolph Bandalier, personal friend of Cushing

E. H. Horsford, provided living and funds for Cushing while he was working in the East during his last illness

Mrs. Richard Levis, provided extra comforts for the Marco expedition, from Tarpon Springs

Professor Hartt, at Cornell, early encourager of Cushing

George Kennan, prominent early traveler, longtime close friend of Cushing

Mrs. Augustus Hemenway, hostess to Cushings, provided financing for Hemenway expedition

Participants in Controversy over Artifacts

George M. Coffin, assistant comptroller of U.S. Treasury

William Dinwiddie, BAE photographer and later Sunday editor for the New York Herald

Boise Penrose, senator from Pennsylvania

H. H. Bingham, congressman from Philadelphia

Robert Adams, Jr., congressman from Philadelphia, regent of Smithsonian, graduate of the University of Pennsylvania

Other Important Individuals

Captain Smith, captain and owner of sloop rented by Cushing for first reconnaissance

Kathleen Alton Bailey, fiancée of Wells Sawyer

2

BIG

MARCO

PASS

WITH A GENTLE splash into the clear, quiet waters of Big Marco Pass, the anchor of the *Silver Spray* sought firm hold on the bottom. Marco at last! Here in this world of water dotted with islands looking like great green buttons, the schooner riding at anchor would serve as living quarters for crew and excavators. With dry quarters cooled by the sea breezes they would be free of the ever-present mosquito, so much better than camping in tents ashore as they had done in Tarpon Springs.

It was a good anchorage. This protected passage behind Marco, running all the way down to Cape Romano between the Ten Thousand Islands and the mainland, created passage and anchorage safe from rough water and storms. Not yet mapped by the Coast Survey, these islands cover an area fifty or sixty miles long and in places as much as thirty miles wide. Mangrove keys are in some places so numerous that it is unsafe to enter them without a guide; they all look alike, and the tide currents running between them flow so swiftly that a person in a boat is soon hurried past

a few of them and then can find no way out of this labyrinth. In most of this area the water is shallow, except in the passes where the rising and falling tides cut deeper passages.

Lying at the head of the Ten Thousand Islands fifteen miles below Naples, Marco was the highest point on the southwest coast of Florida. It had a surprisingly diverse terrain: sand hills reaching an elevation of 67 feet crowded with native vegetation and crowned by tall trees; several hundred acres of sand prairie; a couple thousand acres of high pine forest; and another few thousand acres of mangrove swamp. There were cypress, red mangrove, and some white mangrove in the lower areas, with buttonwood, pine, and gumbo-limbo trees in the higher elevations, leaving the mud flats to the black mangroves.

Six miles of beautiful sand beach on the western side of the island were rich in colorful marine shells, and there were deep natural channels on both the north and south ends of the island. A large bird population including bald eagles, white pelicans, roseate spoonbills, flamingos, ibises, and egrets far outnumbered the human inhabitants of the island.

There were a few miles of road—not really road but mere weedy trails over the sand and shell hills. But there was little need for roads. No road connected the island to the mainland, there were few vehicles of any kind, and all commerce and travel in the area was by boat of one kind or another, as it had always been. The seaward edge of the mainland for some miles inland—low, wet, and covered with a dense tangle of mangrove forest—was almost impossible to travel. Sea travel was the only practical way to move about.

It was to be many years before travel to and about the island would be easy, but once the way was opened, developers of the mid-twentieth century would move in with bulldozers, paving machines, dredges, and big plans. It would not take them long to denude the island of most of its native vegetation, flatten the hills, dredge canals, and cover the island with houses, condominiums, landscaping, paving, and a large hotel, turning it into a "tourist's paradise." By 1980 the Marriott Marco Island would be a big busy hotel where herds of people wearing tags move from one convention to another until late afternoon when drinks are poured, and by the time torches are lighted around the pool the hotel has been transformed into a place to party.

The area's population would soar. From a total of 317 in all of South Florida in 1825, Collier County alone would reach 38,000 by 1970 and 80,000 by 1980. Predictions for the dawn of the twenty-first century would put the population at nearly a quarter of a million.

In 1896, changes were already beginning to take place. In the limited cultivated areas the early settlers had added citrus, coconut, avocado, and mango groves, fields of bananas, pineapples, and melons, and garden crops including onions, tomatoes, cabbage, pumpkins, eggplant, and peppers. For nearly twenty years Marco had been shipping produce and cattle to market in Key West, a thriving city of 18,000, the largest city in Florida, which had to bring in nearly all of its food. The cattle and produce fed the native population and the large contingent of naval vessels based there, and some was transshipped to growing northern markets.

Both land and sea around Marco held abundant native animal life. Mullet was the most common fish in the shallow waters; huge schools two to three miles long were reported in the passes. Tarpon and snook already brought many sportsmen to the island, and food fish were routinely caught in large quantities—pompano, mackerel, bluefish, kingfish, grouper, sea trout, weakfish, snapper, redfish, jewfish, sheepshead, and channel bass. Oysters, clams, conchs, and other shellfish were equally abundant and always had been if the huge and still growing heaps of shells on the island were any evidence. There were alligators in the slough and shallow water areas; the higher land provided homes for deer, Florida wolves, bears, panthers, bobcats, gray foxes, raccoons, opossums, skunks, rabbits, and squirrels. It was obvious that this land had furnished a plentiful and comparatively easy living to all who had made it their home.

In an oft-repeated story, the aboriginal population was not so hospitable as nature to all who came after them. The earliest residents of the Marco area we can identify are the Calusa Indians. Europeans had come early to this area, Ponce de León making contact there on his first voyage in 1513. During the early years of Spanish exploration and attempted colonization in South Florida, the Tequesta and the Calusa were the two dominant tribes in the region, the latter the most important, the least hospitable, and the last to be conquered or displaced.

Most historians agree that Ponce first met the

Calusa somewhere in the area of Charlotte Harbor or Estero Bay. He stopped on one of the small islands to take on fresh water and to careen one of his ships, remaining there from May 23 to June 3. The Indians previously met by the expedition along the east coast of Florida attacked, and Ponce took one of them prisoner to be taught Spanish and used as an interpreter. The Indians Ponce saw on shore in the Calusa area signaled to him to come ashore, but having no trade goods and having already made the acquaintance of Indian darts and arrows, the Spaniards kept to their ships. When Ponce did not accept their invitation, the Indians came out to the ships in their canoes. When Ponce sought to change his anchorage, the Indians thought he was leaving and laid hold of his anchor cables. After some struggle, Ponce and some of his men went ashore in their longboats, captured four women, and broke up two old canoes—not a friendly beginning.

Early historical accounts leave some important questions unanswered. On this voyage in 1513, on which Ponce de León discovered Florida, he is said to have heard rumors of "the Cacique Carlos and his gold" and to have had contact with an Indian who understood Spanish, and the Indians had already discovered the Spaniards' greed for gold (Lowery 1959:142).

If Carlos had gold he must have acquired it outside of Florida through trading with native peoples from other shores. There had as yet been no plate fleet wrecks. Do. d'Escalante Fontaneda, held prisoner by the Calusa for seventeen years, says repeatedly that they had no gold except from the sea. The Collier site yielded no gold.

Twenty-one years had passed since Columbus' first voyage, so it is possible that Ponce could have encountered an Indian who understood Spanish. There was contact among tribes in the Caribbean area so Indians who had crossed the path of one of the earliest Spanish explorers might have made their way to Florida, or a Florida native might have been in the Caribbean on a trading mission where he made contact with Spaniards.

It is harder to explain how a reputation for greed for gold could have preceded Ponce to these shores since the great treasures of Central and South America had not yet been discovered by the Spaniards. It is possible that the Indians did not know what it was that the Spaniards asked for; but no matter what they thought it was, and whether they had it or not, they would have said that they did in order to trick Ponce and his men into staying until Carlos could collect his forces for attack. At eleven o'clock the next morning that is exactly what they did, but they were sufficiently frightened by the crossbows and guns that they maintained a safe distance from the ships, putting the ships out of range of their arrows. Finally the Indians withdrew, and Ponce continued on his journey back to Havana.

In 1516, Diego Miruelo reached the coast in a single ship where he is said to have bartered items of iron and glass for gold, but we do not know where he came ashore because he failed to mark his exact position.

In 1517, Hernández de Córdova sailed from Havana with three ships, one of which had been sold to him by the governor of Cuba with the stipulation that it be paid for in slaves captured from among the Indians. This the crew refused to do, so instead of a slaving expedition it became one of exploration.

There is a possible error in the sailing date above given by Bernal Diaz, who related his memoirs some years later after his return to Spain. He refers to the place they landed as the "bay where Juan Ponce was killed." Ponce was not killed until 1521, on his second voyage. It is not possible to tell if Diaz is confusing the date or if he is merely using this fact to identify the bay where Córdova stopped on Florida's west coast as the same bay where Ponce had anchored and careened one of his ships. In any case, among Córdova's crew were two men who took part in other historic voyages. Anton de Alaminos, the pilot, had been with Ponce de León on his 1513 voyage of discovery, and it was he who identified the bay where Córdova stopped as the same bay where Ponce had anchored.

While Córdova and his men were ashore digging for water in Calusa territory they were attacked by the Indians. Bernal Diaz wrote:

Upon our arrival in Florida twenty of the soldiers whose wounds were nearest healed went ashore. Anton de Alaminos, the pilot, and I went with them. We took such casks as we still possessed, hoes, crossbows, and muskets. As the captain was very badly wounded, and weakened by thirst, he ordered us to be sure to bring back sweet water, or he would die.

We landed near a creek that Alaminos said was the place where Indians had attacked when he was with Juan Ponce de León. We posted two sentinels while we dug deep wells on the broad beach, and it pleased God that we should find good water. We were so overjoyed that between quenching our thirst and washing bandages we must have been there an hour, when one of the sentinels ran toward us crying, "To arms! Many warriors are coming, both by land and downstream in canoes."

The soldier and the Indians arrived at almost the same moment. The Indians were very tall, dressed in deerskin, and carried long bows, good arrows, lances, and a kind of sword. They attacked immediately, wounding six of us and I received a small cut. We answered so quickly with sword and fire that they retreated to the aid of their companions in the canoes, who were fighting hand to hand with our sailors. Our boat had been captured after four sailors had been hurt and Alaminos wounded in the throat. We returned their attack in water more than waist-deep and made them abandon our boat. Twenty lay dead on the shore and in the water and we took three prisoners, who died of wounds on shipboard.

After the skirmish was over, we asked the sentinel what had become of Berrio, his companion. He replied that Berrio had gone off with a hatchet to cut a palmetto, and that later he had heard cries in Spanish, so that he feared Berrio must have been killed. We began to search for him immediately and came upon a palm tree partially cut through and the ground trampled. There was no sign of blood, so he must have been carried off alive. We searched and shouted for another hour before taking the water back to the ships.

The soldiers were overjoyed as though we

had given them life itself. One jumped from the ship into the boat, took a jug to his chest, and drank so much that within two days he swelled up and died.

We took on the boats and set sail for Havana, which we made in a day and a night. Near some islands called Los Martires [named by Ponce on his first voyage, now called the Florida Keys] there are shallows no more than four fathoms deep; here our captain struck, and we made water fast. All the soldiers manned the pumps. We feared we would founder, but somehow we managed to trim the sails and pump until Our Lord carried us into the port where Havana now is, which used to be called Carenas. (Diaz 1956:25–26)

Córdova died ten days later in Cuba.

In 1519, Piñeda sailed the entire coast of Florida and the Gulf, proving that Florida was not an island after all but a part of the mainland. There is no record of his coming ashore anywhere in Florida.

Ponce de León still had dreams of settling Florida. In a letter to Charles V, dated February 10, 1521, he says, "Among my services I discovered at my own cost and charge, the Island of Florida and others in its district . . . and now I return to that Island, if it please God's will, to settle it . . . . I shall set out to pursue my voyage hence in five or six days" (Lowery 1959:158).

Proceed he did, once again to the Calusa territory he had visited before. There he took a group ashore where he had previously stopped; while trying to construct dwellings for settlers, they were attacked by the Calusas and Ponce was wounded in the throat by an arrow. Many of his followers were killed, and the survivors returned to Cuba where Ponce died a few days later.

In succeeding years others sailed along Florida's Gulf coast and stopped somewhere because at least two of them brought back Indian captives, but they left no records of where they had landed. Narváez and de Soto, both of whom made extensive explorations in Florida, began their campaigns farther north, from Tampa Bay, in the land of the Tocobaga.

In 1545 a Spanish vessel was wrecked on the

Gulf coast, casting two hundred souls into Calusa territory. Some of them were killed and the rest enslaved by the Indians. Probably also about this time, there was another shipwreck on the Gulf coast. One survivor, Hernando d'Escalante Fontaneda, a lad of thirteen when cast ashore, spent seventeen years as a Calusa captive. He tells of other wrecks along the coast in 1551 and the one in which Pedro Menéndez de Avilés lost his son in 1563. When Pedro Menéndez came looking for his lost son on the west coast in 1566, he was met, on landing in Charlotte Harbor, by Fontaneda in a canoe. It was probably Menéndez who rescued Fontaneda from his long captivity among the Calusa.

In 1553 a treasure fleet bound from Terra Firma to Spain, carrying over a thousand soldiers, merchants, women, children and five Dominican friars, was wrecked off the Gulf coast. Three hundred of them made shore, most of whom were either killed by the Indians or died of the hardships they were forced to endure. One of the monks, Fray Marcos de Mena, escaped. Seriously wounded by the Indian arrows and seemingly on the point of death, his compatriots did not want to abandon him alive and wounded to the Indians, so they buried him in sand on the bank of a river, leaving only his face exposed so that he might breathe for the few moments of life remaining to him. Then his companions sought safety for themselves in flight. In his weakened and exhausted condition, the monk soon fell asleep; when he awoke he felt refreshed and invigorated, so he dug himself out of his shallow grave and proceeded to follow the trail of his companions. Not far up the river he came upon those who had recently buried him, all dead at the hands of the Indians. He was later rescued by two friendly natives and sent back to Tampico (Lowery 1959:352–53).

Castaways had reason to fear the Calusa. They had a reputation even among other Indian tribes of being fierce and cruel. Those earliest cast ashore had no means of communicating and no understanding of Indian ways. Later captives sometimes had the benefit of earlier captives who could act as interpreters, thus saving the lives of many of them. According to Fontaneda who served many as interpreter:

The natives who took them would order them to dance and sing; and as they did not understand, and the Indians themselves are very mean (for the most so of any are the people of Florida), they thought the Christians were rebellious, and unwilling to do so. And so they would kill them, and report to the cacique that for their meanness and rebelliousness they had been slain, because they would not do as they were told; which was the answer, as I have said, made to the cacique when he would ask them why they had killed them. One day, I, a negro, and two others, Spaniards recently made captives, being present, the cacique, in conversation with his vassals and the great chiefs of his train about what I have just mentioned, asked me, I being "masladino" (better acquainted with the language than any one), saying, "Escalante, tell us the truth, for you well know that I like you much: When we tell these, your companions, to dance and sing, and do other things, why are they so mean and rebellious that they will not? Or is it that they do not fear death, or will not yield to a people unlike them in their religion? Answer me, and if you do not know the reason, ask it of those newly seized, who for their own fault are captives now, a people whom once we held to be gods come down from the sky." And I, answering my lord and master, told him the truth: "My Lord, as I understand it, they are not contrary, nor is it for any evil reason, but it is because they cannot understand you, which they earnestly strive to do." He said it was not true; that often he would command them to do things, and sometimes they would obey him; and at others they would not, however much they might be told. I said to him: "Even so, my Lord, they do not intentionally behave amiss, nor for perversity, but from not understanding. Speak to them, that I may be a witness, and likewise this your free negro." And the Cacique, laughingly, said: "Se-le-te-ga." to the newcomers; and they asked what it was he said to them. The negro, who was near to them, laughed, and said to the cacique: "Master, I will tell you the truth; they have not understood, and they ask Escalante what it is you say, and he does not wish to tell them until you command him." Then the cacique believed the truth, and said to me: "Declare it to them, Escalante; for now do I really believe you." I made known to them the meaning of Se-le-te-ga, which is, "Run to the look-out, see if there be any people coming." They of Florida abbreviate their words more than we. The cacique, discovering the truth, said to his vassals, that when they should find Christians thus cast away, and seize them, they must require them to do nothing without giving notice, that one might go to them who should understand their language. (Fontaneda 1945: 33–34)

Well should Fontaneda have known the fate of captives. During his own captivity he had witnessed the killing of forty-two fellow prisoners from his own shipwreck, one of them his older brother (Lowery 1959:148).

Fontaneda repeatedly says that the Indians had pearls but no gold or silver "and are rich only by the sea, from the many vessels that have been lost well laden with these metals, as was the case with the transport in which Farfan and the mulatto owner were; with the vessel of the Vizcaino, in which came Anton Granado, who was a passenger and was captured; and with the vessel of which Juan Christoval was master and captain, lost in the year '51, when the Indians murdered Don Martin de Guzmán, the Captain Hernando de Andino, Procurador of the Province of Popayan, and Juan Ortiz de Zarate, Distributor of Santa Martha; and there came in her also two sons of Alonzo de Mena, with an uncle, all of them rich. He that brought least was I, but with all I brought twenty-five thousand dollars in pure gold; for my father and mother remained in Carthagena, where they were comenderos, and served His Majesty in those parts of Peru, and afterwards in the city of Carthagena, where they settled, and I and a brother were born. Thence they sent us to Spain to be educated; when we were wrecked on

Florida" (Fontaneda 1945:32–33). Much treasure taken by Indians from wrecks on the east coast of Florida ended up in the hands of Carlos after it was paid to him as tribute by those east coast tribes he controlled.

Pedro Menéndez de Avilés believed there was a water route across the Florida peninsula. He thought that the St. Johns River (then called the San Mateo) emptied into the Gulf of Mexico somewhere along the southwest coast. He wrote the Spanish king from Havana in 1566 that he would go to Florida, auctioning a French prize ship and her cargo to buy supplies, and would explore the lower keys looking for a passage east of the Tortugas which could be used by vessels homebound from Mexico to Spain. Then he would skirt along the west coast of Florida looking for a good harbor in the vicinity of the Bay of Juan Ponce. Menéndez believed he would find the western end of the cross-Florida waterway somewhere in that vicinity, and when he did he wished to establish a fort and a colony at that point.

Early in 1566 Menéndez left Havana with seven ships, led by the *Santa Catalina,* and probed cautiously east of the Tortugas. He was successful in finding an adequate channel there, then continued on, sighting the west coast somewhere in the area of the Ten Thousand Islands. He continued close inshore looking for the Bay of Juan Ponce, then left the larger ships anchored offshore and continued into shallower water to an inlet. There he met Hernando d'Escalante Fontaneda in a canoe. Menéndez hoped to establish friendly relations with the Indians in the area through their cacique, Carlos, and to leave settlers in the area, with Fontaneda, of course, serving as interpreter.

Observers record the meeting between Menéndez and Carlos as one of considerable ceremony. Menéndez was sent ashore to the music of fife, drum, and trumpet, to be received by the ruler of much of South Florida seated in state among his nobles and villagers. He persuaded Carlos to release the thirty-two shipwreck victims still held captive and to conclude a treaty of peace with the Spanish. Among the captives released were five men, five mestiza women from Peru, and one black woman. Carlos also promised to free three other Christians held captive some distance away. Menéndez and Carlos entertained one another with food and drink, and Carlos cemented the friendly relations by granting Menéndez one of the highest honors of his culture: he gave Menéndez his own sister for a wife and insisted that the marriage be consummated forthwith.

At this time Menéndez did not try to establish a religious mission but did try to reconfirm the faith of captives who chose to stay there and to make some small effort to introduce the Indians to the principles of the Catholic faith. He behaved admirably in his relations with the Indians. He took no booty, carrying away with him a single bar of gold, a gift of Carlos. His men, however, traded vigorously with the Indians and gathered treasure estimated to be worth 3,500 ducats before they returned to Cuba.

Menéndez planned to return to Carlos in the spring of 1567, this time to establish a fort and mission. He took with him Carlos's sister, who had been held in Cuba as hostage to her brother's good intentions, intending to return her to her brother. The previous July, Menéndez had promoted Francisco de Reinoso to the rank of captain and assigned him men who would garrison the fort to be built at Carlos (Lyon 1976:165).

Now he took with him two Jesuit priests, Father Juan Rogel and Francisco Villareal, who would establish the first Jesuit mission in Florida. But when Menéndez landed at Carlos, he found that all the friendship of his earlier visit had evaporated; his "marriage" to Carlos's sister helped none at all since Doña Antonia, as she had been named by Menéndez, had reported to her brother that her marriage was unfulfilled. Then Menéndez made a proposal to Carlos that was both puzzling and infuriating: He suggested that Carlos sign a peace agreement with the Tocobaga, his traditional enemies.

Menéndez had a motive: He was still looking for the water route across Florida, and the Indians had suggested that he try a river that emptied into what is now Tampa Bay, in Tocobaga country. Menéndez managed to persuade Carlos to go on an expedition to Tocobaga, taking Fontaneda

along as interpreter. They apparently reached the chief village of the Tocobaga undetected, and Carlos wanted to attack immediately. Menéndez persuaded him not to by promising to secure the release of Calusa prisoners held by the Tocobaga.

The new alliance with the Tocobaga caused tension between factions of the Calusa as well as increasing their ill feelings toward the Spaniards. Since it was obvious they were not welcome in Carlos, Menéndez decided that it would be prudent to move his fort and colony to another island rather than to try to build it on Carlos's main island. Carlos offered to help them make the move to the other island in his canoes, intending to overturn the canoes and drown the Spaniards. Fortunately, the Spaniards who had been captives of the Calusa warned Menéndez in time to avert disaster for the entire group. Fontaneda and the mulatto, who are given credit for discovering the plot, warned Menéndez of the Indians' intentions, and he moved them in his own small boats instead.

So Fort San Anton de Padua was established on a nearby island, the original fort garrison for twelve (six soldiers and six soldier-farmers) reinforced by fifty soldiers, and Menéndez hurried back to Havana to take care of a threat to his authority there. The history of the mission is one of struggle and disaster, which only intensified after Menéndez left in the spring of 1567. The Spaniards dared not leave their blockhouse without armed guard. As the situation worsened, Father Rogel left for Havana to report to his superiors. He had been the mediator between the Spaniards and the Indians, and his departure only made things worse. Soon after he left, Carlos moved his treasure and his women to another island and made plans to massacre the Christians. When Captain Reinoso learned of this plot, he summoned Carlos near the fort and had him executed on the spot.

The new chief, called Philip (or Filipe) by the Spaniards, was more tractable, even allowing Menéndez to confirm him in office as chief and as a vassal of the king of Spain. This change brought new hope to Father Rogel. Realizing that before any of the villagers could be converted he must first convert their leader, he set about to confirm Philip in the Catholic faith but was determined not to do so until the Indian had fully and freely become a convert.

Father Rogel faced a problem. The Indians were willing to accept the cross and the tenets of Christianity as they understood them but only alongside those of their own religion and not to the exclusion of their own long-held beliefs and customs. They particularly objected to abandoning such cultural traditions as sodomy, the required sibling marriage and polygamy of the chief, and the sacrifice of children on occasions that required such things.

Meantime, Father Villareal had gone east to convert the Tequesta, who were said to be more submissive. In April 1568, Father Villareal and eighteen soldiers, the only survivors of the Tequesta mission, arrived at Carlos. A food shortage, abuse by the Spanish garrison, and the killing of one of their leaders had enraged the Tequesta, and they had surrounded the fort and burned it, murdering four Spaniards. The discouraged priests soon returned to Havana (Lyon 1976:203).

Rogel's assessment of the situation was that the Spaniards were their own worst enemies and their own worst obstacle to colonization and evangelization. They demanded food; they beat and killed the Indians and abused their women and children; they were overbearing, harsh, and cruel. They could, he said, succeed only through colonization and example (Lyon 1976:205).

For a long time there were no further efforts to colonize this part of Florida, and because of their reputation as fierce and inhospitable the Calusa were left alone. But while further attempts at colonization were abandoned for a time, the Indians were not forgotten. In 1573, Menéndez petitioned the Spanish Crown for permission to exterminate the Indians in South Florida because they were so bloodthirsty and such a menace to

the Spanish, particularly to castaways. The petition was accompanied by sworn affidavits of a number of Spaniards attesting to Indian cruelty.

By the late seventeenth century some of the Keys Indians had been converted to the Catholic faith. There is a record from 1697 of some Catholic Indians of Matecumbe Key giving refuge to five Franciscans from Calusa territory. The Franciscans had been preaching Catholic doctrine at "Cayo de Carlos" when the Indians attacked them and drove them naked from their territory (Goggin 1964:45).

The late John Goggin, a recognized expert on South Florida Indians, said that the population of South Florida was apparently dwindling rapidly by the early part of the eighteenth century. According to him, Creek sources reported that warfare was carried on against the Indians of Cape Florida, who were reduced to thirty men and moved to Havana with the Spaniards. Bernard Romans says they were driven into the mangroves of the Ten Thousand Islands and to the keys (1962:289).

After the signing of a treaty by Great Britain, France, and Spain in 1762, when Florida was ceded to England in exchange for Havana, all Spanish residents of South Florida were given the opportunity to evacuate to Havana if they wished to do so. Many did, and many Indians went with them. The few Indians who remained were henceforth known as Spanish Indians. According to Romans, the remaining eighty or so families of Calusa on Key Vaca and Key West moved to Havana, ending Calusa residence in Florida (Goggin 1964:46).

It is entirely possible that had the Spaniards really come in peace, as friends, willing to recognize the validity of ways other than their own, Florida's history might have been different. Since they did not, the first permanent white residents of Marco did not arrive until late in the nineteenth century.

3

MARCO'S FIRST RESIDENTS

WHO WERE THESE Calusa, these first recorded residents of southwest Florida? Their origins are gradually being uncovered by archaeologists. They occupied territory in southwest Florida which they called Escampaba (Juan Lopez de Velasco, in Lowery 1959: 445). The Indians called themselves Carlos, which meant in their language, according to one of their long-time captives, "fierce people." Some authorities state that the cacique and the main town of the territory he ruled bore the same name, in this case, Carlos.

There has been some speculation that the name Carlos came from the Spanish monarch, Charles V, but there is evidence that the name predates Spanish contact, and, according to Fontaneda, had been the name of the tribe for some time before his tenure with them. The father of the Cacique Carlos met by Menéndez was Senequene, or Carlos I.

In any case, when the Spaniards first met them, they called their chief Carlos. It was also the name of their principal town, which has been located by various authorities on different islands along the coast in the Charlotte Harbor–Estero Bay area. Goggin and Sturtevant, after careful study, placed it on Mound Key in Estero Bay. We know that it was on an island in a bay in that region, and from historical records and archaeological evidence that location seems the probable one.

Fontaneda says they were called "Carlos," meaning "fierce people," because they were brave and skillful "as in truth they were" (Fontaneda 1945:25). They were also, to some extent, people of legend, frequently described as especially large. Fontaneda describes them as "large and of good countenance" in the keys, and Bernal Diaz describes those on the southwest coast as being "very tall" (Diaz 1956:25).

They lived in a land of plenty, the rich land and sea surrounding them furnishing most materials necessary for the subsistence and defense of the Calusa and their ancestors. That they made most efficient use of materials in their natural environment is adequately demonstrated by the archaeological evidence.

The wooded shores provided pine, cypress, three species of mangroves, and other woods for building materials and for the manufacture of weapons and household utensils, religious paraphernalia, canoes, and paddles. Palms and vines provided fiber from which they made excellent rope, twine, and netting. The woods furnished also their meager clothing: The men wore a breechcloth of woven palm fibers and the women a short apronlike garment of Spanish moss. From the woods also came game animals, which furnished not only food but bone for tools and weapons, and the wild berries and other plant foods that were a part of their regular diet.

To the Calusa the resources of the sea were even more important. They were expert fishermen and reaped a constant harvest of shellfish, a major staple of their diet. They erected their buildings on huge mounds of shells, keeping them above the tide line on these low-lying islands. Out of shells of various kinds they manufactured the tools and utensils of their daily lives. Fontaneda tells us that in the easterly part of the Calusa empire they ate quantities of eels, fish, roots (one was like truffle and was used to make bread), trout, lagartos (alligators), animals like rats, snakes and turtles "and many more disgusting reptiles" as well as deer and birds (Fontaneda 1945:27).

The water also provided the main means of travel, much easier than making their way among the low, swampy areas and the mangrove roots of the outer shoreline. Early historical sources tell us that they not only used the traditional dugout canoe in inland waters and near shore but that they lashed two canoes together, catamaran style, for ventures farther from land. There are no reports of sails.

The Calusa were a sedentary people, nonagricultural, who derived their subsistence largely from the rich marine resources surrounding them. In this area, with such a concentrated food supply, it was unnecessary to make seasonal migrations in search of sustenance. Such an atmosphere fosters centralization of authority and a stratified society with specialized occupations. Time gained from not having to scrape for food

can be spent in experimenting with technologies, ceremonialism, and religious and artistic development. It also leaves manpower free and under central control to build the great mounds and earthworks characteristic of the Calusa area and to wage organized warfare on neighbors. At the time of Spanish contact, the Calusa controlled virtually all of South Florida and the upper keys, a population estimated to have been at least four thousand and perhaps as high as ten thousand, with an estimated one thousand in the main village. The main Calusa area was from Boca Grande Pass southward along the west coast, but, according to Fontaneda, more than fifty towns in the Tequesta area, including twenty-five around Lake Okeechobee and in the keys, paid tribute to Carlos and were under his control. One authority states that in the Calusa area Carlos controlled more than seventy towns as well as the fifty subject villages in Tequesta territory—a sizable domain for a primitive society. Tribute was paid in feathers, mats, fruits and other foods, roots, deerskins, captives, and, later on, in gold and silver from the Spanish shipwrecks.

They had traditional enemies as well as traditional friends. The Tocobaga and Mocoso were in the former category and, as we have seen, Carlos was greatly upset by Pedro Menéndez's insistence that he sign a joint peace treaty with the Tocobaga and the Spaniards.

Military campaigns were conducted to establish and maintain political and economic dominance and to obtain sacrificial victims and trophy heads for ceremonial purposes. They were also conducted to repel the invading Spaniards, and successfully in spite of the superiority of Spanish weapons.

Another product of abundant time was the religious development that accompanied political expansion. Paraphernalia and ceremonialism were developed to a high degree. Paraphernalia included masks, plaques of all sizes, and totemic objects, first made of wood, some elaborately decorated, and later, when metals became available, reproduced in gold and silver.

Incumbent upon the chiefs, as well as political duties, were religious responsibilities. They had special secret religious knowledge, known only to them. When Father Rogel asked Carlos if he believed in the Unity of God and that God was the creator of the universe and the ruler of everything, he replied yes; it was one of the secrets that he and his ancestors, the kings, held secret in their breasts and had not told to anyone except their successors (Goggin and Sturtevant 1964:192).

The Calusa believed that there were three entities who ruled the world, one greater than the other two. This one had domain over the most universal and common matters such as celestial movements and weather. The second, greater than the third but lesser than the first, was the ruler of kingdoms, empires, and republics. The third, and least of all, helped in wars whoever applied to him (Goggin and Sturtevant 1964:197).

The spirits of the dead were also important, though the details of their domain is unclear. According to Father Rogel, one of the "idols" required human sacrifice because he ate human eyes. The heads of victims so sacrificed were later carried in religious dances. At one time one of Menéndez's men counted more than fifty such heads at the base of a tree in the main Calusa town. After contact with the Spaniards, most of their sacrificial victims were Spanish captives except when a chief or member of his family died. Prior to that it is thought captives from other tribes were used as sacrificial victims. When a chief or his principal wife died, some of their "servants" were dispatched to accompany the dead. When the child of a chief died, children were sacrificed.

Various mortuary practices were reported for the Calusa area. Some were thought to have had separate charnel houses where the dead were kept. Others report that the bodies were exposed until the flesh had decomposed, at which time there was secondary burial in common graves. Sir John Hawkins, reported in 1565 that "In these Islands [in southwest Florida] they being a shore, found a dead man, dried in a manner whole, with other heads and bodies of men" (Hawkins 1965:150).

At least in the main Calusa town, religious paraphernalia was stored in a temple built on a mound, to which the chief retired, with a few of

his associates, to perform secret rituals at certain times. To him was credited the fruitfulness of land and sea. Religious paraphernalia was extensive and elaborate. Masks were widely used, and Father Rogel tells of watching a procession of masked figures coming down from the temple on the mound toward the point where he was standing. It was accompanied by singing women as it moved down from the mound in view of the populace. There are many carved and painted wooden boards, amulets, and tablets in the Key Marco collection, most of which are thought to have had religious or ceremonial significance. A number of masks were also found, many still clearly bearing the original designs painted on them.

There was a chief priest and sorcerers or curers. Nobles and captains seem too to have had religious duties as well as political ones. There was a captain general (so designated by the Spaniards) and a second captain, whose duties were apparently important but were undefined in available reports. Carlos frequently consulted the captain general and was unwilling to move against his advice. This captain general was more feared by the people than was Carlos himself (Goggin and Sturtevant 1964:190).

Like most tribes, the Calusa had rules against incest, but, unlike most, they held one exception. Like the Egyptian pharaoh, the Calusa chief was required to take as his principal wife his own full sister (Goggin and Sturtevant 1964:192). He then took as lesser wives women related to the chiefs of other tribes in order to cement political alliances with these tribes and to ensure their subjugation.

Calusa society was stratified with evidence of at least two classes, nobles and ordinary people, and probably some slaves. Some dietary items were allowed to the higher classes and prohibited to the lower ones. Fontaneda says, "Some eat sea-wolves; not all of them, for there is a distinction between the higher and the lower classes, but the principal persons eat them" (Fontaneda 1945:26).

The status of the chief was marked by a forehead ornament (of gold in later years), beaded leg bands, and personal treasure. He was also, at state times, seated on a low stool, the only person so equipped. When he was approached by lesser persons, they knelt before him with raised hands held palms up. The chief then placed his hands on top of the upturned palms (Goggin and Sturtevant 1964:191–92).

The tradition in this area was to build thatched houses on the tops of shell mounds, and evidence suggests that it is what the Calusa did. There are some reports of buildings plastered over with colored mud. They appear to have constructed holding ponds for fresh water and some for holding live fish. So far they are the only tribe known to have caught mullet in nets.

The Calusa are described as great bowmen and powerful archers. The Spaniards are reported to have used Indian divers in salvaging plate fleet wrecks in 1733 (Goggin 1964:46). Spears, spearthrowers, and bows and arrows were all used in hunting; nets, hooks, and spears were used in fishing. Burdens were carried mostly in canoes or, on overland trips, probably on the backs of men.

The Calusa were the most powerful tribe in the area. They had a highly developed social structure and superb technology. Their system of social and political customs worked, for them. When the Spaniards came, the Calusa could see no reason to abandon values and customs that had been successful traditions for generations in favor of principles that they did not understand and that had no validity in their way of life. The Spaniards were not willing to admit the validity and integrity of the Indian culture, and the Indians, who were willing to accept Christianity alongside their own religion and on an equal basis, could not be convinced that everything they did was wrong and that everything the Spaniards did was right. And the Spaniards' behavior did little to convince them.

So, while Calusa hostility to strangers delayed their fate, they eventually were destroyed or driven out by Creek and English raids of the early eighteenth century. There is considerable evidence that the Collier site was at least partly destroyed by fire. Many wooden artifacts are partially burned. Perhaps the village was raided by a hostile force, either Europeans or another tribe; perhaps when defense was minimal because the men were away on a raid somewhere else, attackers put the remaining occupants to flight in their canoes and then put the village to the torch as was the custom of many tribes. Whether humanmade or natural, the cause of abandonment of the site came swiftly. While no whole canoes were found, there was much ceremonial and religious paraphernalia. It is doubtful if any people, in a planned move, would leave all of that behind. It was nearly four hundred years before Marco once again knew permanent residents.

4

MARCO'S

FIRST

WHITE

SETTLERS

FEAR-STRICKEN, weary, and wet, the eleven Colliers huddled together on Indian Key in the Ten Thousand Islands, thankful that all had been spared when their schooner was wrecked in a sudden storm.

Marco's first permanent settler, William Thomas Collier, was no stranger to adventure and danger. The Colliers came originally from North Carolina. They had moved in 1808 to what they thought was Alabama, but the territory had not yet been surveyed; when that was done the Colliers found themselves about a mile and a half over the line in Tennessee. Here, on March 12, 1815, William Thomas Collier was born.

He was well educated for his time, well read, a thinker and a philosopher, a man of action and great resourcefulness, a true pioneer. His formal schooling spanned ten years, from six to sixteen, considerable for his day. His father hoped that he would become a civil engineer and planned to educate him at the university in Huntsville, but he was unable to fulfill that dream after paying a

$10,000 debt he had guaranteed for one of his wife's brothers. W. T. had some private teachers instead of college, the first of whom he says "took to drink and died," but none of these teachers was able to teach him the requisite mathematics for engineering (Collier n.d.). He must have done a lot of reading on his own because, in surviving memoirs, he demonstrates a knowledge of astronomy, other religions, the Bible, and such philosophers and historians as Philo, Pliny the Elder, Pliny the Younger, Josephus, Jacoliot, and Lardner (Collier n.d.). He also apparently had a lively sense of humor.

Denied a college education and a career in engineering, W. T. Collier turned in other directions. For a time he worked in his brother-in-law's carriage business; he didn't like it so he tried his hand at millwrighting. He first built a sawmill for his father, then two more for others. His reputation as a millwright grew, and, building both gristmills and sawmills, he was kept busy. When he became dissatisfied with the wasteful quantities of water required by mills then in use, he began experimenting with improvements and after five years produced an improved wheel using less water.

After both of his parents died within a short time, he moved back to North Carolina where he built many more mills. While there he worked in one of them with a man named Wilfong whose sister went to school in Asheville. One year Wilfong was to transport his sister and a number of other students home for the Christmas holidays in his carriage; as the conveyance was too small to accommodate them all comfortably, Wilfong asked Collier to provide his horse and buggy for additional transport. Collier soon became aware that there was another reason for the request, as Wilfong seemed most anxious to introduce him to his sister. The sister and another young man were driving Collier's horse while Collier rode with Wilfong, but after seeing what he considered mistreatment of his horse by the other young man Collier took it away from him. The sister was offended, and Wilfong's efforts at matchmaking were endangered. After being taken to task by her brother she tried to apologize, but Collier had already decided the girl was not for him.

This girl later married a newcomer from Mississippi who clerked in a store in the county seat. The townspeople liked him, and after living with his bride's family for several months he decided he could successfully open a store of his own. He borrowed $17,000 from his bride plus all he could from others in the community and left for Charleston to buy stock for his store. He never came back.

The resulting suspicions of the townspeople toward all strangers caused difficulties for Collier. Wilfong had a young cousin Collier found attractive, but because of the feeling toward newcomers Wilfong would not introduce them. First he had to prove himself; this he did by letting Wilfong read his letters from home.

Collier pressed his case. He says that one time he saw the girl she was "with a Negro woman making good time after a chicken." He tried to speak to her but she "ducked into a bunch of weeds" and stayed hidden until he left. The young man who was with Collier at the time told him she was the prettiest girl in the county and that she was "raised right" (Collier n.d.). That was in the spring. Sometime that summer he managed an introduction to her at a prayer meeting and she allowed him to walk her home. After that he "rode with her several times to preaching" and finally married Barbara Elizabeth Hedick on April 5, 1849 (Collier n.d.).

Shortly after that he was "taken with a bad cough," and a doctor advised a trip to Florida for his health. It would seem that perhaps the good doctor had a double motive for such a prescription because he asked Collier to look over a mill he owned at Cedar Key while he was down there. Collier went to the mill but says he "saw that Dr. McIlvane [who operated the mill] knew it all so he said nothing" (Collier n.d.).

Collier began building mills in Florida. The third one he built was a sawmill for a Colonel Gibson who was so pleased with it that he offered to sell Collier a half interest. Collier didn't have the money to buy it, so they made arrangements whereby Collier could pay for his half of the mill and fixtures out of the first lumber they sawed—which he did in three months.

A little over a year later Gibson bought out Collier's interest in the mill for $3,200. Collier quickly invested the money. On four hundred acres of pine land he owned near Quincy, Florida, a gale had blown down most of the trees and they were rotting on the ground. He went to New York, bought a mill and engine, and that year sold $6,000 worth of lumber, clearing $4,000. Then he sold that mill. It was during this time that a second son, William David Collier—Captain Bill—was born in Quincy on September 20, 1852.

After the mill was sold the family moved to Clearwater Harbor, where they bought the old Fort Harrison property. Collier also bought a Negro slave and one hundred head of cattle. In addition to his agricultural activities he made trading voyages between New Orleans and Florida ports, carrying freight and supplies of all kinds. His wife and children often accompanied him.

When the Civil War began he decided he could no longer stay in Clearwater. After taking his family to his father-in-law's home, now in Hernando County, and asking him to care for them, Collier joined the army. He served under General Bragg throughout the Kentucky campaign; always detailed to guard a wagon train or bridge, he was in several skirmishes but never in a pitched battle.

After leaving the army he and a John Darby bought a steam mill on the Suwannee River for $4,000. He later sold out to Darby for his cost and bought a half interest in a steam mill on Hatchet Creek near Gainesville. That was all he owned when the Civil War ended. When that mill burned down, he lost everything he had. Shortly afterward he journeyed to New York to buy the mill and engine for a group of men who were planning to build a big mill near Palatka. That mill did well, but there were some unsatisfactory workmen they needed to replace. Collier went to Savannah seeking the replacements, and there he was shanghaied.

As he passed the corner of a plank fence he was struck down, and when he regained consciousness he was in the hold of a ship. He was fed once a day, and after two or three days he was put ashore on a small island, robbed of a good watch, a gold pencil, and a hundred dollars in cash. He later learned that the island was one of the Bahamas. His kidnappers' vessel was not yet out of sight when he saw another ship which he managed to signal. It took him aboard and continued on the way to Veracruz. There he secured passage on a small bark to Galveston. Penniless, he found no work in Galveston, so he traveled on to Houston where he had heard there would be employment. He wrote home from there to tell them what had happened and to assure them that he would be home as soon as possible. He worked in a railroad shop for three dollars a day to earn his passage money.

When Collier did get home he found the mill in poor condition. He repaired it, sawed himself some lumber, built a schooner, the *Robert E. Lee*, and moved his family to New Smyrna. He operated this schooner between New Smyrna and Sa-

vannah but soon discovered that the east coast harbors were more difficult to negotiate than those on the Gulf coast. Also, the family liked the west coast better, so they decided to return to that side of the peninsula to carry on their commerce.

It was on this voyage, as they rounded Indian Key, that they were caught in a sudden storm and wrecked. They were stranded there for five days until the storm abated. The next day they saw a wrecked schooner and 400,000 feet of lumber floating in the shallow water near shore. Another less fortunate craft had also been caught in the storm, leaving no trace of survivors.

The Colliers repaired their boat with some of the lumber and loaded the rest on board. Most of it they sold, but they kept 15,000 feet on board and set sail once more. They first sailed along the coast a short way, then entered the Caloosahatchee River. They sailed past where Ft. Myers now stands and up to Buckingham. The soil there was fertile and it looked like a good place to settle down, so they unloaded the lumber and returned to Ft. Myers.

The family soon decided that they liked neither Ft. Myers nor the Buckingham area any better than they had their home on the east coast. En route to Key West early in 1871, they sailed up Marco Pass and came upon a sight they thought the most beautiful they had seen on the west coast. They landed at Marco Island and decided that it was the place they would call home. In March of that year the lumber they had left at Buckingham, the family's household goods, and the Collier family came to Marco to stay.

The only inhabitants of the entire island were four Negro squatters. Collier bought their claims and paid their way to Ft. Myers. The family immediately built their first home from the lumber they had salvaged. They had everything they needed except shingles for the roof, so they built a temporary roof of palmettos. When it was necessary to sail to Key West for supplies a short time later, Collier brought back shingles. When he reached Marco there was no house to put them on. He found the family living in a palmetto shack. A spark had set fire to the dry palmetto thatch and burned the house to the ground, destroying all the contents as well.

For some time the family lived in the palmetto shack while they set about cultivating some of the land. They raised a good crop of cabbages and shipped them to Key West, then a thriving city of 18,000. The large contingent of naval vessels there at the time helped to provide a ready market.

After a time, more lumber was procured and a new house was begun. A good house, on the same site, it too was destroyed by fire in 1873. This site had been out on the Gulf front, but before they rebuilt again a severe storm made them decide to move to higher ground. The old site was abandoned and the new house was built on a high shell mound. This house, which stood there for many years, became the permanent home of the Collier family. It originally had five rooms, but as the family grew the roof was raised and a second floor added (pl. 1). The Collier family lived in this house until the inn was built in 1895. In late 1964, this original house was moved to Goodland, renamed the Whitehouse, and operated as an eating place and lodge. It has since been renamed the Marco Lodge.

The cabbage patch flourished and other vegetables were added, but it was necessary to people the garden with scarecrows to keep the numerous deer from eating up the profits. Oranges, coconuts, and pineapples were added later. The produce was shipped to Key West and some reshipped to northern markets. The Colliers were the first people in southwestern Florida to ship vegetables for the northern winter market.

All this time Collier's sailing vessel was the only connection between this part of Florida and the rest of the world. There were no roads and no railroads. All of the freight that was used throughout South Florida came on this little schooner from New Orleans.

W. D. Collier, the son born in Quincy in 1852, worked with his father in all family enterprises, and by 1873 he was engaged in building boats as well. That year he built himself a boat, and for three years he sailed it among the islands and along the west coast around Marco Island, gathering curiosities of many kinds, including birds, birds' eggs, fish, and strange seashells. In 1876, twenty-four years old, he took these collections and sailed by himself to Philadelphia to attend the Centennial Exposition.

Some time later Collier returned to Florida and located in Ft. Myers. On January 20, 1880 he married Margaret McIlvane of Cedar Key, daughter of the Dr. McIlvane his father had met at the mill there when he first came to Florida. On October 23 of that year, before they were able to make Ft. Myers in their schooner, the *Emma White*, a daughter was born to them while they were anchored in the Caloosahatchee River. The daughter, named Emma after the schooner, came to Marco at the age of two and lived there until her death January 14, 1977, at age ninety-six. We meet her here as a young girl in her mother's diary.

In 1882, because of his father's failing health, Captain Bill and his young wife moved again to Marco where he remained until 1925. After the death of his father on November 5, 1902, Captain Bill continued his profitable trading, sailing his ship to Tampa, Ft. Myers, Key West, and New Orleans. He brought the first storekeeper from New Orleans to Ft. Myers, and his schooner carried the lumber to build the first church and the first school in Ft. Myers. His vessel was also depended upon to carry products from southwest Florida to market. Farmers came to Ft. Myers from as far north as Ft. Meade in Polk County bringing produce, or driving a cow or a pig, to be shipped to market aboard his schooner.

In addition to his trading ventures and agricultural pursuits, he built twenty ships, some for his own use but mostly for sale to others. He opened a general store in 1883. His customers included not only those coastal residents who came in sailing ships but also Indians who came in dugout canoes to trade their deer and bear meat and hides for the white man's cloth, beads, and other supplies. One of his customers was John Gomez, who claimed to have been a cabin boy on José Gaspar's pirate ship. In 1883 the town of Marco was founded. In 1888 Captain Bill became the first postmaster. Mail was brought from Tampa to Punta Rassa where he picked it up, bringing it to

Marco by boat once a week. Before that it had to come from Key West, a trip that took several weeks.

By 1890 sport fishing in the surrounding waters was becoming an important activity, bringing men from distant places to fish for the plentiful tarpon. By 1895 the demand for rooms was so great that the family was being crowded out of their home by tourists and fishermen so Captain Collier built the Marco Inn. Until its completion the family continued to live in the original house, but upon completion of the inn, with its twenty rooms, parlor, dining room, and bathroom, the family moved there. The inn is now known as the Marco Hotel and, with more recent additions, is still in operation.

When the inn was completed the Colliers sent out invitations to a formal opening, but they wondered if there would be any guests since the only access to Marco was by boat. To their surprise, more than one hundred guests came in small boats from Ft. Myers and Punta Rassa. It was the beginning of another lucrative business for Captain Bill.

Margaret McIlvane Collier died on October 5, 1896, within a year after the opening of the inn, preceding her mother by three years. On March 3, 1898, Captain Bill would also lose three of his sons, George, Thomas, and Wilmer, all at one time. He was sailing one of his ships, the *Speedwell*, from Key West when they were caught in a squall off the Marquesas, eighteen miles from Key West. The ship overturned, drowning the nine people in the cabin, three of them the Collier sons. All six of the others were members of a single family from Connecticut. One other passenger, two deckhands, and Captain Collier were the only survivors. They were on deck and were thrown clear.

Having noted that digging clams by hand limited the activity to shallow water while clams could also be found at greater depths, Captain Bill devised a machine capable of harvesting them in deeper water. By 1904, a canning factory had been established at Caxambas, and seven years later Collier built one at Marco. By 1920, he had improved on his invention. He invited J. H. Doxsee, who had been canning clams on Long Island, to come down to inspect his operation at Marco. A year later the Doxsees moved to Marco where several generations of the family operated the cannery until it closed in 1947.

Captain Collier would serve on the county commission, first as the south county representative on the commission of large Lee County before it was divided, then two years on the commission of the newly formed Collier County.

5

CUSHING,

A MAN

WITH

A DREAM

IT WOULD BE a long journey, nearly two months, before Frank Hamilton Cushing would return to Philadelphia. There would be little time for rest once he left this ship, yet he felt certain that the trip, arduous though it might be at times, would benefit his health. He was excited; he had never been to Florida, and exploring new areas was one of the loves of his life, far more satisfying than writing the dreary reports that must always follow. That part he had to force himself to do and then often only after repeated urgings by his superiors.

Now, in mid-May 1895, as he boarded the Clyde Line steamship in New York, he felt a familiar stir of excitement and anticipation that new adventure always brought. Having been a loner most of his life, he didn't mind that he was traveling alone, and he would have time to think these next several days before he reached Jacksonville. His life had been so hectic in recent years that he had had little time for reflection. Looking back, the trail of events that had brought him aboard

this ship seemed long and full of challenges and obstacles.

He really did hope his health would improve. That was one reason he was making this trip. It was a nuisance to be so often slowed or stopped entirely for a time by illness. He had been sickly all of his life. Always of slight build and rather frail looking, Cushing says he weighed but a pound and a half when delivered by his physician father, Thomas Cushing, on July 22, 1857, in Erie County, Pennsylvania. No one had thought he would survive, and it was uncanny how often his poor health had played a part in the direction his life would take.

As a child, his physical condition prohibited participation in the rough-and-tumble games of other children so he spent many hours in solitary pursuits. From the age of three he used to wander for hours in the woods near his home in Barre Center in Orleans County, New York. It was there he first became a keen observer of nature.

His attendance at school was sporadic and infrequent, but he was a natural scholar with native insight and intelligence. He was not yet ten years old when a projectile point brought to the surface by a plow on his father's farm kindled his interest in the American Indian.

After serving as a Civil War surgeon at such battles as Bull Run, Antietam, and South Mountain, his father had returned to his rural medical practice in Barre Center. By 1870, Dr. Cushing decided to move the family to Medina, New York, so that he could conduct his practice in town and so that Frank might attend an academy. His attendance there was not much better, but it brought him new opportunities to search for Indian sites and to add to his collection of artifacts. He built a hut near the site of an Indian fort he had discovered and went there for days at a time, digging for artifacts during the day and at night, by the light of his campfire, studying them and speculating on their makers' methods of manufacture. Throughout his career he continued to experiment with techniques the Indians might have used in their daily lives, and he became expert at duplicating many of them.

Whenever he could he sought out experts in an effort to learn from them. One of his first such contacts was George Kennan, a noted traveler, who became his friend for life. Archaeology and ethnology were infant sciences with limited available publications, but he read all he could get his hands on and corresponded with some of the pioneers in the field. He was always humble in his approach but was so hungry for knowledge that he was bold enough to contact the best of them.

He began early to try to analyze his artifacts and to try to reconstruct Indian life through interpretation of them. He kept notes and wrote reports on his finds. In 1874, at age seventeen, he sent a report on his collections in Orleans County to the officers of the Smithsonian Institution. The secretary of the Smithsonian, Joseph Henry, and the assistant secretary, Spencer Baird, were sufficiently impressed that they published it in the Smithsonian Annual Report for that year. He later gave the collection described in this report to the Smithsonian. After that he often wrote the Smithsonian for information, pleading his youth and inexperience as reasons for his ignorance. At least once Professor Baird sent him a package of books.

Through one of his early contacts he had an opportunity to visit Cornell University, where Professor Hartt was so impressed with a collection of artifacts he made right on the grounds of the university on the first day of his visit that the professor arranged for him to attend Cornell as a special student in the natural sciences. Hartt also found funds to pay his tuition.

At Cornell he spent most of his time in the library, encouraged in his studies by his father and Professor Baird. His career at Cornell was short. When he heard of a possible opening at the Smithsonian arranging collections, he wrote to Baird saying that he would be pleased at any time to work at the Smithsonian if there should be anything within his limited abilities. To his great surprise, by late November 1875, Baird asked him to report for work.

Cushing was assigned as assistant to Dr. Charles Rau, a Belgian scholar newly arrived at the Smithsonian. One of his first duties was to arrange some collections and prepare them for exhibit at the Centennial Exposition in Philadelphia the following year. He accompanied the exhibit to Philadelphia, living in a boardinghouse for the six months of the Centennial.

During those months he spent at the exposition, his interest in the artifacts and their meaning grew. He had contact with many visiting archaeologists, widening his horizons and sparking his first interest in the Pueblo Indians. When he returned to Washington at the close of the exposition in November, he was appointed curator of the Department of Ethnology of the National Museum. He was then nineteen years old.

Thereafter he did some early fieldwork for the Smithsonian in Virginia, and there began the problems that were so often repeated: he ran short of funds; he had chronic health problems; and because he loved the fieldwork but detested the necessary paperwork, he usually delayed it as long as possible in spite of his considerable literary talents.

Archaeology was a new and intriguing science

that stimulated the public's imagination, creating a demand in the popular press for information and interpretation of archaeological excavations. It was Cushing's first adventure with pressure from the press.

Now, May 24, 1895, he arrived in Jacksonville where the next day, through the courtesy of Colonel J. K. Leslie and Major Joseph H. Durkee, he boarded a smaller riverboat for the trip up the St. Johns River to Sanford. On this first trip to Florida he looked forward to the challenge of the unknown. He was, of course, familiar with work by others in all parts of Florida. Clarence B. Moore had been digging in the sand mounds along this river. There had been an article on Florida pottery as early as 1854, and many observations on various shell heaps had followed Daniel G. Brinton's article in 1859. There had been a few articles on the aboriginal population, one on the use of crania as cinerary urns in burial mounds in Florida and another on fossil human bones. In 1883, Charles J. Kenworthy had explored some ancient canals. There had been two articles on silver and gold ornaments from Florida sites, the earliest one, in 1878, written by his first boss at the Smithsonian, Dr. Rau.

He did not consider himself yet in the realm of the great names of this young science, but the prospects of what he hoped to find in Florida greatly excited him. Perhaps he too would one day make such a contribution to archaeology, and perhaps Florida would provide him with that opportunity.

From Sanford his journey took Cushing across "the low-lying, lake bestrewn pine lands and cypress swamps, so characteristic of southern Florida, to the little town of Punta Gorda on the Pease River, at the head of Charlotte Harbor" (*New York Journal*, June 21, 1896). For some reason Cushing was unable to complete the journey to the railhead at Punta Gorda by train, and he was forced to travel the last thirty miles on horseback. It had not been his first journey by train; he had made four such trips, much longer ones, between the East and New Mexico, but he had never traveled alone on any of those journeys. Nor was it the first trip he had begun by train and ended on the back of an animal. In fact, his first such

excursion—to Zuñi—had ended on the back of a mule.

There were other parallels too. Even though Florida was in the East and growing much faster, it was really still pioneer territory, though so different from the Southwest where he had spent six years studying the Zuñis. That adventure, full of rewards and difficulties and frustrations but in the end a valuable experience, had provided a solid base for all of his future work.

From his early fieldwork in Virginia he had returned to routine duties at the museum, but he had chafed under the routine and longed to return to the field. In July, his opportunity arrived: Baird told him to get ready to leave in four days for New Mexico with Colonel James Stevenson and his wife, Mathilda Coxe Stevenson, who were going on a collecting trip for the museum. Cushing was being sent as an ethnologist specifically assigned to learn as much as he could about a typical group of Pueblo Indians in the three months he could expect to be there. Major John Wesley Powell gave him his detailed instructions.

The party of four—the two Stevensons, photographer Jack Hillers, and Cushing—traveled by train to the western terminus of the Santa Fe Railroad at Las Vegas, New Mexico. From there they rode mules to Ft. Wingate, a ten-day trip that gave him time to explore along the way.

At Zuñi they set up camp outside the pueblo while their interpreter explained to the Indians that they were there to trade and to study the Zuñi way of life. Each day the Stevensons set up a trading operation, and each day Hillers took photographs and Cushing took notes on ceremonies and sketched what he saw. The Indians resented the intrusion, especially on their ceremonies, and complained constantly to Cushing. When he could stand their complaints no longer, he moved into the house of the governor, the headman, thinking that might better his relations with them.

The governor, who had not been consulted, was not pleased. His one comment was "Tuh!" (Damn!) when, on being asked how long he planned to stay there, Cushing answered two months. That evening Cushing tried to build a fire to cook his supper, but "Unsavory fumes rose from my badly burned bacon, and presently the governor's face appeared at one of the openings in the roof. He regarded operations silently a minute, and then vanished. Soon he followed his feet down the ladder, approached the fireplace and without a word shoved me aside. Taking my skillet he marched down to the river. When he returned, every trace of the odious bacon had been removed, and replaced by a liberal quantity of mutton and abundant suet. Poking up the fire, the old fellow dexterously cooked the contents brown. Then, placing skillet and all in the center of the floor, he hastened away, soon to return with a tray of curious paper bread in one hand, while in the other, to my surprise, he held a steaming pot of thoroughly boiled coffee" (Green 1979:63). As the governor climbed back up the ladder he muttered, "Poor fellow!" in Spanish, then reappeared early the next morning to prepare another meal.

Cushing made fair progress in ingratiating himself with the family of the governor's wife, all of whom lived together on the level above Cushing's abode, and gradually he made progress with the other villagers as well. He was, however, still considered as somewhat of a black sheep because of his constant sketching and notetaking. The Indians had also noted some estrangement between Cushing and the rest of the Stevenson party, and it seemed to make them suspicious of him.

When Hillers and the Stevensons made preparations to go on to Moqui to continue their trading, Cushing decided not to accompany them but to further his studies in Zuñi instead. They promised to leave his food supplies with the missionary, but when he inquired for them the missionary told him that nothing had been left.

Dejected he returned to his room. The solicitous governor asked Cushing why he was so sad; and when Cushing explained that his friends had left him nothing, the old chief said, "Little brother, you may be a Washington man, but it seems you are very poor. Now, if you do as we tell you, and will only make up your mind to be a Zuñi, you shall be rich, for you shall have fathers and mothers, brothers and sisters, and the best food in the world. But if you do not do as

we tell you, you will be very, very, very poor indeed" (Green 1979:68). It was not hard for Cushing, in the circumstances, to agree to be a Zuñi, and shortly the governor and his wife appeared with boiled mutton, corncakes mixed with chili, and sliced beef, his first real Zuñi meal.

But there was another side to his life with the Indians. In a letter to Professor Baird of October 29, 1879, he wrote, "Were I to paint you a picture of my daily life here—of my *meals*—you would, I fear, for some days, enjoy yours as little as on all days, does your poor servant his. I am the good Kushie for I take a child, dark with inherited disease, and cleanse and annoint its great sores that they heal. As such, therefore, I am entitled to distinguished courtesy. Hence a woman at a meal picks up from the floor (which is our table) a wooden spoon. It is *not* clean. She therefore wipes it across her moccasin (I do not tell you what that moccasin has repeatedly stepped on today), she draws it along her mantle (which was once white), and bethinking that it is the Good Cushing who is to eat with it, she quickly raises it to her mouth (I will not tell you what that mouth has been used for today—wait till my report comes out) and in a manner most natural and expeditious, cleans (?) and immediately with the most irresistible smile hands it to me" (Cushing 1879). Philosopher that he is, Cushing thinks of it not only in terms of sanitation but as the price of kindness on her part and access to means of satisfying his research needs.

Colonel Stevenson was in charge of this expedition so when he instructed Cushing to send no information east, Cushing felt compelled to comply. After the Stevensons left, Cushing wrote to Baird, alluding to problems with the Stevensons but not saying specifically what they were. It brought a prompt rebuke for not keeping in touch so that Baird might be aware of his problems. He ordered Cushing to write at least weekly from then on. Cushing had been caught between fires, his duty to report to his superior at the Smithsonian—which he had wished to do—and orders from the leader of the expedition not to write and specifically to report nothing about their collections.

Another source of irritation to Cushing was that

Mrs. Stevenson had somehow managed to acquire all the milk and eggs in Zuñi and she refused to share them with anyone.

Cushing had requested an extension of his time in the field, and on their return from the Hopi village the Stevensons brought with them a letter from Baird granting his request.

By this time the governor insisted that Cushing call him his old brother and showed much concern for his well-being and acceptance among the other Indians. When Cushing told his old brother that Washington wanted him to stay among them and write about his children, the Zuñis, and to sketch their dances and dress, the governor was skeptical, wanting to know why Washington should be interested in those things. Cushing explained that it would help stop friction between whites and Indians if they understood the ways of one another. The governor agreed but warned Cushing that he might be in trouble with some of the Indians if he pictured the Ka-ka too much.

After a pause, the old Indian continued, "Well, then, what makes you puff up your face with sad thoughts? Don't you have plenty to eat? When you came here you lived on pig's grease and baked dough, but I threw the light of my favor on you and cooked some mutton. Have you ever had to ask for more? Sister would make all the paper-bread, corn-cakes, and dumplings you could eat, but you will not eat them, and she has grown ashamed. What's the matter anyway? Do you want to see your mother? Pah! Well, you can't, for if Washington says, 'You stay here,' what have you to say? Now go to bed. You had better cut down that hanging bed of strings [his hammock], though, and sleep on a couple of sheepskins, like a man. Some night you will dream of 'Short Nose' [Cushing's mule], and tumble out of that 'rabbit net,' and then Washington will say I killed you. You must wait till 'Teem-sy' [Col. Stevenson] and his beasts [the Mexican cook and drivers] go away, I'll make a man of you then" (Green 1979:78).

A day or two later, Cushing related, "He approached me with a designing look in his eyes, and snatched off my helmet hat and threw it among some rubbish in the corner, producing from behind his back a red silk handkerchief. Folding this carefully, he tied it around his knee, and then placed it on my head. With a remark denoting disgust, he hastily removed it, and disappeared through a blanket-closed door into a quaint mud-plastered little room. After rummaging about for a time, he came out with a long black silken scarf, fringed at either end, which must have belonged once to some Mexican officer. He wound this round and round my head, and tied the ends in a bow-knot at my temple, meanwhile turning his head from side to side critically. Good, Good! There, now, go out and show the Zuñis, then travel down to the camp and show the 'Teem-sy-kwe' [Stevenson people] what a sensible man you are, and how much better an othl-pan is than a mouse-head-shaped hat. The governor also insisted on replacing his 'squeaking foot-packs' [English walking shoes] with red buckskin moccasins" (Green 1979:78–79).

Cushing said he was "heartily ashamed" to walk across the whole pueblo in his "mongrel constume" of blue flannel shirt, corduroy breeches, long canvas leggings, and Zuñi moccasins and headband. The Zuñis approved highly, but the Stevenson crew made fun of him. On returning to the governor's house he asked for the return of his garments, but the governor had disposed of them. His old brother was determined to make a Zuñi of him, and a few days after the Stevenson party left he led Cushing into the little mud-plastered room where he "had unearthed" the black silk headband. "In one corner stood a forge, over which a blanket had been spread. All trappings had been removed, and the floor had been freshly plastered. A little arched fire-place in the corner opposite the forge was aglow with piñon, which lighted even the smoky old rafters and the wattled willow ceiling. Two sheepskins and my few belongings, a jar of water and a wooden poker, were all the furnishings. 'There,' said the governor, 'now you have a little house, what more do you want? Here, take these two blankets,—they are all you can have. If you get cold, take off all your clothes and sleep next to the sheepskins and *think* you are warm, as the Zuñi does. You must sleep in the cold on a hard bed; that will harden your meat. And you must never go to Dust-eye's [the mission], or to Black-beard's [the trader] to eat for I want to make a Zuñi of you. How can I do that if you eat American food?' " (Green 1979:90).

Cushing related that he "suffered immeasurably" that night from cold and from his hard bed, but he told the governor next morning that he had "passed a good night." He insisted on slinging his hammock in his little room, but the governor had other ideas: "It would not be good for it to hang in a smoky room, so I have packed it away" (Green 1979:90).

By November 20 the Stevensons had left to return to the East. They again promised to leave provisions and funds for Cushing but again did not do it. Now Cushing was alone with the Indians. When he told the governor that in another two months he, too, would be returning to Washington, the governor objected, saying, "I guess *not*!" (Green 1979:90). By this time his acceptance was a matter of fact, and he was permitted to observe more and more of their dances and ceremonies, which elated him.

Cushing had become friends with an old Zuñi priest, a frequent visitor of the governor's, who joined the campaign to make a Zuñi of him. He repeatedly insisted that Cushing don full Zuñi costume and have his ears pierced. Cushing resisted, but one day the governor's wife came in with a bundle of dark blue cloth and a long red embroidered belt. Cushing says the bundle of cloth proved to be "a strip of diagonal stuff about five feet long by a yard in width. Through the middle a hole was cut, and to the edges, either side of this hole, were stitched, with brightly colored strips of fabric, a pair of sleeves." She told him to put it on and that his brother would make him a pair of breeches, and "then you will be a handsome young man" (Green 1979:91). He did as he was told, but when the governor entered, the garment came off and was folded and put under the blanket on the forge. Later in the day, the governor returned with a pair of short, thick, black cotton trousers and a pair of long, knitted blue woolen leggings.

The governor instructed him to "Take off that blue coat and rag necklace [his blue flannel shirt and gray silk tie]" and insisted that Cushing re-move his undergarments. He was then told to go over into the corner and don the new trousers and admonished not to wear anything under them. Then the coarse woolen blanket shirt was again put on, this time next to his skin. Discovering that the construction of this shirt was such that it left the sides open a little below the armpits, and the arms down to the elbow exposed, he asked the governor if he could not wear his undercoat. Permission was denied—he was to have his "meat hardened" (Green 1979:92).

Added to this costume was a heavy gray serape, striped with blue and black and fringed with red and blue. Then one of the young men gave him a copper bracelet and the old priest gave him two strings of black stone beads for a necklace. (This is the costume referred to by Mrs. Stevenson [n.d.] in a note on the back of a picture of Cushing in Zuñi dress which reads "Frank Hamilton Cushing in his fantastic dress worn while among the Zuñi Indians. This man was the biggest fool and charlatan I ever knew. He even put his hair up in curl papers every night. How could a man walk weighted down with so much toggery?")

The Zuñis were pleased, Cushing probably less so, but there was nothing he could have done to change it because when he returned to his own room after his first venture into the village in full Zuñi dress, he found that all of his own clothing had disappeared.

Finally he acceded to their demands to have his ears pierced, correctly guessing that there was some reason for their insistence. It was a ceremonial occasion during which he was recommended to the Indian gods as a "son of the Corn People of Earth" and as a "Child of the Sun." He was adopted as a member of the tribe and given his Zuñi name, Te-na-tsa-li, meaning "Medicine Flower," after a magical plant that grew on a single mountain in the West, the many-colored flowers of which were the most beautiful in the world and its roots and juices a panacea for all injuries to human flesh. "That by this name, which only one man in a generation could bear, would I be known, as long as the sun rose and set and smiled on the Corn People of Earth, as a Shi wi (Zuñi)" (Green 1979:93).

Py spring Cushing's health was a major problem. On April 8, 1880, he wrote to Baird that he had "been, during the past six weeks very much prostrated by an attack of lung complaint, brought on by exposure, I presume" (Cushing 1880a). By May 5 he wrote, "I have been for more than two months midway between the bed and my feet, of a pulmonary difficulty from which—although the chances are I may be long in fully recovering—I am certainly rapidly mending. At times I have been unable for two or three days to write anything more than my daily memoranda,—with difficulty, even these—not from suffering, but from general debility. At other times, when better, the Indians have claimed and even compelled, my exclusive attention" (Cushing 1880b). He asked for blue, green, and coral stones for trading with the Indians, stated that he has been living on Zuñi food since January, and asked forgiveness for the poorly written letter (which it was not) because he was writing it at midnight after riding nearly a hundred miles over mountain country in two days.

On July 18, 1880, he wrote another long letter to Baird: "Although my exile here, save for the ethnologic interest which it still has for me—would, from the superstitious character of the natives, the desert character of the country and the absence of all vegetable substance from my diet, as well as the stale character of the flesh, and utter flatulency of most Zuñi cereal preparations—be absolutely unendurable. Yet I am gratified more than I can say with the decision which both yourself and Major Powell have reached regarding my case" (Cushing 1880c). He was again asking for more time in the field, this time adding another aspect to his pleas: "Another consideration of weight is that, should I come to the very close atmosphere of Washington during the warm season, from the extremely elevated region that I am now inhabiting (8,000 to 9,000 feet) it would, I fear, especially in my present weak condition, result very unfavorably for my constitution" (Cushing 1880c).

All the while he suffered constantly from poor food and the intense cold of the winters. He had inadequate clothing and blankets and no way to get more. Then another blow fell. He learned that Mrs. Stevenson, upon returning to Washington,

had been writing articles about the Zuñi for the popular press, scooping his scientific reports and robbing him of some of the reward of his work. His biggest worry was about the effect such publications would have on his relations with the Zuñi when they learned of it, but at least he felt relieved of his obligations to live up to Colonel Stevenson's instructions not to send information east for publication.

He showed a remarkably understanding and forgiving nature when, in reporting to Baird that he had been left with but twenty dollars and had been forced to sell his own rations for needed supplies, he implied that perhaps the Stevensons merely were short of funds and under pressure of expedition problems.

It is remarkable that one of such frail health ever survived to return to Washington. There were times when he was not sure he would. One such time when he was lost for days, afoot, in the mountains in a blizzard, he wrote a note to Baird, leaving it with a prospector with instructions that if he did not return in two weeks he could be considered lost and please notify his friends and family.

By this time the Zuñis were talking openly with him, and he began to learn of their secret societies. The most powerful one was the Priests of the Bow, so Cushing decided to seek admission to this group in order to learn everything he could about the Zuñis. Since he had been adopted into the tribe, his relations with them were good enough to make this move possible.

The price was high; for over two years he endured periods of fasting and much overexposure resulting in frequent chest colds, sometimes forcing him to bed for days or weeks at a time. He witnessed countless ordeals without showing the revulsion he sometimes felt. He faced threats without flinching, knowing that any other reaction would considerably lessen his chances of gaining the admission he sought.

On October 29, 1879, he described his life among the Zuñi to Baird: "I live among them, I eat their food, and sleep in their houses. Because I will unhesitatingly plunge my hand in common with their dusty ones and dirtier children's into a great kind of hot, miscellaneous food; will sit close to them having neither vermin nor disease, will fondle and talk sweet Indian to their bright eyed little babies; will wear the blanket and tie the panier around my long hair, will look with reverence on their beautiful and ancient ceremonies, and never laugh at any absurd observance, they love me, and I learn. On account of this, the women name me Cushie K'ok-shi Ku-shi Tihi Nima (the good Cushing, the sweet Cushing) and the speakers of the dance call me (in Zuñi of course) the little Captain Cuzique. But do not fancy that this is all lightly purchased. Were I to paint you the picture of my daily life, *of my meals* [Cushing's emphasis], you would for some time enjoy yours as little as your poor servant does his" (Cushing 1879). "My living is simply horrible, unmentionable. I thought I couldn't bear too lightly on that subject last autumn; but the spring living of the Zuñis I'd better not mention at all. Until now (July 18) no green thing has appeared in all this valley" (Cushing 1880d). A few days later he wrote:

The rains have at last come, and since the dying away of the sandstorms my health has been on the gain constantly—although I continue to lose flesh very fast. And the only actual depression I ever suffer from is when I see my health failing, and sometimes recognize my inability to fill the time properly with work.

I can sum up in one sentence what my life here has been—physically, so far as the appetites are concerned, paralysis; socially, exile; ethically, theoretically, a feast, a peace of mind unapproached in all my previous experience.

And as to results—probable impaired health during life; a strengthening and development of moral character in *every respect*, and aside from a more practical and cosmopolitan view of humanity and its institutions, I hope and pray (tho sometimes dubiously) that it will make *a worker* of me. (Cushing 1880e)

By July 22, he wrote, "I have been very ill, but tonight finds me better than for many weeks." He asked for books he needed, *Hakluyt's voyages*, volumes 1 and 3, a Spanish dictionary, and Davis's

Conquest of New Mexico, which was very important to him. He continued, "Colonel Stevenson has a copy . . . which he promised to send me last winter, but which he must have forgotten about. If they can't be borrowed, purchase them at any price. In case of my death or indebtedness, they are all works of great rarity and value, standard, and therefore essential to complete the anthropologic series of the Bureau" (Cushing 1880f).

He was a long time recovering. On August 19, he wrote again to Baird, "My health continues, however, to be poor, although not critical—the trouble being principally a very slow but obstinate one with the lungs. I began a few days since to drink whiskey; but finding it of no use, gave it up. I am however, very much better able to attend to my duties now than during the spring" (Cushing 1880g). Ten days later in his letter, again to Baird, he reported, "I have little to communicate in this note save that I am usually well, and of course still making progress in my research, especially in the language" (Cushing 1880h).

His frequent illnesses were a matter of concern to his old friend George Kennan, who wrote on August 23, 1880, "What you tell me about your health alarms me very much. I heard through Joe that you had been sick but I did not understand that it was anything serious and the idea that you have contracted any dangerous disease comes to me with a painful shock. . . . All the facts you could gather would be dearly purchased with a life so dear to your friends and so full of promise to science as yours. . . . You are more absolutely free from all kind of petty meannesses than any person I ever knew with the exception of my wife" (Kennan 1880).

By the end of 1880, Smithsonian officials, having asked him to do special chores for them, such as collecting ornithological specimens and taking a census, satisfied that he was doing a good job of his major assignment as well as those special requests, were content to let him remain in the field as long as he cared to stay. Baird and Powell tried valiantly to supply him with the trade goods he needed and made special efforts to supply the blue beads and green stones most wanted by the Zuñis. Somehow the Stevensons managed to cause a problem there too. They were responsible for Cushing receiving a shipment of imitation turquoise and beads made of wax which melted around the Indians' necks, causing him embarrassment and problems.

As usual, he had money problems. On January 25, 1881, Cushing wrote to Baird, "I am very much reduced in means. The expenditure of the following sums having left me at date, with *one dollar* ($1.00) on hand for emergencies. Bill with trading store $53.00, cost of cave trip . . . $65.00, purchase of commissaries, ammunition and specimens, $20, $5.00, and $7.00 respectively. Will you therefore kindly ask Mr. Rhees to forward me as much as can be conveniently spared, *at once?* as I dislike either to borrow, or to get things on credit" (Cushing 1881a).

Later that year, there was another problem. During his stay in Zuñi, Cushing carried on detailed studies of all aspects of Zuñi life, keeping notes for the detailed reports he expected to write after his studies were concluded. Some of his reports were not reaching Washington, including one of fifty pages on the Zuñi language and numeration and another of some thirty-seven pages. Enough reports were lost to lead Cushing to speculate that perhaps someone on the Washington end might be keeping his reports from Major Powell. At least once, when Dr. Washington Matthews visited from Ft. Wingate, Cushing sent a report with him which Dr. Matthews sent along as his own to Powell. Unfortunately, all of his reports and correspondence were written by hand, making that the only copy.

On June 11, 1881, Cushing wrote to Powell from Zuñi:

I believe you are aware that I am now almost thoroughly familiar with the Zuñi tongue, have been for more than a year an adopted member of the tribe, and of one of the gentes (the latter not, however, to be confirmed until marriage) and one of the head chiefs of the nation . . . .

Learning through a letter to Mrs. and Dr. Matthews, from Lt. Witherspoon of the Department of Arizona, that a cavalry expedition with Dr. Coues as naturalist, left his post five or six

days since for the country of the Kuh-nis; and facilitated by a kind and voluntary advance of money by Dr. Matthews I am making rapid preparations to set out with some of my Indians as interpreters, across the Moqui Desert— in order to secure priority of description and pure results, for the Bureau, and myself. (Cushing 1881b)

He must have done a truly remarkable job, because the Bureau of American Ethnology Annual Report for 1881–82 states that during the four days Cushing was able to pass among these people, he collected a vocabulary of more than four hundred words, recorded some of the myths of the tribe, and succeeded in securing valuable notes regarding the manners, customs, industries, and religion of these people.

In spite of the difficulty of travel and remoteness of his location, Cushing did occasionally have visitors. Sylvester Baxter, a reporter for the *Boston Herald*, wrote Baird on August 3, 1881, "I have just returned from a trip to New Mexico where I had the pleasure of meeting Mr. Frank H. Cushing, of the nature and importance of whose work I wrote an account for the *Herald*. I hope I shall have the pleasure of meeting you while you are in New England. You would probably be interested to hear personally about Cushing from one who has learned to admire him not only for his masterly scientific methods but stirling qualities as a man" (Baxter 1881).

During his stay in Zuñi, Cushing made occasional visits to Ft. Wingate. It was a source of both pleasure and pain. Most of the time he was at least accepted by the officers, with a few he was even popular, and there were other times when he felt an outcast, mostly because of his Indian dress for which the soldiers sometimes ridiculed him. On one trip to the fort he met John G. Bourke, an officer who was to become an admiring friend for life.

Late in the summer of 1881, Cushing got an idea that sounded out of character. He wrote Bourke that "last night" he had "decided to seek an appointment as Second Lieutenant in the U.S. Army. . . . In brief, I wish to enter the army that I may cultivate arms as a profession, and science as a recreation and love." He asked Bourke's opinion of this decision (Cushing 1881c).

As odd as this idea seems, we can follow Cushing's probable reasoning. It was not unusual at that time for army officers to carry on archaeological and ethnological fieldwork. The army was often in the vanguard of those in contact with the aboriginal American population, and many of them made valuable contributions to the fledgling science. They did so while on active military duty, receiving leave for the fieldwork but remaining on the army's payroll. Cushing had perpetual money problems and chafed under the paperwork required by the government officials in a scientific environment such as the Bureau of Ethnology and the Smithsonian. These army officers were more or less free to carry on any way they chose within the limits of the length of their leave.

Cushing's friend apparently forwarded his application for a commission directly to General Philip H. Sheridan, who endorsed it and sent it along. The general replied to Bourke on June 8, 1882, "I had your note about Cushing's application which I endorsed days ago. I sincerely hope he will get his appointment. He will make a clever nice young officer with plenty of ability and a speciality which will with his industry do credit to the service" (Sheridan 1882).

Somewhere higher up, his application was denied. On June 30, 1884, Bourke wrote to Cushing, "I am afraid to say too much lest you doubt my sincerity; but in all truth, assert that to withdraw you from your chosen field of labor among the Zuñis will shortly prove to have been a grievous blunder and a great loss to ethnological science. . . . If you have no other means of livelihood, let me suggest that you return to New Mexico, get the Zuñis to point out to you some good cattle-ranch outside their reservation, but near enough so that you can have their protection and they your counsels. New York and Boston capitalists are now eager to back up just such men as you. You may, possibly, be taken up and encouraged by the Ethnological Bureau. I hardly expect that. Your attainments are too solid and too varied. A congregation of penny-dips will not be disposed to let an electric light enter among them.

You know that I have always distrusted those people and that in our conversations long ago we both concluded not to lean upon them too much. I believe that they were at the bottom of your failure to get a commission" (Bourke 1884).

During 1881, Cushing was invited to join the Bearers of the Bow. He completed most of the many initiation rituals on his own, though the cost may have been personally or psychologically high. One requirement was more than he could bring himself to handle alone—that he acquire three scalps, preferably Apache. He appealed to his father and a Dr. Yarrow, each of whom furnished him with one. It is not known how he obtained the third one, but he did it somehow on his own in the company of Indians. All he reported to Baird (on September 24, 1881) was, "As I informed you in my letter dated Ft. Whipple, 8/25, I left that post on the 4th day following, reaching Zuñi on the 16th instant, after a severe journey—four days of it through country raided by Apaches. This matter, far from being disastrous, enabled me to secure a scalp, which with ones furnished by my father and Dr. Yarrow, enabled me to get a hearing in the secret council" (Cushing 1881d).

During his time in Zuñi Cushing had changed from an ethnologist collecting material to one collecting ethnological data. He wrote to Baird on December 4, 1881:

Having, during the past two years turned my attention almost exclusively to the acquisition of facts, to a great extent, the avidity for gathering *material*, which characterized the earlier years of my acquaintance with you; . . .

My progress is most happy in the study of the Zuñi inner life. Being now a Pithlan-shi-wa-ni or Priest of the Bow, I am secured the privileges of this strictly exotic society, as well as entrance into any meetings of, though not for the present, membership in all the other secret, medicine, or sacred orders of the tribe. I bent all my energies toward this supreme order of the Zuñis, for more than a year, and my success in gaining admission to it, is the greatest of all the achievements of my life perhaps; for it breaks down the last shadow of objection to my gaining knowledge of the sacred rites, not only of this, but of the Moqui tribes and others as well.

Were it not for my membership in this order, the day of my ruin would now be at hand, through the interference of the missionary here. And it now becomes my duty—an unpleasant one—to inform you of some recent relations with him, and to ask you to determine his standing, etc.

He went on to state that *all* published about the Zuñis is either a direct or indirect emanation from his own researches (Cushing 1881e). Again he mentioned money: "Ere long I shall be in need of some money." He wanted silver sent to him at Ft. Wingate and continued, "My expenses for subsistence alone during the presence of Colonel Stevenson and his party was more than ninety dollars ($90.00) as I had to be free with my commissaries, toward one who is, I have reason to believe, now, entirely well disposed toward me" (Cushing 1881f).

On December 24, he elaborated on his problems with the missionary: "I shall continue, nevertheless, to execute my duties as a chief among the Zuñis and as a 'Priest of the Bow' with the recently added rank of Warrior of the Cacique (or Priest) of the House, and in case Mr. Bentley, as Acting Agent, sees fit to interfere, I shall call his attention to the treaty which I now have in my possession, between the U.S. and the people of Zuñi, which recognizes the 'rights and authority of the chiefs and headmen of Zuñi.' In case that gentleman still persists, I shall either follow his own doctrine, and disfigure his cadaverous countenance, or else use my influence with the Indians, openly, yet legitimately, against him" (Cushing 1881g).

More money problems arose. On January 3, 1882 he again wrote to Baird:

I wrote, some time since, a letter to Mr. Graham, the trader here, acknowledging the correctness of his account of more than two years standing with me,—which he informs me he forwarded, according to instructions from Colonel Stevenson, to Major Powell.

As no reply has been received to this communication, I write to ask if you will look into the matter. It is not an unimportant one, as it concerns very vitally my reputation. Had I imagined there would be any trouble in the settlement of this and other bills which Colonel Stevenson authorized me to make, more than two and a half years since, I should not have made them. This, and the bill of Mr. Hopkins, which have been made almost exclusively in the prosecution of my researches in Zuñi, all matter of a private nature save a very few items having been settled for immediately and charged to myself.

I also wrote some time since for some money which I said I would need very soon, but none has thus far come, and I have been compelled to borrow in order to get along.

The expenses of my work at Zuñi may, at times, seem large, to Major Powell and yourself, but the *results also* are large, larger than I can say or you can realize, as I hope you may come to know ere long.

And in the end, if these results seem to you not what I have represented them to be, I shall be glad to reclaim them, and bear from my own salary as I am enabled to do the expenses I underwent in securing them; doubting not that, with the material I have already on hand, to say nought of that which I am daily amassing, I shall be able to reimburse myself.

I am quite sure, however, that such will not prove to be the case, and meanwhile I beg the hearty support of the Institution and Bureau.

My work in Zuñi, while voluntary, is *not* a pleasure, nor is it for *myself*. It is for the Smithsonian Institution and the Bureau of Ethnology; and I have never responded to the many tempting and liberal offers I have had for even the roughest press notes, nor have I willingly given the smallest scrap of information to representatives of the press. The various notices of my work which you may have seen have been unavoidable and have been ingeniously gathered either from my friends or from my unconscious conversations; or else enthusiastic acquaintances, in their kind zeal to aid and please me, have published them personally, from their own observations. I have never, either morally or in the matter of etiquette once forgotten my honor, in my relationships with you and Major Powell. (Cushing 1882a)

In October 1881, he had written to his superiors asking permission to come east and bring four or five Indians to Washington:

With this view, I have begun negotiations for securing free passage for myself and party via Omaha and Chicago. Some excellent connections which I have made during the past two years, will, I think, render this easy. Some of my enthusiastic friends in the two cities mentioned will aid me strongly; and the ladies of Boston have extended cordial invitations to me, to bring my party on, if not to Boston, as far east as New York and Washington, promising their aid, etc.; also I wish to make this move principally to advance my future work in Zuñi, as the Indians have for each day, more than a year, spoken of this, begging that I should bring it to pass. They wish to see my great Cacique's house; see what we will do with their things, and if, in the end, they prove satisfied, they promise to furnish me a series of their sacred costumes for the dances, etc., than which nothing can be more interesting, beautiful or valuable for an ethnographic museum. Inasmuch as after the new sun festivities and ceremonials, nothing save the night Ka-kas,—which I have faithfully seen for two seasons—occurs during the months of January, February, March and April I have hoped I might remain in Washington during those months, retaining my brother, the head chief, working with him on the dictionary and grammar, and a part of the ethnography getting together material for the final work in Zuñi of collecting and observing and finally returning.

Through the promised aid of Col. Stevenson and my friends the completion of this scheme would not involve great expense, would be the last remaining policy stroke with the Indians, and, according to the Colonel, would aid immensely in popularizing—not more mine than

his own part of the ethnographic work. (Cushing 1881e)

He received no answer. In January 1882, he renewed his request. By now the Indians had heard much about Washington and, looking upon it as a person rather than a place, somewhat in the vein of a superchief of Cushing's tribe, their curiosity increased with their friendship. In reply, he was instructed to obtain an estimate of the cost to bring two Indians, a male and a female.

Cushing reminded them that "When we first arrived at the pueblo, Colonel and Mrs. Stevenson encouraged the head men to believe that some of them would, through your agency, be enabled sooner or later to go to the Eastern country;—a matter they have ever since held me responsible for." He continued, "I would find it difficult to induce two Indians alone, to come to Washington; first, for reasons of their own, and secondly, because they are detained by the chiefs and caciques; who are determined to accompany me themselves."

Besides, he said, the railroad had promised passes for "a group" of Indians and would not grant them for only two since it would lessen the public relations value to the railroad. He wrote that it would not cost more than $500 for the whole party, and if the bureau could not afford it, couldn't it *lend* the money to him? He also had a desperate personal reason for making the trip. The Zuñis, who had tried previously to get him to marry Zuñi girls, had given Cushing notice that he had to choose between making the trip east with them or of marrying a Zuñi squaw. He would pay for the trip himself if the Smithsonian would not or could not, he said (Cushing 1882a).

In the end, Cushing brought six Indians, but once again Mrs. Stevenson managed to get into his act. She managed to see to it that one of the Indians to come east in the group was a Hopi rainmaker who had been adopted by the Zuñis, an Indian she knew. We can only guess at her motives.

The Indians toured Washington and Boston and Chicago along the way. While in Washington, Cushing spent much time over his reports at the

Smithsonian. Baird, anxious to record all he could while Cushing was there, wrote a note to Powell on April 25, 1882: "It has occurred to me that you will be most likely to get out of Mr. Cushing what he has learned in regard to the Zuñis by making some arrangements for the use of a phonographer for a few weeks in taking down what he has yet to say on the subject. He is primed with important facts and many desired generalizations and conclusions; but, like many persons, he is a little constipated and requires loosening, so as to effect a proper discharge. I saw him last night and he was anxious that I should speak to you on this much-by-him-desired subject. His best plan, I think, is to evolve paragraphs in regard to what he knows on any point without regard to order and then, when they are written up, they can be systematized. Should he have to go away, or should anything happen to prevent *his* doing this, the notes will still be on hand for elaboration" (Baird 1882a).

During his stay in Washington, Cushing introduced his Zuñi friends to Miss Emily Magill. The Indians wanted him to marry her right away, and he did so in July before returning to the West. In late July, Cushing was again ill and confined to bed for a time. On July 24, he wrote to Pilling, "I have been suffering during the past three weeks intermittently with a difficulty of the bowels. Toward the latter portion of last week this difficulty became more aggravated and constant. Last night it entirely prostrated me and I find myself today unable either to visit the Bureau or to work" (Cushing 1882b).

In preparation for his return to the west, Cushing wrote a long letter to Baird,

I have the honor to inform you that my work in Washington is now so nearly completed as to render my departure with my Indians for Zuñi advisable and possible.

Under existing rules of the BAE and the Treasury Administration, it became impossible for the Director to refund the expenditures made by me during the years of 1879 to the present inclusive. I am therefore greatly in need of an advance of money which shall enable me to make purchases and preparations

for a continued residence in Zuñi, of at least three years. In the anticipation of some funds which shall be placed at my disposal by the Century and Atlantic magazines some time during the autumn months, in payment for articles already written for and accepted by those magazines. I make bold to ask that the Institution aid me if convenient, by the advancement of $225, which I promise to refund on or before the end of November 1882.

By causing such assistance to be extended to me, you will not only confer upon me a personal obligation of great weight, but also, enable me the sooner to resume my already much neglected researches in Zuñi.

His last request was that he be assigned a stenographer to go with him to Zuñi if they can afford it, and he made suggestions as to who might be available and suitable for the position (Cushing 1882c).

Apparently Baird thought Cushing had a good idea because he passed the suggestion along to Powell the same day: "I wish to place before you for careful consideration the matter of assistance to be rendered Mr. Cushing in his further work among the Zuñis. In view of his peculiar characteristics it would be well, I think, to give him the services of an assistant, who could serve as a stenographer, especially for the purpose of taking down the Indian myths. The period of Mr. Cushing's stay among the Indians is quite uncertain, and I have no doubt that the aid recommended would materially increase results even for a single year.... Mr. Cushing informs me that he can secure the services of such a man for about $60 a month. I think that his own salary should be increased to $100 per month" (Baird 1882b). Before leaving the East, Cushing, his wife, and the Indians went to his boyhood home in New York, visiting the nearby Seneca tribe. While there, Cushing and his Zuñi guests were all adopted into the Seneca tribe. When, having rested his sick Indians, Cushing left for the West on September 12, 1882, he was accompanied by his new bride and her sister, Margaret. They arrived at Ft. Wingate on September 19.

During the summer of 1882, while Cushing

was in the East, Senator John Logan and his son-in-law, Major Tucker, visited Zuñi. Whether intentionally or accidentally, they sought to check up on Cushing by questioning the Indians. Their interpreter was incompetent, understanding but little of the Zuñi tongue. They concluded, on the basis of what they learned in this way, that Cushing was an impostor, labeled him such to the Zuñis, and determined that they would expose him to his superiors.

Enter Colonel Stevenson again: On December 12, 1882 he wrote to Baird, "I beg to call your attention to a conversation I had a few days since with Senator Logan, in which he referred to an article which had been shown him, from the Boston *Herald* of a recent date, post marked Zuñi, New Mexico, severely criticizing him as a United States Senator. The Senator stated that he believed it was written, or instigated by Cushing of the Bureau of Ethnology. Senator Logan seemed to be so incensed that I have deemed it proper to call your attention to the matter. I assured Senator Logan that the fact had never come to your attention, and that you did not allow anything of the kind to occur" (Stevenson 1882). On his return from an expedition to Oraibi, Cushing received a letter from Baird asking for explanation of the Logan matter. Cushing promptly denied any knowledge or responsibility in the affair.

The previous October, during a visit to Cushing at Zuñi, Powell had ordered him to proceed with J. Stanley Brown as soon as possible to Oraibi to take charge of a party for the collection of ethnological material for the Bureau and the United States National Museum. On November 5 he set out for Moqui, a trip that took nine days. While detained by a snowstorm at Walpi, he met an adopted Oraibi who offered to make arrangements for them. In Moqui they met objections to their collecting and were ordered to leave before daylight on pain of death if they refused. He, as well as his interpreters and accompanying Zuñi chiefs, were insulted and maltreated. All of the latter fled, but Cushing stood up to them, and during the four days he managed to stay in Moqui to wait for the wagons he succeeded in secretly collecting some two hundred pieces. He did make extensive collections in Oraibi during the

three weeks he spent there. On the return trip to Zuñi he was once more detained by snowstorms along the way.

Soon after his return to Zuñi on January 31, 1883, he was kicked in the thigh by a mule and so disabled that he was confined to his room. Later, as a result of exposure during the return from Moqui, he succumbed to influenza; pneumonia threatened, and he was confined to bed until the end of February. During his recuperation he worked on correspondence and research notes. He also had a visitor, Adolph Bandalier of Boston.

Some time later there were reports in the East of army officers claiming land around Las Nutrias Springs, traditionally Zuñi land, and implicating Logan and Tucker. An error in the original survey setting apart the reservation was discovered and corrected. Logan was sure Cushing was responsible for their loss of the claim and threatened to have funds for the Bureau of Ethnology cut off by Congress unless Cushing was recalled to Washington immediately. Baird asked Cushing for a statement on the matter; Cushing promptly and emphatically denied that he had had anything to do with it and upheld the Zuñi right to land held by the tribe for centuries. The matter was not finally settled until 1885 when all claims on Zuñi land were canceled. Cushing was not recalled.

Another person who tried to have Cushing removed from Zuñi was the Presbyterian missionary schoolteacher at Zuñi who complained that Cushing encouraged the Zuñis in their pagan ways. His efforts were equally unsuccessful.

Problems of a smaller nature also came his way. Lieutenant Witherspoon had written Baird accusing Cushing of losing a mule. When Baird asked for an explanation, Cushing replied, "The mule in question, was neither lost nor injured during my trip. It was required by Captain Bourke for recovery of stray ambulance mules. It was lost at Las Nutrias by a Private of the 13th Infantry during the search" (Cushing 1883a). Bourke gave him an affidavit to this effect, but it apparently did not reach Washington so, when the snow would permit, Cushing would go to Ft. Wingate to get another. Somewhat later Cushing reported to Baird that he had learned at Ft.

Wingate that the man who lost the mule was then a military prisoner at Ft. Leavenworth, Kansas. He got affidavits from this man and from Bourke, but he had temporarily lost his own and would send it along as soon as he found it.

Money problems were constant. Cushing was not able to repay the $225 loan by the end of November as he had promised because he had not been paid for the magazine articles. He suggested to Baird that he keep Cushing's December pay as part payment but that he would need January's pay. By February 3, 1883, he wrote again to Powell, "I find, somewhat to my disconcertion, that neither my expense of travel from Washington to Zuñi last summer—nor my pay account for November, December, and January have been settled. I hope you will see that the matter is attended to at once, as I am at present entirely without means" (Cushing 1883b).

He did not make rapid recovery from his illnesses. In March he complained of "almost constant illness from a pulmonary difficulty which has at times shut off even my lighter correspondence and reading" (Cushing 1883c).

Another of Cushing's ideas was to become postmaster at Zuñi. There was no post office closer than Ft. Wingate, and the government decided eventually that one was not needed at Zuñi. By the time the government reached that decision, Cushing had already decided he didn't want the job anyway.

Emily tried her best to make an attractive home for her husband, but she never really liked having given up her comfortable home in Washington for the adobe walls of Zuñi. Her sister's reaction was the opposite; she enjoyed life there and entered into it wholeheartedly. As Cushing was often sick, Emily wrote to his superiors to explain why he was again delinquent in his reports and government forms. Emily was ill too and had a miscarriage. Finally, probably at the instigation of his Washington superiors, Cushing was visited by Dr. Matthews from Ft. Wingate, who diagnosed Cushing's difficulties as the result of poor food and unhealthful surroundings.

On May 1, 1883, on advice of Dr. Matthews, Cushing left Zuñi for a short trip of exploration, eight to fourteen days, to the southwest. It was an effort to restore his health. He would make a hasty reconnaissance of several ruins and localities mentioned in Zuñi traditions. He would take one or two Zuñi Indians with him and pay for the trip himself. He reported discovery of what he termed fissure ruins varying from a few hundred yards to half a mile in length.

Once again he asked for money, this time repayment for horses hired from the Zuñis. One of his horses had gotten sick en route from Moqui to Zuñi; he had to leave it behind, and it was later missing. He paid $65 to its Zuñi owner. An interesting note dated July 1, 1883, and signed "J.D. McC" reads, "Don't see how we can reimburse Mr. C. the value of this horse *$65.00*—but can pay him for hire of animal which he charges for in his expense acct. *52 days hire of a horse @ 75c/ per day $39.00*. Congress alone can afford relief to claimant" (Anonymous 1883).

Because of his illnesses, Cushing decided that if he were to finish his researches in Zuñi he would have to have better housing. On August 20, 1883, he wrote to Powell that at the approach of cold weather he must abandon the better portion of the house he was occupying for two reasons: the Indians' increase in family meant they needed it because their present quarters were inadequate for cold weather, and Dr. Matthews said his ill health was due to water-poisoning and the unhealthfulness of his quarters. He received no answer to his request to add a room to his quarters but proceeded to build anyway. His room became quite a large building costing more than $1,000 (Cushing 1883d).

Cushing's friend E. H. Horsford in Cambridge, Massachusetts, was becoming concerned about Cushing's health. On November 19, 1883, he wrote to Powell:

I enclose to you a letter recently received from Mr. Cushing. I am moved to this in part, and very largely, I may say, in the interest of your department of Ethnology, in which I have from the outset, and indeed from the date of my early acquaintance with Lewis H. Morgan, permitted my sympathies to take very deep root.

From Bandelier I have learned, as well as

from Cushing and others, of the immense amount of material Cushing has accumulated —the value of it, properly digested and put into form for preservation must be very great. In its present condition if he were to turn it over to others, it could not fail to lose very greatly. It would be substantially a loss and a loss that in all human probability, could never be regained.

I am afraid we are in danger of losing it!

Cushing has repeatedly written me of his terrible suffering from *dyspepsia*. In his letter I see a little of the martyr spirit which alarms me. We cannot afford to indulge in such sacrifice.

With this preliminary, I ask you to read his letter and judge whether it does not show that he is in a condition requiring his immediate call home—first to his home in the East for a rest, and then for systematic writing up his work—and then if later—he feels like resuming it—you will promise whatever you deem wise.

If it be necessary for someone to advance a little aid for this purpose—assuming of course that you act on my suggestion, having seen with your other means of judging that I am justified of the facts in making it—draw on me for $250 without hesitation. I do not care to be known in this matter to anyone. I have no scheme of notoriety at all.

I remember how Nicholai's vast accumulations were lost to science—*30 years* of work among the Indians—simply because he put off the day of writing. I know in my own case how great a mistake I made in delaying to write up my papers.

Now if I have made a mistake in coming to you rather than to Dr. Baird, be kind enough to lay the matter before him.

I will thank you to return me Mr. Cushing's letter when you have read it. (Horsford 1883)

By early 1884, perhaps influenced some by Horsford's letter, Cushing's superiors at the Smithsonian reached a decision. Baird was ill, so on January 19, on Baird's instructions, Chief Clerk James C. Pilling wrote to Cushing:

It is thought best that the valuable ethnologic material collected by you at the Pueblo of Zuñi should be put in shape for publication at as early a day as practicable and that progress to this end would be facilitated by your presence for a time in the East. As soon, therefore, as you can settle your affairs at Zuñi, and make the necessary arrangements, not later than February 15th, if possible—you will proceed to Washington and report to the Director.

Passes for three (3) over the A&P and AT&SF railroads will be sent you at an early day; also transportation orders from Kansas City to Washington, via St. Louis. Such shipments that you may have to make as will admit of delay, can be sent through the Quartermaster's Department. Your manuscripts, however, it is thought wise to trust to the custody of the express company. By order of the Director. (Pilling 1884)

By January 29, 1884, when Cushing had been building his house for four months, he heard indirectly that Powell did not disapprove but that the department might not pay for it. The cost overrun of the project compelled Cushing to do his own carpentry. Now he had been two weeks in his new home and already his health was improved. So far his house had cost $697. He still owed $75 for freight, $275 for lumber, windows, doors, and fittings, $37 for labor, $35 for paving stones, a total of $412. He added, in reporting this to Powell, that he would have to pay these expenses before leaving Zuñi (Cushing 1884), and ended rather sadly, "I regret that by building (under the impression that I could *monograph* Zuñi and live to do it!) I made a mistake. The error has, however, been committed! and alas! I am compelled to write you as I do. If the above considerations seem either uncalled for or insubordinate, I beg earnestly you will forgive the liberty I have taken in submitting them, bear with and support me during the necessary preparations and correspondence accompanying my final withdrawal from the services of the government, and accept as heartfelt, my profound gratitude for the many kindnesses and opportunity I have received at your hands" (Cushing 1884).

On March 30, he received the passes and drafts for his return to Washington. His leaving was delayed by heavy rains and again by illness, but Cushing, his wife, and her sister finally left Zuñi on April 26, 1884. His Indian friends were sad because they did not think they would ever see him again.

Cushing took sick leave on returning to Washington and did not report to his desk at the Smithsonian until early June. By then he was getting a great deal of public recognition and was doing considerable speaking.

The first half of 1885 was spent in alternating periods of illness and work. He did much writing and was reminded by his superiors that he still had not written the report on his early work in Virginia. By summer he was ill once again and spent the summer in Barre Center recuperating and trying to devise means of bringing two Zuñis east to help with the writing of the dictionary and grammar. From Barre Center he went, under the care of a new physician, to Long Island for treatment and further recuperation. On October 31, 1885 from Prospect Grove, Shelter Island, Suffolk County, New York, he wrote Powell:

I have written you no fewer than three letters since your return from the Southwest, in vain effort to express moderately, yet adequately, my thanks for your repeated kindnesses. . . .

I do thank you for authorizing the advancement of my salary when I so much needed its augmentation—yet was so little able to earn it, for allowing me the long vacation I also needed so much—yet also gave so little promise of speedily making good return for; and for doing all you have to facilitate the bringing East of the Zuñi Indians. . . .

Doubtless not a little of my hesitation has been due to the embarrassing thought that I had not, after all these months, gained sufficiently in health to be enabled to lay before you more substantial proof of my appreciation, in the form of work well done. . . .

Withal, I am glad to tell you I have at last

gained somewhat. I am physically stronger, certainly; and attacks of my illness resulting in faintness and mental prostration are far less frequent lately, and of shorter duration with each recurrence. I therefore hope yet to be worth something during the winter.

The kindness of my most noble friend, Professor Horsford, has been delicate and constant. He has spared neither means nor pains to get me in working order again. I mention this here because my obligations to you and to him are identical. They mean work, or weight.

He then went on to suggest means for bringing the Zuñis east (Cushing 1885).

By Christmas he had been transferred to the care of a Boston specialist, further extending his sick leave which was already almost six months. During the early part of 1886 he was back again at his writing. That summer he and his wife were invited to spend some time at the Maine summer home of Mrs. Augustus Hemenway, an invitation they eagerly accepted.

Cushing quickly saw Mrs. Hemenway as a potential sponsor for further expeditions into the field and carefully cultivated her for the purpose. She was an avid listener, and he gladly supplied her with information. It was not long until she agreed to sponsor an archaeological expedition to the Southwest.

Cushing was ecstatic as he set about preparations. He easily secured the necessary permission from his superiors and put together an impressive staff, including Charles A. Garlick, a topographical engineer who would be field manager; Frederick Webb Hodge of the Smithsonian Institution staff, who would be his field secretary and personal assistant; Herman F. C. ten Kate, a noted anthropologist, who would join him later; and Emily and her sister, Margaret, who would go as curators of artifacts. In December, accompanied by the three Indians brought east as tourists by Cushing's brother Enos during the summer, the party left with the blessings and cooperation of the Bureau of American Ethnology.

In February 1887, Camp Hemenway was established in the Salado Valley. Cushing was excited by the number and extent of the sites there to excavate.

By summer he was ill again, very ill. He was unable to work and finally consented to travel to the West Coast to recuperate. On October 27, Charles Garlick wrote to him in San Francisco, "Am sorry to hear your trip has not benefited you to the extent hoped for. And greatly sympathize with you in having to suffer one relapse after another" (Garlick 1887). After some months in San Diego and San Francisco he returned in better health and worked hard until the summer of 1888, when he again fell ill. By October, he had decided that he must return to Washington for hospitalization and treatment for an indefinite period. Hodge was to manage the expedition in his absence. As usual, rumors were rampant. Cushing wrote to J. Walter Fewkes on May 10, 1889, from Garfield Hospital, referring to "those who supposed he was down in Washington 'playing sick'" (Cushing 1889).

By the summer of 1889, Mrs. Hemenway was becoming concerned about the expedition because Cushing's ill health was compelling him to be so long absent from the field. Since she had developed considerable confidence in Walter Fewkes by this time and trusted his judgment, she asked him to travel to the Southwest to check on the state of the expedition and report to her. He was dismayed by what he found and recommended to Mrs. Hemenway that either the expedition be reorganized or disbanded altogether. She decided that it should be reorganized under the direction of Fewkes.

By this time Cushing had been absent from the expedition for some months, and Hodge had been left in charge. At some time Cushing became dissatisfied with Hodge's performance; in a letter to Charles Garlick on November 20, 1896, he says, "And I know very well that until Mr. Hodge was offended by my deposition of himself for failing to send in accounts, and my placing of yourself in charge, such ideas never entered even his mind, foolish and resentful as it has ever since been" (Cushing 1896). These things may have played a part in the controversy that was to haunt Cushing the rest of his days.

In letters to Mr. and Mrs. Cushing during 1889, Garlick often expressed his concern over Cushing's health. On May 15 he wrote, "While I am very sorry to hear of Mr. Cushing's continued illness I am very glad to hear from you. I know, Dearheart, you must be very much worn out with your duties by the sick bed" (Garlick 1889a). Later, when Cushing was despondent over his replacement as director of the expedition, he wrote, "I am very sorry to hear Mr. Cushing takes the breaking up of the expedition so much to heart" (Garlick 1889b).

During 1890, Cushing was still sick and despondent most of the time. He accomplished some writing, but he was discouraged because so much of the time he was not well enough to do anything. But by the early months of 1891 he improved enough to work again on the Zuñi manuscripts.

He apparently lived any way he could. A note in the Bureau of Ethnology files commented on Cushing's work: "It will be remembered that an indefinite leave of absence, *without pay*, [author's emphasis] was granted to Mr. Cushing in December, 1886, in order that he might organize and conduct the important exploration in Southern Arizona and the Zuñi country, of the Southwestern Archaeological Expedition, established by Mrs. Hemenway of Boston.... His successful fulfillment of this work was, however, suddenly interrupted, in the winter of 1889, by a severe and prostrating illness which continued disabling until the summer of 1897" (Anonymous n.d.c). It would seem that neither his salary from the Bureau nor that from Mrs. Hemenway had been resumed. He spent much time as a guest of one friend or another, moving from place to place as he had been wont to do before. A memo from one E. T. Coann dated July 16, 1891, read, "Cushing has been a very sick man for two or three years and for the last year or more a good portion of the time an inmate of my family—By assiduous care he has become convalescent and for six or eight months able to do a fair but limited amount of work.... Having lost the whole of his personal investment in the [Hemenway] expedition (not an inconsiderable sum) left with impaired health and without a dollar or means of support, in common humanity—if not in common honesty—should he be required to assume this labor with no arrangement for means for his current support?" (Coann 1891).

By 1892, Cushing was back working full time on his reports, and some of them had been published. In 1893, he made the acquaintance of Stewart Culin of the Museum of the University of Pennsylvania, a friendship that would prove important to Cushing. The years 1894 and early 1895 produced a great deal of writing and publishing. Cushing was still hard at work on his Zuñi materials.

He had been denied access to any of the materials he had recovered on the Hemenway expedition, and he became embroiled in another controversy over one of the artifacts. Charges were brought that he had fabricated a jeweled toad with intent to defraud authorities and the public by passing it off as a genuine antique. Hodge, by this time married to Margaret Magill, Cushing's wife's sister, made the original accusation.

Cushing, still plagued by ill health, was now under the care of Dr. William Pepper, a physician who was also president of the Archaeology Department of the University of Pennsylvania in Philadelphia. Cushing was traveling there for consultation and treatment, making one such trip in April 1895. Once again his poor health guided the hand of fate, this time to send him on to Marco Island.

6

A JOURNEY

OF

EXPLORATION

TWO EARLY TOURISTS to the Naples area were catalysts in the Marco drama: Charles Wilkins of Rochester, New York, and C. D. Durnford, a lieutenant colonel in the British Army, both coming to Florida's mangrove coast to fish for tarpon.

Early in the spring of 1895, while digging the rich organic muck to fertilize the island's sand and shell soil where he grew orange trees, Captain W. D. Collier accidentally dug up strands of fiber which he thought at first were rootlets. Then he saw more fibers and, on closer examination, concluded they were twine of some sort. His continued digging produced a beautifully shaped and highly polished ladle or cup made from shell, followed by a curious block of wood, sliced in two by his shovel, that he decided was an article made by human hands.

At about the same time, Colonel Durnford had organized a small group of men to explore the mounds and canals in the Naples area. Charles Wilkins was one of them. When Wilkins sailed to Marco in search of tarpon, he heard of Collier's recent finds. He asked to see them, became quite excited over them, and made a small excavation near where Collier had made his discoveries. In a short time he had unearthed two cups cut from conch shell, several wooden cups of various sizes, one hollow, openmouthed animal head of wood, bones of fish and various animals, fragments of pottery, a post or maul, what he thought to be a necklace of fish bones in a cup, several shell tools (two with wooden handles), one bone gouge (or chisel or oyster knife), several sinkers of shell and stone, one carved wooden board, and one wooden pin (probably a float peg) (Wilkins, cited in Durnford 1895).

Wilkins rushed back to Naples to show Colonel Durnford what he had found. Durnford, accompanied by his wife, immediately set out for Marco. He made a small excavation as near as possible to the spot where Collier had made the first discoveries, and in a short time he too had uncovered some amazing things: a wooden trencher, oval, with carved handles, measuring ten by eighteen inches, extremely well made; a "clam shell funnel"; netting of three-ply cord varying in thickness from three-sixteenths to one inch in diameter; a series of twenty to thirty float pegs joined with twine at about one-foot intervals; small, well-made pieces of board with holes drilled in them; and more netting with about a two-inch mesh (Durnford 1895).

The colonel was cautious and not yet willing to state unequivocally that these things belonged to a much earlier day, but he was sufficiently convinced of it to take his finds with him when he left the Naples area. En route to England in April, he and his wife stopped in Philadelphia to call on Mr. Henry Mercer, curator of the American section of the Archaeological Department of the Museum of the University of Pennsylvania, whom he had met a year or two earlier in southern Europe. Mr. Mercer was not in, but Stewart Culin, the director, heard Durnford's story. That same day, Cushing, who was on sick leave from the Bureau of Ethnology, was at the museum paying a call on Dr. William Pepper, president of the Archaeological Department and Cushing's personal physician. Thus Cushing heard the account of Durnford's and Wilkins's finds, and later that evening he and Dr. Pepper visited the Durnfords in their room at the Bellevue Hotel to inspect the articles themselves.

Mercer would have been the logical person to pursue any investigation of the area that produced these articles, but he was loathe to leave Philadelphia because of other pressing work there. His health having improved, Cushing eagerly volunteered, and he was given consent by the director of the bureau, Major J. W. Powell.

On April 22, 1895, Dr. Pepper had written to Powell reporting that Cushing "is in a very serious condition of health" and that he regarded it as "quite certain that he would break down permanently unless he secures radical relief by strict scientific treatment without delay. Nothing but extraordinary will power and constitutional tenacity would have enabled him to work under the wretched conditions of digestion during the past ten years." Once again it was hoped that a change of climate might produce improvement (Pepper 1895a). After Cushing was granted leave from the bureau, Dr. Pepper made the necessary

arrangements for the preliminary survey of the Marco area, including the necessary funding as well as transportation passes all the way to Punta Gorda.

Less than a fortnight after leaving New York, Cushing found himself at "the little town of Punta Gorda, near the mouth of the Pease River, a deep tidal inlet, on the gulfward side" of the state. The journey had not been as simple as it had sounded. He had reached Jacksonville on May 24, 1895, and proceeded up the St. Johns River to Sanford; there he boarded the train to take him "diagonally down through the pine lands and the tropic lowlands of Florida" (Cushing 1897:329) (see map). For some reason he was unable to go the entire distance to Punta Gorda by rail even though it had become the railhead two years previously. His letter to Pepper upon arrival there on May 26 began, "I am writing to you after having ridden thirty miles in the saddle" (Cushing 1895b).

There were no roads and no railroads to take him on the last leg of his journey. He would have to find a boat of some kind to reach Marco. He had thought to ride the mail boat but changed his mind and instead hired the little sloop *Florida*, her owner, Captain Smith, and his man named Thomas Parkerson, so that he might be able to explore along the way on some of these drowned lands belonging to Disston. Cushing left Punta Gorda at 7:30 P.M. on May 28 on "the little fishing sloop and sailed one glorious evening late in May" (Cushing 1897:331), intending to explore as many as possible of the islands and capes of Charlotte Harbor, Pine Island Sound, Caloosa Bay, and the lower, more open coast as far as Marco, ninety miles southward. On May 29 he made his first exploration on Cashio Key, the "very first encountered of these thicket-bound islets," and he described it in some detail:

> After wading ankle deep in the slimy and muddy shoals, and then alternately clambering and floundering for a long distance among the wide-reaching interlocked roots of the mangroves—held hip-high above the green weedy tide-wash by myriad ruddy fingers, bended like the legs of centipedes—I

dimly beheld, in the somber depths of this sunless jungle of the waters, a long, nearly straight, but ruinous embankment of piled-up conch shells. Beyond it were to be seen... other banks, less high, not always regular, but forming a maze of distinct enclosures of various sizes and outlines, nearly all of them open a little at either end or at opposite sides, as if for outlet and inlet.

Threading this zone of boggy bins, and leading in toward a more central point, were here and there open ways like channels. They were formed by parallel ridges of shells, increasing in height toward the interior, until at last they merged into a steep, somewhat extended bench, also of shells, and flat on the top like a platform. Here, of course, at the foot of the platform, the channel ended, in a slightly broadened cove like a landing place; but a graded depression or pathway ascended from it and crossed this bench or platform, leading to and in turn climbing over, or rather through, another and higher platform a slight distance beyond. In places off to the side on either hand were still more of these platforms, rising terrace-like, but very irregularly, from the enclosures below to the foundations of great, level-topped mounds, which, like worn-out, elongated and truncated pyramids, loftily and imposingly crowned the whole, some of them to a height of nearly thirty feet above the encircling sea.

All this was not by any means plain at first. Except for mere patches a few feet in width, here and there along the steepest slopes, these elevations, and especially the terraces and platforms above the first series, were almost completely shrouded from view under not only a stunted forest of mulberry, papaya, mastich, iron-wood, button-wood, laurel, live oak and other gnarly kinds of trees, mostly evergreen, and all over-run and bound fast together from top to bottom by leafy, tough, and thorny vines, and thong-like clinging creepers, but also by a rank tangle below, of grasses, weeds, brambles, cacti, bristling Spanish bayonets and huge spike-leaved century plants, their tall sere flower stalks of former years standing bare and aslant, like spars of storm-beached shipping above this tumultuous sea of verdure.

The utmost heights were, in places, freer; but even there, grew weeds and creepers and bushes, not a few, and overtopping them all, some of the most fantastic of trees—the trees 'par excellence' of the heights of these ancient keys, the so-called gumbo-limbos or West Indian Birches—bare, skinny, livid, monstrous and crooked of limb, and, compared with surrounding growth, gigantic. To the topmost branches of these weird-looking trees, brilliant red grosbeaks came and went as I climbed. Long ere I saw them, I could hear them trilling, in plaintive flute-like strains, to mates in far away trees, perhaps on other groups of mounds—whence at least answers like faint echoes of these nearer songs came lonesomely back as though across void hollows.

The bare patches along the ascents to the mounds were, like the ridges below, built up wholly of shells, great conch-shells chiefly, blackened by exposure for ages; and ringing like thin potsherds when disturbed even by the light feet of the raccoons and little dusky brown rabbits that now and then scuttled across them from covert to covert and that seemed to be, with the ever-present grosbeaks above, and with many lizards and some few rattlesnakes and other reptiles below, the principal dwellers on these lonely keys—if swarming insects may be left unnamed!

But everywhere else it was necessary to cut and tear the way step by step. Wherever thus revealed, the surface below, like the bare spaces themselves, proved to be also of shells, smaller or much broken on the levels and gentler slopes, and mingled with scant black mold on the wider terraces, as though these had been formed with a view to cultivation and supplied with soil from the rich muck beds below. Here also occurred occasional potsherds and many worn valves of gigantic clams and whorls of huge univalves that appeared to have been used as hoes and picks or other digging tools, and this again suggested the idea that at least the wider terraces—many of which proved to be not level, but filled with basin-shaped depressions or bordered by retaining walls—had been used as garden plats, some, perhaps, as drainage basins. But the margins of these, whether raised or not, and the edges of even the lesser terraces, the sides of the graded ways leading up to or through them, and especially the slopes of the greater mounds, were all of unmixed shell, in which, as on the barren patches, enormous nearly equal-sized whelks or conch shells prevailed.

Such various features, seen one by one, impressed me more and more forcibly, as indicating general design—a structural origin of at least the enormous accumulations of shell I was so slowly and painfully traversing, if not, indeed, of the entire key or islet. Still, my mind was not, perhaps, wholly disabused of the prevalent opinion that these and like accumulations on capes of the neighboring mainland were primarily stupendous shell heaps, chiefly the undisturbed refuse remaining from ages of intermittent aboriginal occupation, until I had scaled the topmost of the platforms. Then I could see that the vast pile on which I stood, and of which the terraces I had climbed were, in a sense, irregular stages formed in reality a single, prodigious elbow-shaped foundation, crowned at its bend by a definite group of lofty, narrow and elongated mounds, that stretched fan-like across its summit like the thumb and four fingers of a mighty outspread hand. Beyond, moreover, were other great foundations, bearing aloft still other groups of mounds, their declivities thickly overgrown, but their summits betokened by the bare branches of gumbo limbos, whence had come, no doubt, the lone-sounding songs of the grosbeaks. They stood, these other foundations, like the sundered ramparts of some vast and ruined fortress along one side and across the farther end of a deep open space or quadrangular court more than an acre in extent, level and as closely covered with mangroves and other tidal growths at the bottom as were the outer swamps. It was apparent that this had actually been a central court of some kind, had probably been formed as an open lagoon by the gradual upbuilding on attol-like reefs or shoals

around deeper water, of these foundations or ramparts as I have called them, from even below tide level to their present imposing height. At any rate they were divided from one another by deep narrow gaps that appeared as though left open between them to serve as channels, and that still, although filled now with peaty deposits and rank vegetation, communicated with the outer swamps, and, in some cases, extended, between parallel banks of shell like those already described, quite through the surrounding enclosures or lesser courts, to what had evidently been, ere the universal sand shoals had formed and mangrove swamps had grown, the open sea.

The elevation I had ascended, stood at the northern end and formed one corner of this great inner court, the slope to which from the base of the mounds was unbroken by terraces, and sheer. But like the steepest ascents outside, it was composed of large weather-darkened conch-shells and was comparatively bare of vegetation. Directly down the middle of this wide incline led, from between the two first mounds, a broad sunken pathway, very deep here near the summit, as was the opposite and similarly graded way I had in part followed up, but gradually diminishing in depth as it approached the bottom, in such manner as to render much gentler the descent to the edge of the swamp. Here numerous pierced busycon shells lay strewn about and others could be seen protruding from the marginal muck. A glance sufficed to show that they had all been designed for tool heads, hafted similarly, but used for quite various purposes. The long columellae of some were battered as if they had once been employed as hammers or picks, while others were sharpened to chisel or gouge-like points and edges. Here, too, sherds of pottery were much more abundant than even on the upper terraces. This struck me as especially significant, and I ventured forth a little way over the yielding quagmire and dug between the sprawling mangrove fingers as deeply as I could with only a stick, into the water-soaked muck. Similarly worked shells and sherds of pottery, intermingled with char-

coal and bones, were thus revealed. These were surprisingly fresh, not as though washed into the place from above, but as though they had fallen and lodged where I found them, and had been covered with water ever since.

I suddenly realized that the place, although a central rather than a marginal court or filled-up bayou, was nevertheless similar in general character to the one Colonel Durnford had described, and that thus soon my conclusions relative to the typical nature of the Collier deposit, were, in a measure borne out. Here at least had been a water court, around the margins of which, it would seem, places of abode whence these remains had been derived—houses rather than landings—had clustered, here it became choked with debris and vegetal growth; or else it was a veritable haven of ancient wharves and pile-dwellings, safe alike from tidal wave and hurricane within these gigantic ramparts of shell, where through the channel gateways to the sea, canoes might readily come and go. (Cushing 1897a:331–35)

The following day, May 30, Cushing and the crew of his sloop explored three more sites. The first was Josslyn's Key:

It had been cleared and cultivated as a fruit and vegetable garden many years before, but was now abandoned and desolate and again overrun by brambles and weeds and vines, with some few massive gumbo limbos and rubber trees standing on its heights. . . .

Near the mouth of the principal canal, leading forth from the southeastern corner of this court, and still invaded, as were two or three others of the canals, by high-tide water, my skipper and I dug a deep square hole. The excavation rapidly filled with water; not, however, before we had found in the yielding muck a shapely plummet or pendant of coral-stone and two others of shell, many sherds of pottery, worked bones, charcoal, and, more significant than all, a pierced conch-shell, still containing a portion of its rotten wooden handle. Again here, the relics were more abundant than on the heights above, and the structural nature of the entire key was abundantly evident. (Cushing 1897a:337)

The same day, a little over a mile away, he explored Demorey's Key, which he found remarkable:

It also had been cleared to a limited extent, by the man whose name it bore, but, like the first, had long been abandoned and was even more overgrown by vine-smothered trees and brambles—among them many pitiful limes and a few pomegranates run wild, but still faithfully bearing fruit—so that here, too, the knife was constantly requisite.

It was in some respects the most remarkable key encountered during the entire reconnaissance. Its elevations formed an elongated curve five hundred yards in length, the northward extension of which was nearly straight, the southward extension bending around like a hook to the southeast and east, and embracing within its ample circuit a wide swamp thickly overgrown with high mangroves, which also narrowly fringed the outer shore, so that the whole key, when seen from the water, presented the appearance of a trim round or oval, and thickly wooded island. The lower end or point of this key consisted of an imposingly massive and symmetrical sea wall, of conch-shells chiefly, ten or twelve feet high, and as level and broad on top as a turnpike. This wall had evidently once encircled the entire lower bend of the key, but was now merged in the

second and third of a series of broad, comparatively level terraces, that rose one above the other within it, from a little terminal muck-court westwardly to the central and widest, although not highest, elevation of the key, at the commencement of its northward extension. Occupying a point midway along the inner curve of this elevation, that is, directly up from the mangrove swamp it encircled on the one hand, and from the terraces outside on the other, stood a lofty group of five elongated mounds. These mounds were divided from the embracing terraces by a long, deep, and very regularly graded way, which led, in straight sections corresponding to the inner margins of the first three successive terraces, up from a canal formed by shell banks or ridges in the swamp, to the highest of the terraces—the one forming the wide central elevation. Another and much steeper and shorter graded way led up from yet another parallel canal farther within the swamp, to this longer graded way near the point of its ascent to the high central terrace. This foundation, for it proved to be such, arose very steeply from the here sharply curved edge of the mangrove swamp, to an almost uniform height of about twenty-three feet; was from twelve to fourteen yards wide, and thence sloped more gently toward the outer or western shores. The northern extension of the key was occupied by two or three elevated and comparatively inconsiderable mounds, beyond which it was terraced off toward the extreme point, as was the lower point—though less regularly—to a short, similar sea-wall extension eastwardly, that partly enclosed, not a muck-court, but a low, bordered garden-plat, containing two or three round sinks or basins.

The most remarkable feature of this key was a flat, elongated bench, or truncated pyramid, that crowned the middle elevation. I discovered this merely by accident. In order to gain a general idea of the key, which was almost as much overgrown with luxuriant and forbidding vegetation as had been the wilder key first explored, I climbed high up among the skinny and crooked limbs of the gigantic gumbo-limbo that grew directly from the inner edge of this elevation. Luckily, great festoons of tough vines clung to the lower limbs of this tree, for in shifting my position I slipped and fell, was caught by these vines, to the salvation of my bones probably, since by the force of the fall some of the vines were torn away, revealing the inner side of this platform and the fact that it was almost vertically faced up with conch-shells; their larger, truncated and spiral ends, laid outward and in courses so regular, that the effect was of a mural mosaic of volutes. I hastily tore away more of the vines, and found that this faced-up edge of the platform extended many feet in either direction from the old gumbo-limbo. I may say here, that on occasion of two later visits I cleared the facade of this primitive example of shell architecture still more; was enabled, indeed, when I last visited the place—since I was then accompanied by a consider-able force of workmen—to entirely expose its inner side and its southern end. Thus was re-vealed a parallelogrammic and level platform, some three and a half feet high and twelve yards in width, by nearly thrice as many in length. It was approached from the inner side by a graded way that led obliquely along the curved ascent up from the mangrove swamp, to a little step-like subsidiary platform half as high and some twelve feet square, which joined it at right angles. . . . The top of this lesser step, and the approaches to either side of it, were paved with very large, uniform-sized clam-shells, laid convex sides upward, and as closely and regularly as tiles. The lower or southern end of the main platform was rounded at the corners, and rounded also on either side of the sunken ascent midway, in which the longer of the graded ways I have de-scribed terminated. Contemplating the regular-ity of this work, its central position, and its evi-dent importance as indicated by the several graded ways leading to it from distant points, I could not doubt that it had formed the foun-dation of an imposing temple-structure, and this idea was further carried out by the pres-ence at its northern end of two small, but quite prominent altar-like mounds.

Descending from the end of the platform down along the main graded way—the one which divided the terraces from the central group of high mounds—I found that at more than one point, the sides of this deep, regular path, had also been faced up with conch-shells, though none of the courses were now, to any extent, in place.

At the foot of the inner and parallel sided, sunken or graded way—the one descend-ing from between two of the great central mounds—I caused an excavation to be made between the two straight banks or ridges of shell that extended thence far out into the man-grove swamp, in order to ascertain whether this supposed canal had really been such; that is, an open way or channel to the sea for ca-noes. It became evident that it had been this, for we were able to excavate through vegetal muck and other accumulated debris to a depth of more than four feet, although much incon-venienced by inflowing water. I thus found that the shell banks had not only been built up with a considerable degree of regularity, but that, well defined as these ridges were, the portions of them visible above the muck were merely their crests. The excavation was made near what may thus be regarded as having formed the original landing, and in it we found a con-siderable number of well-preserved relics, similar to those I had found in the court on Josslyn's Key. Another excavation made near the termination of the two embankments, how-ever, revealed fewer artificial remains, other than blackened and water-worn sherds of pot-tery. But I found that here also, the artificial banks or walls, so to call them, had been built up with equal regularity, almost vertically, from a depth of between four and five feet. In ex-tending this excavation an interesting feature of the original foundations of these out-works was revealed. It consisted of a kind of shell breccia formed of the first layers of shells that had been placed there—that were composed of conchs, some of which had been driven or wedged, smaller ends first, into the original reef or bar, and had apparently been further solidified by a filling or packing in of tough clay-like marl, now so indurated that shell, sherds of pottery, and here and there bits of bone and charcoal formed, with it, a solid mass well progressed toward fossilization. Indeed, when large fragments of this time-hardened cement were pried up and broken open, the shell, sherds of pottery and bones contained in them appeared already like fossils. I found by making yet other excavations in the contiguous and almost untraceable courts or enclosures, that they, too, had been built up from an equal depth, as though to serve rather as fish pounds than as breakwaters or as courts to the quays and houses, for the crests of these enclosures so slightly protruded above the surface of the muck and weedy carpeting of the mangrove swamp in which they occurred, that I had at first quite failed to observe them. Thus it appeared that this half-enclosed swamp, no less than the swamps surrounding the first key I had examined, contained similar sorts of enclosures, only these had been lower originally, or else had since been more filled in with muck, vegetal growth and tide-wash. The low-bordered terrace or garden plot, the margin of which faced this swamp within the northern end of the key, was wide and comparatively level, except that in one or two places toward the slopes of the terraces next above it, there occurred in it the circular holes I have mentioned as basins, one of which looked almost like a well. The like of these I later encountered on many others of the keys, and they seemed to be catch-basins for rain or places for water storage, artificial cenotes, as it were, like the spring-holes or sinkholes on the mainland and in Yucatan. (Cushing 1897a:337–40).

Cushing's third exploration on May 30 was at Battey's Landing on Pine Island; he

approached by wading a long way, for the tide was low. And as we neared it we were greeted by the barking of a small colony of hounds and other dogs. A solitary man appeared, who occupied one of the two small huts that stood some way up from the shore. His name was Kirk, and he was most hospitable and helpful to me. He and his partner, Captain Rhodes, worked the place as a vegetable farm, and were now again most profitably cultivating its ancient gardens. . . . The foundations, mounds, courts, graded ways and canals here were greater, and some of them even more regular, than any I had yet seen. On the hither or seaward side many enclosures, overgrown of course by mangroves, flanked wide benches or garden platforms through or over which led paths, mostly obliterated by cultivation now. The same sorts of terraces and great foundations, with their coronets of gigantic mounds. The inner or central courts were enormous, nearly level with the swamps on the one hand, and with the sand flats on the other, these muck-beds were sufficiently extensive to serve (having been cleared and drained as far as possible) as rich and ample gardens; and they were framed in, so to say, by quadrangles formed by great shell structures which, foundation terraces, summit-mounds and all, towered above them to a height of more than sixty feet.

There were no fewer than nine of these greater foundations, and within or among them no fewer than five large, more or less rectangular courts; and, beyond all, to the southward, was a long series of lesser benches, courts and enclosures, merging off into scarce visible fragments in the white, bare stretches of sand flats. Suffice it, if I say, that this settlement had an average width of a quarter of a mile, and extended along the shore of Pine Island—that is from north to south—more than three-quarters of a mile; that its high-built portions alone, including of course, the five water courts, covered an area of not less than seventy-five or eighty acres. (Cushing 1897a: 341–42)

He traced the great canal for more than a mile, and although it narrowed he found it traceable beyond that narrowing and was told that it extended completely across the island to similar works and shell elevations on the other side.

Cushing said he learned later that the canal and

mounds on Naples Island were not unlike these, although smaller, and that equally gigantic works occurred far up the great rivers of the coast, as far up as the Caloosahatchee, Lake Okeechobee, and the Everglades.

From Battey's Landing, Cushing proceeded down the sound to St. James City on the southern end of Pine Island, arriving there on May 31. He carried a letter of introduction from Colonel J. M. Kreamer of Philadelphia to Captain E. Whiteside, the most prominent resident of St. James City. Captain Whiteside welcomed him hospitably and offered any help he might be able to give.

Cushing explored the extreme southeastern point of Pine Island as well as the southwestern point where he found a "single long and throughout the lower portions of its course, double-crested shell embankment, from four to nine feet high . . . more than 3500 feet in length" (Cushing 1897a:344). At both places he found shell ridges and structures comparable to those described earlier. From the structures on the southwestern point Captain Whiteside had removed great quantities of shell to construct a boulevard around the southern end of the island and crossroads through the marshy space it enclosed, altogether several miles of road, and had not exhausted the shell heap in doing so.

A third exploration was made on one of the inner marginal reefs of Sanybel (Sanibel) Island where he found well-defined structures similar to those discovered on other keys. He found also what he considered to be almost unmistakably the outer coating or plastering of a temple or some other kind of large building on one of the flat terraces or mounds.

Further exploration was carried out at another location on the northeast side of Sanibel Island, a place called Ellis' Bay. Here Cushing had heard that a few days previously Captain Ellis, the long-time resident of the place, had found some human bones near his quaint palmetto huts on its southern shore. On visiting Ellis' Bay, Cushing found thatched houses irregularly set on the low, flat stretch of sand, amid clumps of native palmettos and luxuriant groves of lime, orange, and other tropical fruits; Captain Ellis offered hospitality and aid to Cushing during his hasty excava-

tion. The surface of the large mound there was under cultivation, and it was in an effort to remove tree roots that Captain Ellis had dislodged the bones. Excavating nearby, Cushing found the whole mound to be permeated with human bones and succeeded in carrying away eleven whole skulls, leaving behind great quantities of broken skulls and other bones.

After leaving Ellis' Bay, Cushing explored Charlotte Harbor, Pine Island Sound, Caloosa Entrance, and Matlatcha Bay, and he discovered more than seventy-five additional sites, forty of which he described as gigantic.

From there he decided to sail the open Gulf to Key Marco because he felt he did not have time for further explorations along the way. He did stop on June 2 at Mound Key (or Johnson's Key, as it was also known), which he found to be extensive. His diary for June 2 reads, "Explored Mound Key. (Frank Johnson living there) took 5–6 photos, Johnson gave maul, plummets, 3 great groups of mounds, one 60' high, 100' × 75–80', truncated, canals and lagoons, sand burial mound to east, 'distinct canoe-ways and canals' some relics—shell sinkers, stone—including pot sherds—trials at photos. Spanish remains abundant" (Cushing 1895a).

Cushing later described Mound Key in some detail in his paper to the Philosophical Society:

It consisted of a long series of enormous elevations crowned by imposing mounds, that reached an average altitude of over sixty feet. They were interspersed with deep inner courts, and widely surrounded with enclosures that were threaded by broad, far-reaching canals, so that this one key included an area of quite two hundred acres, within which area may be reckoned only such surface as had been actually reclaimed by the ancient key builders from this inland or shore-land sea. I was told by Mrs. Johnson, wife of the owner of the place, to whom good Mrs. Ellis had kindly given me a characteristic letter of introduction, that burial mounds, not unlike the one on the Ellis place, but larger, occurred in the depths of the wide mangrove swamps that lay below to-

Pl. 1. Early house (possibly the Collier house) on Key Marco (watercolor by Wells Sawyer).

Pl. 2. The mangrove shore of Key Marco (watercolor by Wells Sawyer).

Pl. 3. Area of excavations on Key Marco (watercolor by Wells Sawyer).

Pl. 4. Frank Hamilton Cushing aboard the *Silver Spray* (watercolor by Wells Sawyer).

Pl. 5. Wells Sawyer and other illustrators of the Edward Everett Hayden U.S. Geological Survey Expedition in 1896, after the expedition to Key Marco. Sawyer is second from the left in the back row. Photo courtesy Smithsonian Institution.

Pl. 6. Wells Sawyer at his easel, date unknown. Wells M. Sawyer Papers, P. K. Yonge Library of Florida History, University of Florida.

Pl. 7. Excavators at the Key Marco site (watercolor by Wells Sawyer).

Pl. 8. George Hudson, the expedition's cook (watercolor by Wells Sawyer).

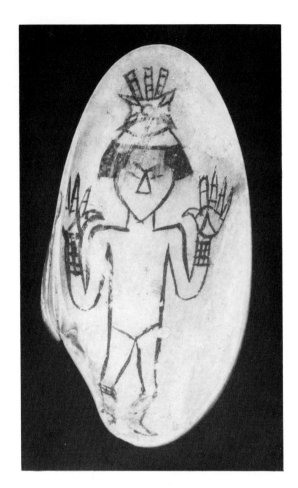

Pl. 9. The controversial painted figure in a shell. Documents and statements from members of the expedition strongly support its authenticity. Photo courtesy University Museum, University of Pennsylvania (negative number 88350).

Pl. 10. Wells Sawyer's photograph of the expedition's camp at Hope Mound. He probably sent a copy of this print to his family. Photo courtesy Smithsonian Institution.

Pl. 11. Carved wooden feline figure, 15 cm high. The original is in the collections of the National Museum of Natural History, Smithsonian Institution (catalogue number 240915). Photograph courtesy Smithsonian Institution.

Pl. 12. Wells Sawyer's photograph of the wharf and docks at St. James City, Pine Island, Florida. Photo courtesy Smithsonian Institution.

Pl. 13. Wells Sawyer's photograph of a grove of coconut palms as seen from Key Marco. The building is unidentified. Photo courtesy Smithsonian Institution.

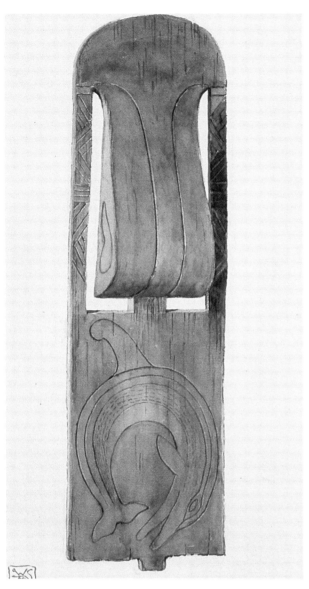

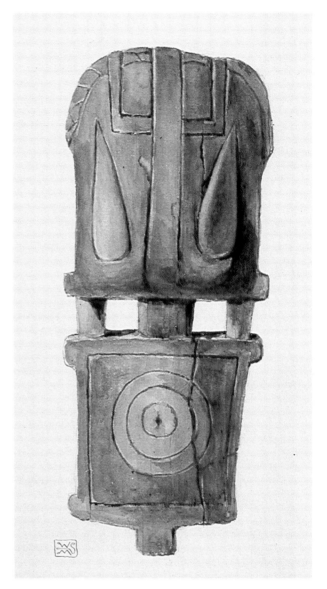

Pl. 14. Wooden tablet or amulet with a dolphin on the lower portion. The cross section of the upper part is in the shape of the head of a spoonbill duck. After excavation, the amulet decayed badly. Wells Sawyer's watercolor (shown here) is the only visual record of it. Only two fragments from this tablet and one shown in plate 15 remain; the largest is about 10 cm long. Both are in the collections of the Florida Museum of Natural History (catalogue number 40682). Painting courtesy Smithsonian Institution.

Pl. 15. A second wooden tablet or amulet carved with a spider motif identical to that found on metal specimens from other South Florida archaeological sites. Like the dolphin tablet, the specimen rapidly decayed after it was removed from the muck, but Sawyer painted this watercolor before it deteriorated. Painting courtesy Smithsonian Institution.

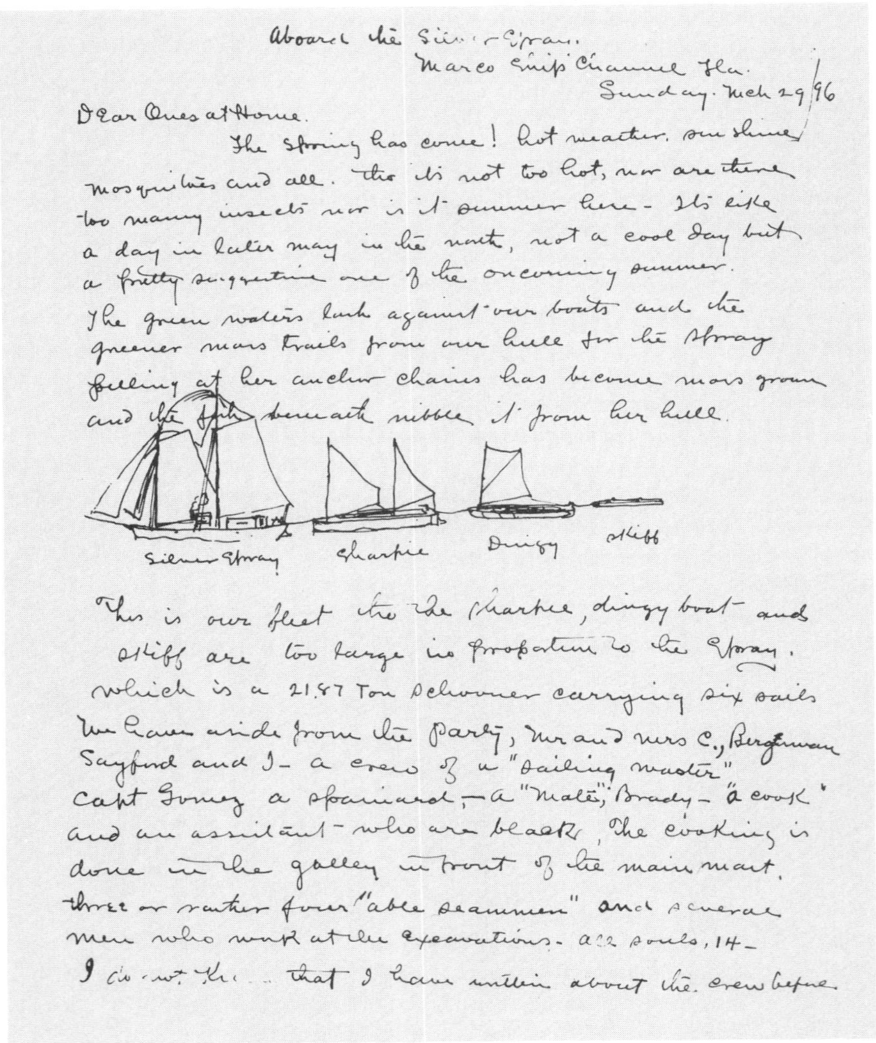

Pl. 16. Wells Sawyer's letter of March 29, 1896, to "Dear Ones at Home" (Sawyer 1896d). Original letter is written on both sides of a sheet from a writing tablet. Wells M. Sawyer Papers, P. K. Yonge Library of Florida History, University of Florida.

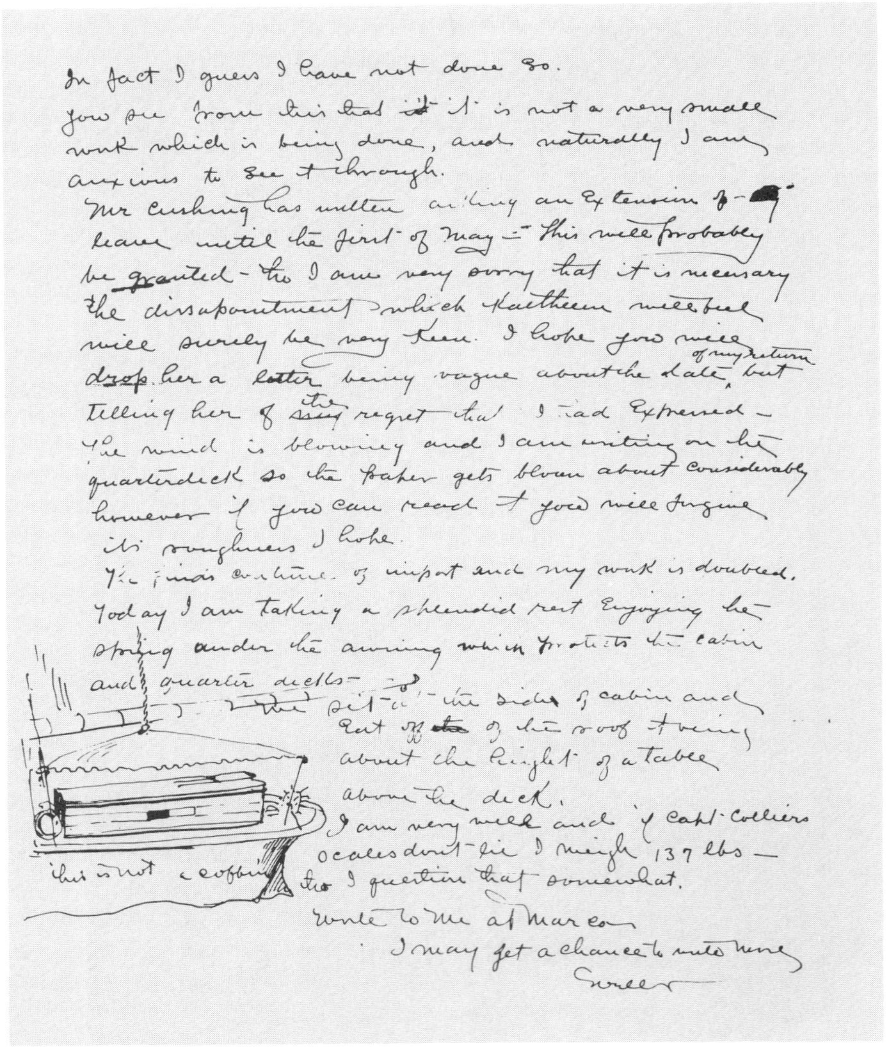

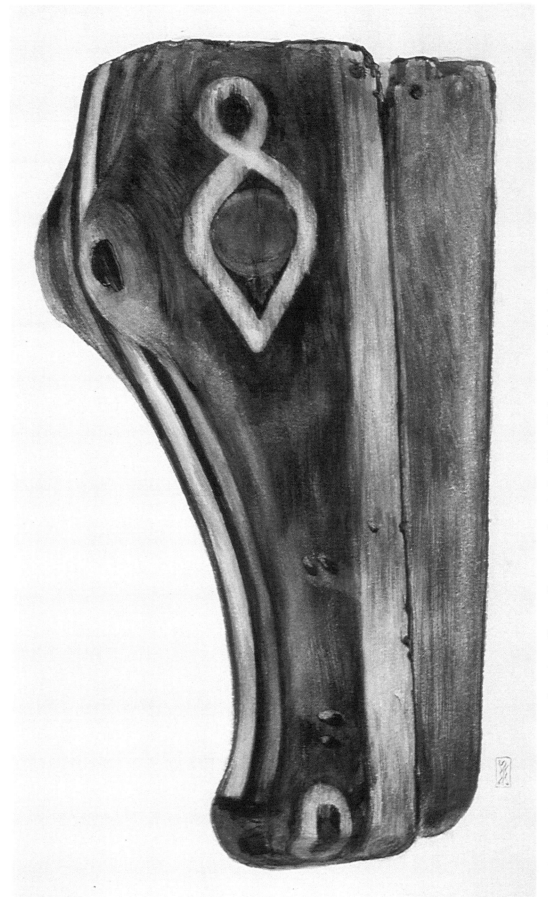

Pl. 17. Wells Sawyer's watercolor of an alligator figurine with articulated jaws. Today only the black pigment can be seen. Lower jaw is 24 cm long. Original in University Museum, University of Pennsylvania (catalogue number 40718). Painting courtesy Smithsonian Institution.

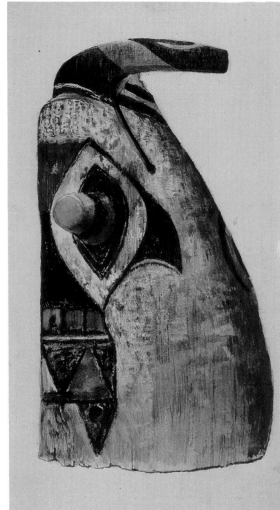

Pl. 19. Wells Sawyer's watercolor of a sea turtle head figurine. The figurine is 17 cm long and is painted in black, blue, white, and red pigments. It is in the collections of the University Museum, University of Pennsylvania (catalogue number 40715). Painting courtesy Smithsonian Institution.

Pl. 18. The wooden masks in plate 18, a–c, were painted in watercolors by Wells Sawyer after the masks were excavated. None of the three survives except perhaps as unidentifiable fragments. There are field photographs of the masks shown in 18a and 18b. Calusa ceremonies involving masked processions were observed by the Spanish in the sixteenth century. The masks were kept in a temple built on a mound (Goggin and Sturtevant 1964: 197, 199). Painting courtesy Smithsonian Institution.

18a

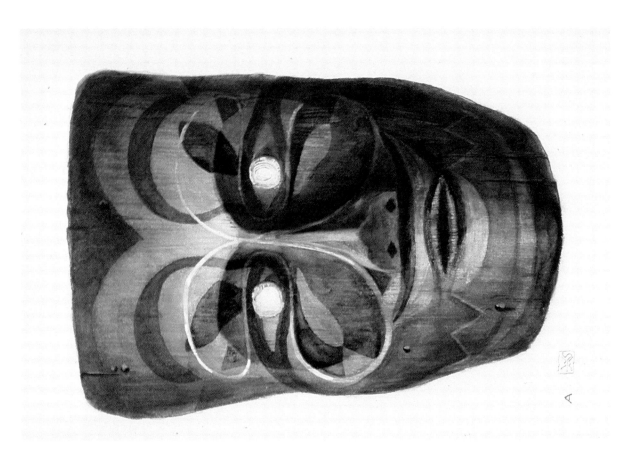

A

18c

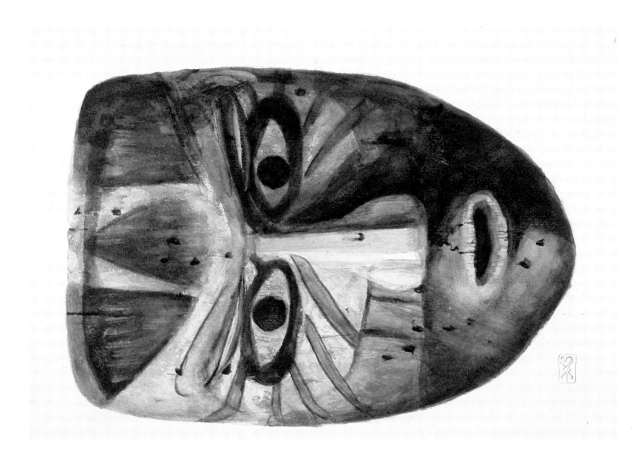

18b

Pl. 21. Wolf figurehead, perhaps a mask or part of a costume, made of wood. The upper jaw is about 16 cm long, and the ears and shoulder attachments can be removed. When excavated, these items were detached and all of the parts were in a bundle wrapped with green palmetto strips. Wells Sawyer did this watercolor and also a painting of the bundle. The figurehead is in the collections of the University Museum, University of Pennsylvania (catalogue number 40700). Painting courtesy Smithsonian Institution.

Pl. 20. The wooden tablet with a woodpecker painted on it in black, white, and blue pigments, 43 cm high. In the years since Wells Sawyer did this watercolor, the pigments have faded. The tablet is in the Florida Museum of Natural History (catalogue number 40697). Painting courtesy Smithsonian Institution.

ward the mainland, and that here on the heights, many Spanish relics had been found— Venetian beads, scraps of sheet copper, small ornaments of gold and silver, and a copper-gilt locket. She showed me this. It contained a faded portrait, and a still more faded letter, written on yellow parchment, apparently from some Spanish Grandee of about two hundred years ago to a resident colonist of that time.

. . . . Around the lower courts, and on the old garden terraces, I found abundant specimens of shell and coarse pottery, characteristic of the key dwellers proper who had anciently built this island, and since returning I have carefully examined an interesting series of both kinds of relics gathered here by . . . Mr. Joseph Wilcox, which offer even better evidence of this, and are now I am happy to say preserved in the University Museum. (Cushing 1897a:347–48)

Cushing's diary for June 3, 1895, read, "All up early. Captain butchered and took quarters of [illegible] turtle. At breakfast fine eating, better than steak which [it] is like. Tried to make start but men afraid. Provoking. Laid until at least half past nine. Came out in nearly a calm. Progress poor until wind freshened at about 11. Then so good that at 12 reached Naples" (Cushing 1895a).

With him he carried a letter of introduction to Captain Large, who received him courteously and showed him the nearby site of the ancient canal explored by Colonel Durnford. This canal, which Durnford had described to Cushing, was found to be much like the one on Pine Island, except that it was deeper and narrower, and, like that at Battey's Landing, it connected two areas of ancient shell works on opposite sides of the island.

From Naples to Marco it was a short sail but apparently not an easy trip. His diary for June 3 continued, "Under way at one. Fine breeze, later storm of rain and wind, sea rough but reached Marko Pass at four" (Cushing 1895a). Elsewhere he noted that "squalls were rising out over the Gulf, making its opalescent waters tumultuous and magnificent, but to my sailors, terrible, driving us now and anon furiously fast through the

rising billows, what though our sails were reefed low. Big Marco Pass opened tortuously between two islands of sand; the northern one narrow, long and straight, backed by mangrove swamps, the southern one broad, generally flat but undulating, and covered with tall, lank grasses, scattered, scrubby trees, and stately palmettos. The mangrove swamps, sundered by numerous inlets on the one side, this wide, straight-edged sandy island on the other, bordered the inlet that led straight eastward a mile or more to the majestic coconut grove that fronted Collier's Bay and Key Marco" (Cushing 1897a:348–49).

Reaching Marco on Monday, June 3, at 5 P.M. he ended his diary entry of that date, "Captain Collier very civil (but bursting with irreligion). Has superb shell and netting, sinkers, stool, (Caribbean type). Very willing for digging, probably keen, but most civil and interested beyond question. Will show me about in morning." The diary continued:

Tuesday, June 4, 1895. Rained all day. Went with Capt. Collier seeing great shell settlement on his and Capt. Cuthbert's place. As extensive as any I have seen, and has abundant surface relics. About fifty acres in all with at least nine canals leading radiatingly from waters of the broad peninsula occupied to centers of groups—(of irregular size and with at least three lagunes 2 small and one very large, through which canals communicate). The outermost of lagunes small and muck bed where the Wilkins and Durnford finds were made. Covered with water surface and brackish backed up by tide. Great prospects, and despite water shall excavate tomorrow with two men. Capt. Collier's very courteous and invites me to dine with them tonight. Has also secured men and offers to take me out to numerous [illegible] and mounds. Have milk and venison brought in today. Very close evening and more mosquitoes than ever saw before.

[June 5] Up very early. Bright morning. Took camera and Smith and went ashore between half past 6 & 7. Took numerous views of canals and lagunes and in particular one to excavate.

Fortunately water little lower. Had man before 8. Located place for him and had enough dam made within which to work. Found place to dig for self. Smith *helped*! We struck relics almost immediately and found from time to time all day. Worked myself with men until 6 p.m. Splendid success. Capt. Collier went off on business and has not returned.

Excavations alongside the diggings made by Mr. Wilkins and Col. Durnford and still further in toward the center and one side of the muck bed although made under water mostly (for the rainy season had set in) revealed within a few hours ... other relics of the kind Col. Durnford has described, net pins, seine stays, small fragments of netting, rope made of palmetto and agave fibre and the like, as well as burnt thatch, a long and beautifully finished spar or post, fragments of a burnt mud hearth and of pottery, some highly finished wattling plummets and sinkers, two beautifully shaped fish clubs, 5 mounted busycon shells, one of which was edged to serve as a celt, several of the shell funnels which proved to have been mounted on handles as spoons, many necklace pendants, etc. etc." (Cushing 1895a)

On June 6 he "settled accts, took some photos, sailed north at 8. To Punta Rassa" (Cushing 1895a).

Explorations among border islands within a radius of fifteen or twenty miles of Key Marco revealed that, on average, about one out of every five of them was an ancient shell settlement.

Before leaving Marco he secured permission from Captain Collier to bring men and excavate the place more thoroughly another year. He returned to St. James City, and, with Captain Whiteside's help, he secured the services of "an intelligent and interested" Scotsman, Alexander Montgomery, and of Johnny Smith, whom he described as "an active and bright young pilot of the place." With them he reexamined and excavated to some extent in the keys he had already seen, returning to Battey's Landing on June 9, Demorey's Key on June 10, and some other sites around Pine Island.

The rainy season had set in, the heat was excessive, and the mosquitoes and sand flies swarmed forth from the mangroves in such clouds that, wherever they dug, except in one or two of the most barren and lofty keys, it was necessary to build smudge fires all around to be free of the insects. These additional explorations convinced him that in these tropic islands lay a vast, comparatively new, and promising field for archaeological research. Well satisfied and impatient to reach his destination, he set forth to return to Philadelphia to report to Dr. Pepper.

7

ORGANIZING

THE

EXPEDITION

CUSHING REACHED Philadelphia on the night of July 2, 1895. His colorful report, accompanied by the artifacts he brought with him from Marco, immediately stirred interest in further exploration. Dr. Pepper, together with several of his friends and associates, hoped to fit out an expedition under the direction of Cushing for the following winter. Cushing would have to obtain leave from the Bureau of Ethnology, expedition arrangements would have to be made, key staff members hired, financial sponsorship secured, and transportation arranged for matériel and staff.

On July 2, 1895, Dr. Pepper wrote to Major J. W. Powell, director of the Bureau of Ethnology and Cushing's immediate superior, stating that as Cushing's personal physician for the past three months he advised that Cushing go to Florida for his health. Pepper said he also hoped Cushing would be granted leave to come to Philadelphia in September for treatment and that he would be allowed to go to Florida later in the year to direct the work at Marco (Pepper 1895b).

Major Powell quickly granted permission, and the next few months were spent making the necessary arrangements and securing financial sponsorship for the expedition. Several associates of the Archaeology Department of the University of Pennsylvania contributed to the original expense fund, estimated at $3,000. A further contribution was promised by Jacob Disston (of the same Philadelphia industrial family), who also offered the use of his schooner, the *Silver Spray*, one of a fleet of sponging vessels at Tarpon Springs.

It is evident that Cushing made every effort to secure donations of needed equipment and supplies, thus holding to a minimum the necessary cash appropriation. In a copy of an undated letter, perhaps to Dr. Pepper, he reported that "Major Powell, through the Coast and Geological Survey, furnished more than fifty dollars worth of detail charts covering literally every road on our way, and am to have a plane table . . . and other topographic aparatus. . . . Thus for the sum of $397 as above estimated for although large, is much smaller than it would be were it necessary for me to buy the charts and topographic instruments. I shall also be supplied gratis by the Interior Department with nearly all the stationery, including sketch and letter press books and trunks for assorted material that will be required in the regular work" (Cushing n.d.a).

The Bureau of Ethnology and the Archaeology Department of the University of Pennsylvania agreed to be joint sponsors of the expedition, and according to the original agreement there would be equal division of the artifacts between the two institutions. The two collections were to be as nearly identical as possible; it was hoped that the two institutions would receive duplicate collections, and at the time these arrangements were made there was little doubt in anyone's mind that this could be accomplished. The collections would become a major problem later because Cushing signed a memo at the University of Pennsylvania before the expedition set out that put a different interpretation on the disposition of the artifacts, especially when they turned out to be so exotic and to contain so few duplicates. This interpretation Cushing reiterated frequently in his correspondence with Dr. Pepper, and there is little doubt that he was aware of the problems it could cause.

Joint sponsorship, with equal division of the artifacts, seemed highly satisfactory to Powell, and he so informed Cushing on October 18, 1895:

> In response to your oral statement I take pleasure in assuring you formally that your plan for archaeological and ethnological researches in Florida, under the joint auspices of the Archaeological Association of the University of Pennsylvania and the Bureau of Ethnology, is approved. It is understood that your field and incidental expenses and the cost of collections, etc. will be borne by the Archaeological Association, and that the objective material obtained by collection will be divided between the institutions represented, the moiety allotted to this Bureau to be placed in the United States National Museum under the terms of law. In making the division you will be expected to represent the interests of this Bureau, as well as those of the Association.

> With respect to publication, it seems desirable that the arrangement with the authorities of the Archaeological Association should be made somewhat more definite. As a collaborator of the Bureau of American Ethnology you are a public officer, and the product of your creative genius is public property, and the right of the government to such property cannot legally be surrendered. There is of course every possibility that the cooperation contemplated between the two institutions can be so arranged as to meet the legitimate requirements of the public service, without injury to the interests of the Archaeological Association and at this time I desire merely to call special attention to the condition herein mentioned as one requiring full consideration when your plan more nearly approaches maturity. (Powell 1895)

With this letter in hand Cushing called on Dr. Pepper; the following documents resulted from their meeting. The first was a letter addressed to Cushing from Dr. Pepper, dated November 9, 1895: "I beg to state that you have placed in my hands the letter of Major J. W. Powell, Director of the Bureau of American Ethnology of the Smithsonian Institution addressed to yourself, and stating the conditions upon which the approval of the Bureau is given to your undertaking the conduct of an Exploration, Archaeological and Ethnological, of certain portions of Florida, at the expense, and primarily in the interest of the Archaeological Association of the University of Pennsylvania. As fully explained by you, the conditions stated in the letter above referred to are satisfactory, and are hereby accepted" (Pepper 1895c).

The conditions of agreement sounded somewhat different in the second document, a memo of the same date, signed by Cushing:

> Mr. Frank Hamilton Cushing calls upon me, ten P.M., Nov. 9, 1895, and presents a letter from Maj. Powell, Director of the BAE of the Smithsonian Institution, Wash. (q.v.)
> Mr. Cushing made a verbal statement to the

effect that this letter was rendered desirable, and even necessary, in order to place his connection with the Exploration upon a proper and official basis, in case inquiry might arise in connection therewith. He stated that there was no intention to enforce the provisions expressed in the letter to the detriment of the interests of the Department of Arch. or to the interference with its desires in connection with its exploration. Mr. Cushing stated his understanding to be that the Archaeological Department should receive not only the most full series, but also all unique specimens and choice of duplicates; the series furnished to the Bureau being such series as could be supplied consistent with the above.

He further stated his understanding that the dept. of arch. desire as many duplicates as possible, to enable them to exchange, and also to enable them to make special studies of points of particular interest. (Note here that Dr. Pepper promised Col. Durnford a representative series in return for his generous treatment of the Dept. in communication of his discovery and the contribution of some of the objects first secured.)

In regard to the matter of publication, Mr. Cushing stated that there would be several ways in which the wishes of the Dept. of Arch. to bring out the results of the exploration so as to secure the fullest credit and priority therefore (while acknowledging fully the services of Mr. Cushing as an officer of the Bureau especially permitted to conduct this work) could be observed. If the Dept. should desire to bear all expense of such publication, it could be so arranged that it should appear as a publication of the Dept., full recognition being given to the Bureau, with an adequate account of the duplicate series in possession of the Bureau. Mr. Cushing observed that the last clauses referring to recognition accorded to the Dept. were graceful but not obligatory. If, however, the Dept. should desire the Bureau to assume the expense of publication, he was confident it could be arranged so the interests of the Dept. of Arch. should be protected fully. (Pepper 1895d)

Those agreements provided sponsorship, both financial and institutional. Once again Cushing appealed to the source of earlier passes for transportation. On November 15, 1895, he wrote to Colonel J. M. Kreamer, engineer of the Atlantic and Gulf Coast Canal and Okeechobee Land Company of Florida, asking for passes for himself and his crew: "It is not improbable that Mrs. Cushing will accompany me; but in any case I have so much proofreading to get through with before leaving that I shall in all likelihood have to go by quick train as far as Jacksonville—meanwhile sending the rest of the party around by boat—and meeting them at the latter place. But if you can arrange without too much trouble for our passage from Jacksonville to Sanford by that most beautiful of all routes, the Clyde Line up the St. John's, I shall be very glad.... I do not believe it will be possible for the expedition to return before the latter part of February. Possibly, if we make unlooked for finds, we may not return before the middle of March" (Cushing 1895c).

In a letter to Jacob Disston on November 24, 1895, he wrote, "We shall leave on the first of December, and expect to be aboard your vessel within a few days after that date" (Cushing 1895d). The next day he wrote to inform Dr. Pepper that he planned to leave December 1 and would spend three months in the field (Cushing 1895e).

He was pleased to have arranged for three men with special training to go with him; he would hire excavators in Florida. He told Kreamer in the November 15 letter that "Having with me a competent artist who is also a cultivated writer, I am quite certain that this time I can secure ample results of a generally interesting nature and that thus wide publicity will at the proper time be given our work" (Cushing 1895c). The men who accompanied him were Wells M. Sawyer, an artist in the employ of the U.S. Geological Survey; Irving Sayford of Harrisburg, Pennsylvania, who would serve as field secretary; and Carl F. W. Bergmann, who had previously been trained as a preparator at the museum in Philadelphia. On December 4 these men left Washington for New York, where they began their sea journey by Clyde Line.

On December 5, Pepper received notice from Joseph Morris, treasurer of the Archaeological Department of the University of Pennsylvania, that $1,500 had been placed in the National Bank of the State of Florida at Jacksonville for Cushing to draw against for expedition expenses. The next day, December 6, Cushing and his wife began their overland journey to Jacksonville; there they were to meet the rest of the party and continue their journey up the St. Johns to Sanford, then to Tarpon Springs, where they were to board the *Silver Spray* for the remainder of the journey to Marco.

The journey from Jacksonville to Tarpon Springs gave Cushing his first opportunity to become acquainted with the key members of his crew. He was sure they would all contribute immeasurably to the success of the venture. Bergmann and Sayford both had experience in what they would do in the field, and he counted on his wife to help in whatever way he might need her. She too had gained experience during those months in the Southwest.

As Cushing became acquainted with the thirty-two-year-old Sawyer, he became more and more pleased with his good fortune in having secured the services of this young man. Son of a merchant and farmer, Wells Moses Sawyer was born in Koekuk, Iowa, on January 31, 1863. Traveling to the Philadelphia Exposition with his family as a lad of thirteen, he was so deeply impressed with the art exhibit he saw there and with the Lennox Library Collection in New York, as well as sketches he saw in the *New York Graphic*, a newspaper, that he decided then he would study art.

After finishing high school he studied law for three years, passing a week's test at the conclusion. While in law school he studied art at night, a practice he continued for fifteen years while pursuing other full-time careers during the day. He was nineteen years old when he began to study with his first master art teacher in 1882. Needing the means to support himself in his studies led Sawyer to specialize in pen drawings which he sold as a free-lance artist to the *Chicago Daily News*, *Chicago Tribune*, *Orange Judd Farmer,* and *Arkansas Traveller*.

His merchant father was a pioneer in the chain store business who, in his most prosperous years, had stores in Wisconsin, Illinois, Missouri, and Iowa. In 1884 he moved his only surviving store to Aurora, Illinois, and asked Wells to join him for a time in getting the business started in the new location. It was there that Sawyer met Frank Vanderlip, who became a close friend and associate for the rest of his life and considerably influenced the direction Wells's career would take.

In the early part of 1885, Frank Vanderlip joined the staff of a newspaper, apparently in a small town because his duties as editor also included the soliciting of advertising from Aurora merchants. It was in the process of soliciting advertising from Wells's father that the two men met.

Both men apparently traveled frequently between Aurora and Chicago in the course of their work, Sawyer to sell his illustrations and Vanderlip to look for advertising. They discovered many mutual interests in the course of their trips together. One of these interests was photography. Wells had learned wet plate photography in 1882, and they often experimented together with early snapshots and with dry plate photography when that came into vogue. Vanderlip later became editor of the financial page of the *Chicago Tribune*, a post that allowed frequent meetings with Sawyer who often sold illustrations to the same newspaper.

Sawyer found his illustrating to be so time-consuming that it left him no time to pursue his painting, so he accepted a position with the Phoenix Furniture Company of Grand Rapids, Michigan. His assignment was to develop a system of decoration for furniture. Here he developed talents in design, materials, woodcraft, and mechanics and became involved in the construction of high quality furniture. When this assignment was finished he planned to go to New York to study art at Columbia University. Again he planned to add to his income by making pen illustrations, this time of scientific items.

A friend who knew of Sawyer's legal training heard of his plans. This friend owned a large tract of land in Arlington, Virginia, to which the titles were not clear. He offered to defray Sawyer's expenses if Sawyer would go to Washington long enough to do the necessary legal work to clear the titles to his land. Sawyer had never visited Washington, was intrigued by the proposition, and accepted the offer. While there he developed a deep interest in the city and decided in 1891 to make it his headquarters.

Looking over the situation in Washington, he decided that government service offered the optimum conditions for employment that would leave time to paint. He sought the aid of his congressman, A. J. Hopkins, who introduced him to Major Powell of the United States Geological Survey and the Bureau of American Ethnology. Fortunately for Sawyer, the Geological Survey was in need of an illustrator (pl. 5). He carried samples of his work, together with letters of recommendation, one of them from Vanderlip, which convinced Powell that he should be given the job. Before he was even officially on the payroll a "cart load of objects" was sent to his room for him to illustrate on a piece-work basis until he could be appointed officially.

It was not long until his appointment came through; he was an expert paleontologic draftsman at a handsome salary of $75 per month, $900 per year, much less than he had been earning. His profit came in the time left him for pursuing his landscape painting (pl. 6). His working hours were 9 A.M. to 4 P.M. so he was free to paint during those late afternoon hours precious to landscape painters.

He and Vanderlip continued to correspond, and their friendship remained warm. Vanderlip asked Sawyer for some of his paintings which he hoped to sell to aid Sawyer's finances. On a visit to Chicago to see the World's Columbian Exposition in 1893, Sawyer ran short of funds for his return to Washington, and Vanderlip loaned him fifteen dollars to buy his ticket. Later, instead of repayment in cash, Vanderlip took some of the paintings. Sawyer was greatly appreciative.

When Grover Cleveland was elected to his second term as president in 1892, the *Chicago Tribune* sent Vanderlip to Washington to gather material for a special edition. During this visit he stayed with Sawyer in his studio, then in an old building across from the State, War and Navy Building at Seventeenth and Pennsylvania avenues. It was not very comfortable so Sawyer arranged for Vanderlip to be accommodated elsewhere at the home of a friend, another illustrator in the Geological Survey.

Because of his press status, Vanderlip had cards for the Inaugural Ball to which he took Sawyer as his guest. At this splendid affair they both noticed a lovely girl dressed in an empire gown of green trimmed with ivy. Years later Sawyer introduced this girl to Vanderlip as his bride-to-be.

While he was working in Washington, Sawyer enrolled in night classes in painting at the Corcoran Gallery School of Art. Soon he was invited to join the Washington Art Students League, later becoming a member of the board and ultimately president of the group.

In the fall of 1895, Sawyer was granted leave from the survey to make a journey by sea to Florida with Vanderlip and another friend. They traveled as far south as Tampa. Florida had not yet recovered from a recent disastrous freeze which had caused almost complete destruction of the orange groves, so the Florida they saw was undergoing an economic depression.

It was later this same fall that Sawyer's services were loaned to Frank Hamilton Cushing for the expedition to Marco. His notes and services, as well as his paintings and photographs, became invaluable to anthropology and to the history of the island.

8

DIGGING

UP

THE

PAST

SO IN MID-DECEMBER 1895, Cushing and his companions reached Tarpon Springs to be faced with the disappointing news that the *Silver Spray* had been sent recently on another sponging cruise and was not expected to return for some time. While awaiting the return of the schooner from its voyage, the Cushing party was installed by Messrs. Cheyney and Marvin in comfortable quarters in one of their hotel cottages in Tarpon Springs.

There was no way of knowing how long it would be until the *Silver Spray* returned, and Cushing was not one to sit idle. He was aware of the mounds successfully excavated by Clarence Bloomfield Moore (who also at times used a camera). On the day of his arrival in Tarpon Springs, he met Leander T. Safford, the adopted son of one of the founders of the city, who conducted him to an ancient burial mound lying at the foot of the village on land belonging to the Safford es-

tates. Cushing lost no time setting about excavating it:

But fortunately this pretty little winter resort was not far from the open Gulf, on a picturesque bayou of the Anclote River. Around it were vast forests of pine, live oak and palmetto, interspersed with cypress bordered lakes and tidewater fenlands and abounding on every hand in prehistoric remains.

It was in this land, too, that De Soto encountered the fierce Hirrihigua and only a few miles further northward, the redoubtable and mysterious Appalachees—the land through which De Soto's predecessor, Narvaez, had striven so hopelessly to pass; through which with better success, yet all disastrously, he marched his mail-clad knights and dauntless soldiers more than 350 years ago. The brusque yet picturesque chronicles

of these expeditions read today like ro-
mances of the days of chivalry, and tell us
that in those times populous nations of dusky
fairly civilized natives, ruled by kinglike chief-
tains, held all the land both to the north and
to the southward.

According to these records and the chronicles of later travelers, these people must have
been closely related (certainly in their ways
of life) to the Muscogees, Choctaws and
Creeks, Natchez and other historic or tribal
confederacies of our southern States. The
Spaniards tell us that they marched day after
day through fields of corn, beans, melons,
pumpkins, potatoes and yams, ever and anon
coming upon the well-built "cabins and ham-
lets" of these people, or desperately storming
some one of their greater central towns or
shapely thatch-roofed houses. Some of their
towns were set in the midst of wide mo-
rasses, approached only by narrow canoe
channels or hazardous causeways, often leading over bridges of floating logs. Where these
cities stood are marsh-bordered hummocks
today.

Others stood on headlands near rivers, or
in the midst of the tide water plains, clustered around great mounds or platforms,
aloft upon which were perched alike the
massive temples and the huge assembly halls
of their Micos or rulers and priestly counselors. These towns were surrounded by heavily timbered palisades, plastered inside and
out with painted clay stucco, as indeed were
the similarly built houses, some so large that
they could shelter all of the families of a numerous clan or ward, others built separately
but in groups for lesser households.

The great elevated public squares of these
towns so amazed the early discoverers that
they have left us many instructive particulars
regarding them. The platforms or flat pyramids on which the squares stood were approached by graded ways, some of them
overlaid with wide stairs formed of flattened
logs. Four halls, each closed at the rear and
ends, but open toward the square, stood at
the four sides of the summit, or sometimes

each of these great buildings stood on a
"mount" of its own.

The principal one of them was divided lon-
gitudinally by a partition enclosing in the
rear a mystic shrine or sanctorum entered by
three small arched doorways, to pass which
was death to any other than the Mico, the
chief warrior, and certain priests. And here in
this dark and secret place were kept the fetiches, medicines and "physic pots," masks,
rattles and sacred paraphernalia of the tribe.
The open front, however, was (as in the case
of all the other buildings) divided by half
partitions of stucco into broad ascending
steps or benches, covered with gorgeous
mats, upon which, according to their ranks,
the "senates" of native rulers and counselors
were seated on occasions of state.

Great pillars of wood, according to Bar-
tram, ingeniously formed in the likeness of
vast speckled serpents ascending upward and
supporting the front or piazza commanded
the entrance ways to these great houses.

Grander and loftier edifices called rotun-
das sometimes stood apart, we are told, on
other elevated mounds, and contiguous to
them were deeply walled-in open-air gymna-
sia and drama-courts. I can only mention the
temples of dead—guarded on every hand by
great wooden idols of fierce aspect, armed
with strange weapons—wherein for long periods the bodies of the chiefs and priests
(awaiting burial in mounds) were preserved
with chests diversely figured, containing also
their weapons and treasures. It has been suggested that the early accounts from which
these notes are gathered were exaggerated,
but my researches at Tarpon Springs, and especially further down the coast, led me to believe that even a higher order of aboriginal
life previously existed there than these
chronicles have pictured.

At the edge of the village of Tarpon
Springs on lands belonging to the Safford estate I found a mound sixty feet in diameter
that had been ruthlessly dug over by relic
hunters, and was said to have produced only
a few human bones and some broken frag-

ments of pottery. But the character of the debris of these diggings encouraged me to have a slight excavation made, and this revealed the fact that the mound was many centuries old and had originally been built within a deeply hollowed basin—a make-believe lake, as it were—and when used had been surrounded by a water-filled channel, or moat.

I therefore surmised that beneath these casual diggings many undisturbed human remains and relics of the objects sacrificed therewith would be found, and that these would reveal to me later an inland phase of the life of the old Key Building People of the Gulf. I at once secured men and began trenching the mound from side to side. Objects of rare interest were speedily found that encouraged a prosecution of the excavations for more than two months. Thus the little mound was explored from border to border. As a result more than 600 skeletons were encountered and perhaps the largest quantity of pottery, stone and other objects of art ever gathered from a single mound of equal size.

But it was not merely in material remains that this place proved rich. The observations I was able to make during the progress of the work formed data so significant that from them many customs and much of the sociologic and governmental organization of its builders can be clearly made out. That they buried their dead at long separated intervals, saving them meanwhile for occasions of ceremonial interment, was made plain by the fact that there were distinct strata, each defined by the accumulation of years of forest growth, traceable throughout the mound.

The remains of the dead were variously buried in accordance evidently with relative rank. Some few, presumably those of chiefs or priests, were buried entire, either extended or trussed up in close bundles like Peruvian mummies. These were accompanied by fetiches, queer concretions or medicine stone and keen-edged dirks of flint, sets of arrows, highly finished stone axes and exquisitely formed plummet-shaped pendants of

various rare and beautiful kinds of stone. As could be seen by nicks in the tangs of the dirks and the arrows, all these personal possessions had been violently broken in order that they might be "slain," and their ghosts be thus liberated for use by the ghosts of the dead.

But by far the greater number of interments had been promiscuously made, so to say. These probably represented the ordinary clans-people, the bones of whom were disarticulated and heterogeneously mingled, old and youth alike, in particular areas of the mound. There were with them, however, not a few skeletons which, although so disarticulated previously to burial, had been kept together in close little packs, the long bones below, the small ones on top, and over all, the skull.

By the dust that surrounded these bone-packs it was obvious that they had been wrapped in soft fur or matting and enclosed in boxes of thin boards or cane splints, and by the objects which accompanied them it was further evident that they were the remains of clan elders or matrons—heads of households, as we would say.

Being anxious to test these observations, and particularly to learn whether the strata in the mound really represented periods of interment, I sent a large party, under Mr. Sawyer, to a burial mound nine miles northward, which, being on the land owned by Captain Hope, of Anclote, I named "Hope Mound." It speedily developed that this also was made up of at least two or more strata.

A remarkable feature was revealed here, as afterward in Safford Mound. Over and around the remains of one or two skeletons Mr. Sawyer found disposed in effigy-like figures (which I recognized as probably symbolic) many beautiful sherds of pottery and unbroken vessels; and others of these entire skeletons had been buried extended, in graves lined, bordered and overlaid with the sherds of many broken vessels. I called these "Pottery Graves," as being in some sort like the "stone graves" of Tennessee. Within one were the remains of a middle-aged woman upon the breast of which we found some admirably wrought copper plates and spangles, which once had been suspended on strings of large and beautiful pearls (many of which were still undestroyed), together with traces of delicately spun tassels and fine cloth, preserved by the oxide of copper.

I was reminded by this find of the sometimes questioned incident related by De Soto's chroniclers—that of his meeting with an Indian Princess who was rowed down to his encampment in a great canopied canoe, and who, as an offering of friendship, took from her neck a many stranded necklace of pearls to which various pendants of bright red and golden metal were attached.

In both of these mounds were other sorts of burials. I was greatly interested to observe, for example, that all those who had died as victims of war (as indicated by the arrow points still clinging to their bones, or by the marks of war clubs or hatchets on their skulls) were invariably buried (or at least their heads were buried) underneath inverted bowls, every one of which, however, had been "killed," and this in turn covered by a large shell drinking cup, also punctured, or "killed."

Then again the remains of very small infants were buried within large shell cups, and these were the only objects found which had not been in some way or other purposely injured, or "killed," for sacrifice, since they had been buried not for use by the dead, but as coffins, so to say, for them.

The ceremonials which manifestly took place on occasions of the great tribal burials must have been elaborate and wonderfully impressive. It was evident that the dead of each clan were buried not only together and within a quarter of the mound by themselves, and that when thus deposited enormous sacrifices had been made of all kinds of earthen vessels violently broken and cast by near of kin, still reeking with food and drink, into

the fires which were kindled over these remains while the sand was being heaped upon them, but also that each procession of these dead had approached the mound from a special quarter—as shown by connected lines of pot sherds. We soon found that all these fragments of pottery occurring in a given area or leading to it could be with patient effort fitted together, and that by saving every sherd many a unique example of primitive American art could be well nigh perfectly restored.

After all these clan burials had been completed—probably the dead chiefs of previous years were last, and with the most elaborate ceremonial observances laid in their graves by all the assembled tribesmen and women—and as a final act in this festival of the dead, rich sacrifices of pottery, unbroken save for the customary puncturing, were made. Each of them contained, curiously enough, five different kinds of vessels, one for each of the quarters of the world and one for this City of the Dead—for such the mound was unquestionably held to be by the builders.

Apprehending this I had no sooner observed one of these multiple sacrifices than I was able to infer and speedily to find three others, making, with the one before mentioned, one group for each of the four quarters of this World of the Dead.

If the Indians encountered by the Early Spaniards had works in stone and clay comparable at all with those of earlier date, I do not wonder that the explorers so often marveled at the beauty of the things the natives possessed. The plummets, pendants and other ornamental and ceremonial objects of stone which we found were among the best products of the aboriginal lapidary's art I have yet seen. They were made of a great variety of material, from soft soapstone and spar to hard diorite and rock crystal, from hematite, polished like burnished steel, to clean cut plates of mica and elaborately wrought symbolic objects of copper.

The range of commerce that these things

indicated was enormous. There was a fine grained stone derived from the far West Indies, a shell from the Gulf of Campeche, the mica and rock crystal were of the Georgia and Carolina kinds, and the copper had been brought both from Lake Superior and from Cuba, while the hematite and galena nodules were of the kind so often found in Missouri and Iowa.

The most interesting objects that we found, however, were the vessels of pottery. Many of them were imitations of gourd utensils or vessels made from the hard rinds of various other kinds of fruit. Much of the pottery was obviously in imitation also of wooden ware—probably survived a time when the ancestry of the people had no other sorts of dishes or vessels than those of gourd and wood.

The surfaces of some were elaborately decorated with involuted concentric designs of the so-called "Caribbean" type but which I determined were developed from the strongly marked graining of well-worn objects of wood, and may thus, as to art motive, have originated from the oft observed impressions on the clay forms while still wet of coarse, curly grained paddles of wood.

There were tall vases highly finished, cylindrical and tapering, open at both ends, and so worn at the rims as to show that they were once like their almost exact counterparts found in Central America, used as drums. In proof of this there were delineated on one of these at top and bottom the round symbols of sound, with the song marks in the shape of conventional drum sticks issuing from them, while between, over the center of this terra cotta drum, was painted and incised in chrome yellow and bright red colors the great square of the world, with the trails or song lines, of the four quarters pointing out toward the corners.

But to me one of the most significant facts in regard to these collections of pottery was that their owners in "ornamenting" them had thought to "make them alive" (we have seen how they used to "kill" them) by painting or otherwise impressing upon their surfaces somewhat of their own personality—in other words, by tattooing, or painting, around the necks of these vessels some part or the whole of their own totemic or clan and name symbols.

This was singularly exemplified in one instance, where the red signs of a bloody panther's claw had been depicted down the side of a splendid, highly finished water jar, which was otherwise decorated almost precisely as was the face and costume of an old Florida Indian, pictured in one of John Whyte's water colors more than 300 years ago by that artist of Sir Walter Raleigh's expedition, a reproduction of which had luckily been given me by Professor G. Brown Goode, of the Smithsonian Institution, prior to my departure for Florida.

Yet other vases had horse-shoe crab and sea-shell designs tattooed upon them. Another had symbols of water (to hold which the jar had been made) in form of the nautilus and of gracefully curved lines, and also the symbol of the clay worker's craft in shape of a single wasp—the only workers in clay besides man known to these ancients—no doubt that the jar might be better suited to hold the sweet waters of life.

Some of the vessels were carved, and in this they were unique and showed plainly in common with the stamped forms their descent from carved wooden dishes, such as we later actually found to the southward. Upon one of them was represented the fish-like mask of the fisherman who had owned it, and also two scenes symbolizing all the modes of taking fish known to its owner—in order, no doubt, that drinking from it he might fare the better in his quest for food of the sea.

Now a study of these curious forms of ornamental investure, so to call it, will go far not merely toward telling us the story of the lives and thoughts of these old-time potters and of how they derived their art, but also toward telling us the meaning of savage or primitive art on the utensils of early folk everywhere; and for this reason I saved every scrap of pottery we uncovered, and shall spend months in putting it together and working out these fruitful designs. (Cushing 1896b)

Still in Tarpon Springs, the expedition was already attracting the attention of the press; reporters for at least two papers visited the site. In an account in the *Washington Post* of February 3, 1896, its reporter wrote, "Your correspondent while on a visit to the cottage had an opportunity to observe the treatment of these remains. Probably the busiest of the party was Mrs. Cushing, who was employed in matching the various fragments of pottery,... Prof. Bergman buries himself in the mass of human bones, emerging only to attend meals and to sleep, and even while sleeping he is still amid them" (Anonymous 1896b).

The *Jacksonville Citizen* of February 2, 1896, reported:

The secretary is employed in labelling the various remains and relics, as our grandmothers did when putting up the season's preserves.

Mr. Sawyer, the artist, keeps busy with his camera arranging the skulls in smiling groups, and also photographing them individually. He has secured some excellent photographs but these are guarded from the public view.

Mr. Cushing superintends the work in all of its branches, and applies himself to fathom the mysteries of some of the most interesting specimens.

From Tarpon Springs the party will go to the Charlotte Harbor country, where they expect to make further valuable discoveries, although they do not look for anything so interesting as that which they have just found. (Anonymous 1896a)

Sawyer's thoughtful comments were contained in letters home and in a fragmentary unpublished manuscript:

The days fly by. Today I am glad to get your letter. We will be here (Mr. and Mrs. Cush-

ing, Mr. Sayford the private Secretary, Mr. Bergmann a museum Expert and myself—(We compose the party)) about a week longer. The boat we are to take is out on a voyage and will probably not be in before that time. The place however is very comfortable and pretty. We have a cottage near the hotel, one of the cottages belonging to that building, and take our meals there.

The land and trees hereabouts are beautiful, great oleander trees some of them very high, line the streets and our yard is filled with pine trees 70 or 80 feet high.

Only a block from here is the pretty river with its boats—but for all of these beautiful things and all of this beautiful air I would gladly exchange a few days in Washington....

This reminds one of a cool September day tho I fancy later it will warm up some. We have a pitch pine fire here in the fireplace and it is comfortable enough too.

We have opened one mound not far from the hotel where we have found fragments of pottery and some skulls. The boy who just came in says that last night we had "a big white frost" so you see we have a little winter down here. I hope it was not heavy enough to hurt the orange trees tho I am sure any white frost would cut the tomatoe plants which are very common hereabouts....

It is so nice of all of you to remember me and to write to Kathleen. Dear ones at home how I should like to see you. Do not try to send any Christmas to me. It is so far and so expensive—I will gladly overlook it.

My health is pretty good and I am gaining some in flesh. Weigh 128. Which is getting back to normal. Was down to 118 at one time.(Sawyer 1895)

I am sending today a photograph of our camp at Hope Mound which will interest you not a little. The palmetto trees back of it are beautiful. The mound itself is only a short distance from the tents of which there are three. Mr. Sayford, Mr. Bergmann and I occupied this tent while the boys had another and our cook and his assistant a third. Mr. and Mrs. Cushing were at the Hotel here—he superintending this splendid mound and I in charge under his direction of the one at Camp Hope [pl. 10].

Today we have made wonderful finds— one a *rock crystal* ornament beautifully wrought into a shape like this [sketch] only much more symmetrical. It was perfectly round and very clear—some four inches long. The boat is all ready for us yet we do not sail. There is some more work to be done here and another letter would reach me at this point. Later I think our address will be Marco but of that I will inform you [before] our departure. I am quite well and most enthusiastic. (Sawyer 1896a)

Today I have been on a long horse-back ride way out into the forest. A beautiful ride through great pine groves and big palmetto hammocks.

We found three mounds and I had them dug into but nothing came so we let them go. Our work here is getting pretty nearly completed so that in a few days we will be off to Marco where we will undertake some important work.

The results here have been *very* valuable— and in conjunction with the observations of early Spanish voyagers will be most conclusive. I have been studying the development of design from the arrow to the beautiful scroll which sometimes is used and find the steps here complete from [sketch] to [sketch] or from the arrow to a design like this [sketch] running around a vase. The results are not entirely conclusive and are somewhat incomplete yet they are good. We are so apt to think we know it all that it is lovely to find the "poor" savages of the long ago fixed as happily and as satisfactorily as we find the people of today. They too thought that they were the most enlightened people, that their systems of weapons and boats and war ships and fishnets and fabrics were for the most part the best while their religion and their

prophets were the greatest. Theirs was the God of Gods and their life was given to his service, how beautiful the contemplation of these people, how small it makes one feel the step from yesterday when we too stood on the edge of the earth naked and savage yet having potentially all knowledge and seeing God in everything down to the present when the lightnings which once were His fiery serpent are chained and made to haul us about in bumpy trolly cars.

How short the step—and yet how significant when we have seen all that is to be seen how much of this story will be read.

The men are all white. They are sons of leading men hereabouts. My health is perfect. (Sawyer n.d.a)

The first stop made was at Tarpon Springs where a splendid collection of pottery and worked stone was secured, from two burial mounds, one situated almost in the heart of the picturesque winter resort and the other at Finley Hammock. No scrap amongst the thousands of fragments unearthed suggested contact with the early explorers, this taken with the condition of the bones goes far to establish the absolutely prehistoric nature [of the site]. . . .

The designs were for the most part either incised into the vessels after they were partially hardened or else imprinted in surprisingly regular lines of dots often curved and delicately covering the upper portions of the vessel with a lace-like tracery of "punctate" character. One of the vessels found in a group of five which constituted a tribal sacrifice, was perhaps the gem of the entire collection, for in the delicate simple gracefully curved lines which encircled or swung round the body of the jar there was much of the cleverness one sees in the good old Japanese treatment of lines and masses. And all these lines ended in a charming backward or scroll-like sweep enclosing conventions of a univalve shell.

Mr. Cushing was inclined to believe the

work that of the ancestors of the Indians found here by De Soto as these people possessed a remarkable culture having at their head a ruler who held his office by inheritance, a political condition which was unique in the territory now covered by the United States.

The stone work as well as pottery was very skilfull and substances such as pure rock crystal, diorite and other hard stones were worked into those delicate problematical little objects called "sinkers, plummets, dipsies and bobbets." The use of which no doubt ranged from a fish line sinker to a weaving bobbin and then again to ceremonial objects even in some cases going so far as to rival the crystal in Ryder Haggard's "She" from employment in divination itself. (Sawyer n.d.b)

Some time during the stay in Tarpon Springs, Sawyer suffered a bout with malaria, but, while he was solicitous of the health of those he left behind, he never mentioned his own illness in his letters home. It appeared only in a reference Cushing made in a note of a much later date.

Cushing of course was enthusiastic, and in his letters to Pepper from Tarpon Springs can be seen not only his enthusiasm but the beginnings of his future troubles as well: His persistent financial problems began, and there was a foreshadowing of the difficulties over division of the collection.

He wrote to Dr. Pepper on January 13, 1896, of finding articles in stone, copper from Lake Superior, galena from Missouri, and rock crystal, hematite, and mica from Georgia. There were, alas, few duplicates (Cushing 1896c). He lamented to Pepper in a letter of February 7, "I have in this whole collection of hundreds of specimens *only 8 or ten* actual duplicates. I believe the case almost unparalleled and ordinarily it would have filled me with joy to get a collection so rich in types. I hope for greater redundancy below, that I may yet be enabled to worthily return the goodness of my institution in giving my time to this work and officially sanctioning it. For

as I promised you the main series of our collections *shall not be broken.* It must be kept together if only because it is monographic in a very high degree" (Cushing 1896d; Cushing's emphasis). He mentioned the possibility of later collaborating with Clarence B. Moore on a joint publication of their Florida mound excavations, but it never materialized.

Cushing again wrote Pepper on February 21, "Friends of yours who have been here or are now here and have seen my later finds and my work will abide by me I am sure in saying that I have done (as I shall continue to do) all in my power for the University Department to the neglect of my own institution (for alas there are but few duplicates)" (Cushing 1896e).

The work at Tarpon Springs, while interesting and fruitful, was not included in the original plans or the original budget, and Cushing requested an additional $500, above the original $3,000, to cover this phase of the work. Apparently his request for additional funds was received by Dr. Pepper while reports on his excavations and the results were not. He received no reply—and no money.

Cushing's troubles were just beginning. He wrote to Pepper, "The *Silver Spray* did not return until after Christmas. . . . She was not fully prepared for sailing until late in January and then a bad pilot grounded her on a sand-bar. The low tides came, consequently we could not get her off until the day before my sailing" (Cushing 1896f). It was not until late February that they were able to complete preparations and set sail for Marco.

The Key Marco excavations were expected to take three months, and the expedition had been provisioned for that length of time. Now nearly three months had been consumed by delays. But through additional contributions by Mrs. Hearst, the expedition was provisioned for two more months with the best materials obtainable on Florida's west coast, though Cushing said these would have been inadequate. Fortunately, however, Mrs. Richard Levis, a winter resident in Tarpon Springs who was a member of the University Archaeological Association, and a friend provided the needed supplies. They also financed some extra comforts which provided a small measure of luxury to their otherwise meager existence at Key Marco.

Cushing, perhaps as insurance against future disasters, obtained captain's papers before leaving Tarpon Springs, and he was in command of the vessel when it finally sailed down the Anclote River on the way to Marco. The party now consisted of Cushing, Mrs. Cushing, Sawyer, Sayford, Bergmann, sailing master Antonio Gomez, mate Thomas Brady, Alfred Hudson, Robert Clarke and Frank Barnes (sailors who doubled as excavators), chief excavator George Gause, a black cook, George Hudson, and steward George Dorsett, also black. Cushing later hired John Calhoun permanently and others from time to time to assist in the excavation.

When, on February 23, 1896, the *Silver Spray* again weighed anchor and finally set sail for Marco, Wells Sawyer toasted the sailing with an original verse:

The Health
Oh Captain Cushing's in command,
The *Silver Spray*'s afloat,
A glad farewell unto the land,
A Bon Voyage to our boat.

For Oh! we sail the Southern Seas
Bound for an isle remote,
Where neath the old Mangrove Trees
There lies an ancient moat,
Built by the men of the olden time,
Men of a bronzy race
Who dwelling in this sunny clime
With nature face to face
In all about them thought they saw
In bird and stream and flower
The workings of a nature law
Embuing all with power,
To them the world went not around,
To them the flowing sun
Shone brightly, on the camping ground
The Greatest living one,
And all else lived as well, they thought,
Was so endowed with life,
That now when forth their works are brought

With story they are rife,
Then let us search this ancient quest
Beneath the mangoes spread
And from it's hidden Treasures wrest
The secrets of the dead:
Again to see the huntsman brave
The warriors call to hear:
The life they ended at the grave
Will open to the seer.

Then a health to Captain Cushing,
A health to the *Silver Spray*,
A health to the breezes pushing
Us on to the sea today" (Sawyer n.d.b).

The voyage from Tarpon Springs to Marco, including a stop at Pine Island (pl. 12) for mail, fuel, and water, took less than three days, and, with a steady Gulf breeze and unusually high tides, they made the difficult pass into Marco Inlet without hindrance. Just northeast of the key, they anchored sufficiently far offshore to protect themselves from the mosquitoes. There the *Silver Spray* rocked at anchor for the duration of the expedition, serving as living quarters for the crew. For exploration of nearby keys Cushing used a light-draft, double-sailed sharpie that had been fitted up and turned over for his use by Mr. Cheyney.

In a letter to the "Folks at home" Wells Sawyer described the expedition's situation soon after arrival at Marco:

Sunday here is a quiet placid day like one in June. This is a change. The coconut groves and mangrove swamps and all the tropical land of Florida is here [pl. 13]. In a few days it will be beautiful tho it is now like midsummer and I have been picking tomatoes, and eating fresh pumpkin. Then sweet potatoes and cabbage and all sorts of things are fresh here.

Our anchorage is in a beautiful bay some miles in extent running behind the keys down to the Cape Romano, below which are the Ten Thousand Islands. We will probably not get to the Everglades at all—the delay at

Tarpon Springs was really serious. Our hotel bill alone being $600. Somewhat over that figure.

This is a wonderfully interesting place—It was entirely built by the Indians and contains many lagoons and canals such as are seldom met with. Never before in this country. (Sawyer n.d.c)

In another, unfortunately fragmentary, manuscript Sawyer's description continued:

It is a world of water dotted with islands which look like great green buttons on the beautiful sea—for the colors of the Gulf are unlike those one sees on the Atlantic and these islands or keys differ too from those of the northern waters. There is no land upon them excepting where the people who lived there many centuries ago have built it. They came in canoes and lived on the oyster bed eating the oysters and throwing away the shells until out in the sea they reared a bit of land made of shell . . . . [The next page is missing.] his arts, his carving and painting, proclaim him the most dexterous of our prehistoric peoples.

Much in the art would be creditable had it come from the valley of the Nile or been dug from Etrusca's mysterious treasure houses.

But let us look at the land or rather the place which these Indians were to inhabit. The lower part of Florida is, geologically, very new, much of it having grown within what is called a recent period. The vast area known as the "Everglades" is filled by swamp grass growing to a height much taller than that of a man—here and there within this area are islands where the land is some higher and on these grow willow, rubber, and other trees which are found in fresh water countries. Near the coast the land is higher and for a distance of several miles in some places it protects the Everglade area from the tide or salt water from the sea. Along the border of the mainland is generally an almost uninterrupted fringe of mangrove which extends outward into the Gulf either as a vast swamp or as a mass of small islands the surface of which are covered with mangrove trees [pl. 2].

Mangrove keys are in some places so numerous that it is unsafe to enter them without a guide as they all look alike and the tide currents running between them flow so swiftly that a person in a boat is soon hurried past a few of them and then having entered this labyrinth there is no way out. It is not generally known that the mass of these islands lying south of Cape Roman and called the Ten Thousand Islands have never been mapped by the Coast Survey, the area being some fifty or sixty miles long and in places thirty miles deep, that is extending for that distance from the Gulf line back toward the mainland.

On the west coast the barrier keys stretch nearly all the way from the northern end of the state to Cape Florida and within them there is an almost passageway for a small boat for the entire distance.

So inside of these barrier keys the depth is very slight excepting in the passes which are deep cut by the rising and falling tides. Between the barrier keys and the mainland the distance varies from [blank] to thirty miles and it was here that the savage found the natural conditions favorable to his needs. Each mangrove key bordered by an oyster fringe and here and there a flat on which the oysters grew in beds, the mangrove key also often the rookery of cormorant, curlew or other bird.

The waters alive with fish and on the mainland the deer very plentiful, while the possum and coon followed everywhere the shore.

So it was that given land to live upon the Indian could thrive here. But there was no land, the mangrove grows above the water standing with its trunk well above the tide so almost must the man who builds a home raise it from the rushing waters.

To live in the swampland was well nigh impossible for within the mangrove clad island the mosquitoes are legion and likewise the sand fly. So it became necessary to live at certain times as much in boats as possible and these boats were anchored on the oyster beds, the shells of the oyster furnishing the first resting place for the foot of the savage, or for the support of his lodge.

The shells were deposited in lateral rows— making two or more ridges—along which the sea dweller lived and between these rows was ample water for the canoe. As the hurricane season (June to November) came on the settlements would probably be abandoned for fierce squalls daily lash the waters with considerable force and frequently tidal waves roll over the country so that during this season the shells were largely rearranged— offering in the fall a better foundation than the year before.

Greater energy would be employed and more substantial structures reared until after several years, no doubt, the paralel ridges were enclosed by a sea wall on the most exposed side and within its ample dimensions were included safe harbor for boats, lagoons for fish preserves, high structures for their priest or council houses and extensive areas of land which from its present fertility and character must have been used agriculturally. These key building peoples mixed a large quantity of fish with their shells on the farm land so that in digging today there is a brown powder composed largely of them, our farmers know the value of a fish compost fertiliser, so also probably did the men of old.

The shell settlements which were examined were obviously "laid out" upon a plan which was well thought out and were not the work of a single man but of a large commu-

nity working together, and in the effort to work toward a common end developed much of that altruistic philosophy which gives us the golden rule.

Is it indeed remarkable that the progress which these people made, was much greater than where the natural surroundings made it better for the people to live in scattered localities? The answer surely is that greater progress is to be expected of these Floridians because of their "communal" (working together) life, and it is borne out by their arts for therein do they wonderfully excel.

Some of these shell keys are very extensive one of the largest which we visited was I should say one mile long in its greatest dimension while the central mound was sixty-three feet high all composed entirely of shell. Some of the early travelers in Florida tell of the prosperous dwellers on these lands saying that their houses were of mats and that they were plastered inside and out with a red and glutening cement, that their council houses stood high above the others and that they were reached by a long gradually ascending way leading up from the water.

They tell us too that these Indians were peaceful and hospitable, as for that matter were most of the red men, before they were so deceived and misused, and indeed it is a matter of history that no war occurred in Florida for about two hundred years.

When the Spaniard came these settlements were probably, many of them at least, abandoned for the most careful search in one of the principal ones at Marco ship channel fails to reveal the slightest trace of European contact, not even a bit of glass, a bead, or bit of metal was found altho practically everything relating to the arts of life was unearthed.

The objects of the temple, dwelling, kitchen, chase, fishing tackle, the kit of a medicine man, the tools of the artezan, the gods and house-gods of the people and the paraphernalia of the sacred dance including many masks.

We have seen that where people work together for a common end they reach a much

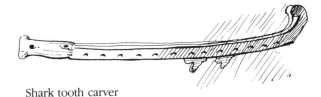

Shark tooth carver

higher state of culture than when working as individuals, as also in their arts these people progressed out of all proportion to the other tribes of the United States. Standards of excellence result from comparisons and where people live in close relationship the criteria more rapidly produce aesthetic ideas. Which ideas in turn tend to produce a higher quality of workmanship so long as these ideas remain pure and are not vitiated by scholastic thoughts of technique, treatment and preconceived convention.

The tools too have much to do with progress in art and amongst these people a very large variety of tools are found. For delicate carving the tooth of the leopard shark offered a cutting edge which surpassed any other primitive implement employed by the American Indian.

The cutting edge of flint flakes compared with this tooth are but rude knives compared to fine rasors. Then too the line which the tooth cuts is long, clean and continuous, either as a straight line or as a curve and the line which can be rubbed by the flint is rough, irregular and broken.

So the tool which the Floridian used was to an extent an explanation of his superior workmanship.

In a small carved statuette of a "mountain lion god" the workmanship is so exquisite that the best Swiss carver of today could scarcely give it a better finish and the design was so dignified and the convention so subservient that the best Egyptian work was suggested. The little figure is scarcely eight inches high yet it has the dignity of a colossus. It is made of a light colored wood which upon drying has checked but slightly . . . [pl. 11].

This statuette differs in the style from ex-

amples of American Indian art found in other localities and its characteristic features are directly traceable to the technique resulting from the tools employed. The long smooth sweeping lines sharply cut by deep clean edged incisors could only have been produced by tools of shell and tooth or by those of metal.

As long periods had passed during which the hand had been trained in the use of those tools a character of line developed which was a direct resultant of those tools.

Yet another unpublished Sawyer manuscript set the stage for excavation:

When the party reached Marco arrangements were made to proceed with the digging without delay and as the court where the work was to be done was below the level of the surrounding tide swept mangrove swamp it was with difficulty bailed out enough for the

Mountain lion or panther

work to progress uninterruptedly. Indeed shifts of men had to bail constantly while others dug [pl. 3].

I shall never forget the first impressions of the muck hole in Marco, which, under the same magic touch, became the famous court of the pile dwellers. The little shoots of mangrove coming up here and there, many curious weeds growing not more than twelve or sixteen inches high, all underlaid by foul-smelling black muck, into which a few trenches had been dug. These were filled with water, and indeed, the whole place was like a thick sponge saturated with water holding a great quantity of salt and a large variety of smells.

We had brought a crew of workmen from up the coast, but almost to a man they looked with absolute revolt upon the unpromising hole. Each face showed the feelings of its owner, and in the group of faces only one was lighted by enthusiasm as we stood on the edge of the Court of the Pile Dwellers.

Captain Cushing waded into the mud, moved boards about and in a short time the men, who reluctantly began work, were following him and working with an enthusiasm and will which hardly flagged through the weeks of wading in mud and slime and of working under a semi-tropical sun in a muck-covered swamp, where the mosquitoes were plentiful and the sand-flies almost like the sands of the sea, the annoyance of the insects alternating with the smoke of the smudge supposed to bring relief. Squatting on their knees in the slime, with hands and arms covered with mud, these men worked day after day, bringing forth treasures which, if seen now as we saw them, would command the attention of every student of American archaeology.

Mr. Cushing says, "I deem it unnecessary to give further details of our operations, save to say that three or four of us worked side by side in each section, digging inch by inch, and foot by foot, horizontally through the muck and rich lower strata, standing or crouching

the while in puddles of mud and water; and as time went on we were pestered morning and evening by swarms and clouds of mosquitoes and sand-flies, and during the midhours of the day, tormented by the fierce tropic sun heat, pouring down, even thus early in the season into this little shut-up hollow among the breathless mangroves. After the first day's work, however, I was left no longer in doubt as to the unique outcome of our excavations, or as to the desirability of searching through the entire contents of the court, howsoever difficult the task might prove to be; for relics not only of the kind already described, but of new and even more interesting varieties, began at once to be found, and continued to be found increasingly as we went on day after day, throughout the entire five weeks of our work in this one little place" [quoting Cushing 1897a:357] [pl. 7].

At Marco the conditions for the preservation of the remains were most remarkable. To the south of the great central mound are several lagoons leading in from the sea or connected with it by canals. On most of these the bottom layer is of shell and is overlaid by a homogeneous and very compact clay. In this and in the peaty deposit above it the specimen bearing strata occur whilst overlying all is a growth of muck some two feet thick the surface of which is at tide level, and finally on the muck dense mangrove forests were growing.

Here all was changed, for instead of digging in mounds for the remains, the men worked in muck holes. The entire character of finds was also changed [from those at Tarpon Springs]. . . .

Mr. Wells Sawyer painted facsimiles of a large number of the most important finds and photographed a typical series of all the different varieties which were dug up [pls. 14, 15, 17–21]. Casts were also made of some of them and various methods of preservation which were within the means of the expedition were resorted to.

Mrs. Cushing watched carefully in the cabin of the *Silver Spray* over the choicest

Kingfisher tablet

objects found and happily succeeded in drying many a treasure of ancient American art any one of which will fill the soul of the archaeologist with joy [pl. 4].

Since the collection is practically unique it is almost impossible to cite a single thing without doing the rest an injustice but amongst the most noteworthy examples are the mountain lion god and the kingfisher god.

These two present entirely different phases since one is a statuette in the round and the other is painted on a board tablet.

The mountain lion, is a small wood carving about seven inches high and represents the seated or kneeling figure of a man masked as a god with a panther face, the splendid dignity of the convention is in no wise marred by the diminutive size of the figure. The forepaws stretch down to the base with a sweep which reminds one of the best Egyptian art and the pose of the head with its delicate modeling would do credit to that famed land upon which the archaeologists have feasted since the time of Herodotus.

The little image is a gem and will stand in the University Museum as the finest example of American carving ever yet found. The wood from which it was made is very hard, light colored and fortunately has checked but little.

When the first example of painted work was brought forth from its bed of clay all of the party were astonished. Tho one had to look closely on the black mask for the faintly tracable design but in a day or two the Kingfisher god came to light and then the wonder was unlimited. Immediately a facsimile of it was begun in water colors and when it was finished a photograph made lest exposure to the light should destroy this piece of ancient painting. But like the colors of Pompeiian frescoes these held their own and now the board and painting are nearly dry—only slightly cracked and but little of the brilliancy destroyed.

The kingfisher god pictured is on a slab of board cut by hacking with shells and dressed down on the paneled side with a shark tooth scraper, the board is eighteen inches high by half as wide [pl. 20]. The bird is conventionally treated yet departs but little from life and lacks as does all art work from the place that grotesqueness which characterizes the work of the northwest coast Indians or the Central or South American people. The element of the grotesque seems almost lacking from all of this work and as Mr. Cushing remarked "It is

Mask

the most rational art of antiquity yet found." And here is a point of greatest interest, the speech of the kingfisher falls as four pearls from his mouth. Obviously he speaks to the four quarters, named north and west, east and south, behind him he holds the double paddle, symbol of his authority over the sea and beneath his feet, under a dark bar which may represent the land, he holds the raccoon, land animal par excellence of the Keys. It is this which reveals to us the fact that he was one of the chief deities of these ancient painters.

The character of the painting and of the symbolism is so astonishingly like the old codex pictures of Central America that at first one is led to say that these people had contact with those of Yucatan at some point, but just where future investigation alone can determine. As it stands this art is more pure, more native, less grotesque, simpler and more rational in every way. And besides not a fragment was found in this muck hole which might not have been of local origin, nothing pointing to extensive commercial or other relations. No gold or silver ornament, only such things as man with skill could have procured within easy distance.

There are a set of masks [pl. 18] which are also very remarkable and which will throw light upon the curious copper plates found further north (shell gorgets and carved bone tools of all sorts from a shell hammer to a surgeon's knife of fish bone).

The most potent factor in the development of the arts of these people was the shark's tooth, from which they made knives and cutting implements of many kinds. The tooth of the leopard shark particularly afforded a knife with which the most delicate work could be carved. In practical experiments made[,] the tooth was found to be admirably adapted to cutting long clean edged lines either in curves or straight ahead. That the superiority of the tooth over the flakes of flint used by the more northern Indians has much to do even is responsible for the progress made by these natives is beyond doubt. Mr. Cushing has in papers published some time ago established the importance of hand craft in the progress of culture and here the tool aided the hand by its natural adaptation to the uses required of a cutting implement. So it was that the rise of the arts along these key settlements was particularly favored. It was not alone in painting and carving wood that the Florida Indians were superior for progress with a people manifests itself not along one or two lines but universally.

The long finely carved shark tooth sword with from six to twelve of the keen edged teeth set into a grooved trough on the under edge was frequently met with. The spear thrower or atlatl with its finger holes was also found. Dirks were made from bone, sometimes carved as in one which had the head of a buzzard conventionally represented on its hilt. This Mr. Cushing said was a sacrificial dagger. The buzzard being in the mythology of barbarians superior over death since he eats the dead and yet lives. The finish and cleanness of this bone carving is remarkable and the surface is as smooth as tho polished by a modern buffer.

Other killing implements were knives of bone, fish hooks of bone and wood, [gouges] with double prongs made from bone, long spears with barbs of fish bone or the sting of the sting ray. Some of them too were probably barbed with deer bone points.

In the shell work the art is of great variety as along other lines. Gorgets, quartered and plain, ear plugs, pendants or bobbets, beads and other ornaments such as the fashion of the times decreed.

Tools were often made from conch shells and include the chisel, gouge, adze, hammer, pick and in fact many differentiated implements quite as limited as to the variety of uses to which they could be put as are their counterparts in steel. Those who have not experimented with shell cannot realise its adaptability. Such employment but showed that they take a conch shell and use it for hacking a shrub or tree it will be found to cut readily and when sharpened to an edge by grinding it serves the purpose of a hatchet.

These by no means exhaust the interesting specimens in the collection. Enough has however been said to show that this is a great discovery in that a pile dwelling, key building people who attained a degree of culture hitherto undreampt of as living within the boundary of the U.S. once flourished on the reefs about Florida.

Their culture status is about the same as the pre-Columbian inhabitants of Yucatan, of whom much has been written. In architecture the same demands were not made upon the Floridian Indian but in planning his city with reference to the sea in building his fish lagoons and canals, in constructing his high mound with reference to the adjacent ones this newly found man has left ruins which place him amongst the brainiest of the prehistoric peoples. After leaving Marco the *Silver Spray* sailed to a great number of such shell settlements finding always the same type features tho varied, at one place an old conch wall faced the sides of the level where once stood the council house as Mr. Cushing said. In others evidence of such conch facing seemed plentiful enough.

Few of the keys have inhabitable land other than such as the Indians built. Wherever they were are now shell hammocks and the farmer or gardener takes advantage of the soil born of an ancient occupation to raise his Bermuda onions, tomatoes and other vegetables for the winter market. The population required to have reared such a number of important settlements must have been considerable; the transportation of quantities of shell such as would build a mound, as at Mound Key or Pine Island more than sixty feet high, merely as the central structure of a settlement surrounding its base, and having several other encircling mounds of from twenty to thirty feet involves a labor which no few men could complete. The region must have been densely populated by an enterprising race upon whom the enervating heat of summer had but little influence, of this the vast remains speak for themselves as do the ruins of the old world. Maj. J. W. Powell visited the settlements during the progress of the work and was also profoundly impressed by the obvious antiquity and extent of the sites which he most happily called ruins of a vast empire.

So it is that American archaeology has been enriched by this discovery and has given a new light on the history of man in the ethnic status below the development of the heiroglyph in so far as writing may be a determinant of culture periods.

Of the collections which resulted from this kind of work it is not surprising that Prof. Putnam should say that he marvels at the explorers ability to have recovered a collection of objects so remarkably unique, in that the perishable things if left in mounds or above ground are here preserved and throw a powerful light on the old culture of Florida. From out the mud at the bottom of the "Court of the Pile Dwellers" many painted objects were taken, some of them still preserve their color very well while others have suffered greatly by the drying, but all came out as fresh to appearance as tho only deposited recently yet in consistency they were hardly more firm

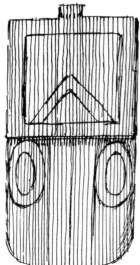

Altar tablet

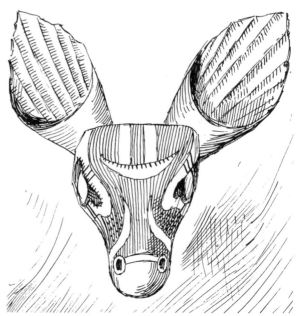

Deer figurehead

than the mud from which they were taken.

Amongst some of the more important finds are those figured on the margin tho the house is fanciful. Yet many piles and masses of palmetto and heavy timbers were found to corroborate Mr. Cushing's claim. [There is a photograph of one heavy timber in situ, probably as a doorsill, but no other posts or pilings existing today would have been large enough for such purposes.]

Toy canoes were also found with markings on bow and stern and a great variety of bowls and cups made from wood. No bow was found but several throwing sticks with short spears such as were used in that manner.

Long spears were also found—so too were fish hooks made of bone, carved bones of various design and a curious class of objects which are called "alter or ancestral tablets" exhibiting two eyes and a triangle either above or below. These were sometimes several feet long. The seated figure of a "panther or mountain lion god" is regarded as the gem of the art collection. It was found by Mr. Cushing at a depth of some twenty inches between the overlying muck and the peat marl.

The little deer's head is the finest example of combined painting and carving which was found. The head of a young deer or doe is a

little under life size, the face markings were perfectly symetrical, the cheeks are gray blue merging upwardly into black and the two lateral bands over the forehead are divided by a deep black band and were themselves a deeper blue.

The eyes had been set in with tortoise shell and the ears were supplied with pegs so that they were movable.

The painted tablet with the "kingfisher" or "jay" is another of the gems of the collection. Many masks were found and Mr. Cushing very convincingly shows the relationship between the mask and the animal from which it was taken, as curiously enough the collection includes in many cases both the animal and humanized form.

This portion of his report is very ingenious and throws much light on conventionalized face painting and markings amongst all peoples. The masks were often found bunched with the animal head from which the semblance had been taken as tho they had fallen together into the court. The little pelican head is an example of this and the mask alongside of it. "It was unquestionably designed to represent the human, or mangod counterpart of this bird; for not only was the chin protruded and the under lip pouted to symbolize the pouch of the pelican, but also, the rear and tail of the body (painted in white on the chin). The trailing legs (in gray-blue and white lines, descending from the nostrils around the corners of the mouth), at the wings and shoulders, (in dappled white over the cheeks), and the huge bald head (in white on the forehead of the mask), were all most distinctly suggested. Moreover, on the upper edge of the mask (at the terminal point of the bird head painted on the forehead), were perforations, indicating that either an actual beak, or an appendage representative thereof, had been attached. With this in mind, if the mask be reversed and a comparison of the design on it be made with the figurehead, or with the imagined form of a flying pelican seen from above, the almost ludicrous resemblance of the design to its supposed original will readily enough be seen" [quoting Cushing 1897a:425].

The general conclusion that this Court of the Pile Dwellers was wrecked at some time, possibly from certain evidences destroyed by fire; that the objects fell into the mud at the bottom of the shell paved lagoon and had been left there for ages until they had almost ceased to be wood; that the salt water and marly clay served as a pickeling element in which to retain the woody fiber until these days when we are beginning to know the value of such pages from the history of the past. All of this is well brought out and the questions of who they were, these Key dwellers, has received attention, indeed Mr. Cushing claims that the mound builder derived his impulse to build mounds from some such environment as these people had. That the building of mounds was at first necessary—for without them these Floridians would have had no place whereon to rest their foot, and that subsequently mounds were built in like manner because of the survival of the old idea.

So it is that the Pepper-Hearst expedition carried on by the University of Pennsylvania Museum of Science and Art conjointly with the Bureau of American Ethnology has brought to light a rich, new field for the investigator and has added much data to the world's knowledge of primitive life on the western continent.

Such specimens, paintings, maps, and photographs with field notes and careful study over the collections can not fail to in the end make the material for a final report which should do credit to the indomitable energy of the veteran explorer, his aids and supporters in the work. (Sawyer n.d.b)

The chronicle of the excavation is best told by those who were there and described it from day to day in their diaries and letters. A high degree of interest and enthusiasm is evidenced throughout, sometimes for attractions other than the artifacts, exotic though they were. The diary of George Gause (1896) reveals him to be a vigorous, unlettered man, but it is worth quoting, leaving intact his misspellings, abbreviations, and punctuation (or mostly lack thereof). On February 6, 1896, he "comenced work" for Cushing:

Left Anclote on the 23 sailed for Marco 2-1/2 days to Pointrosa. Stopped 1/2 day shopping went ashore I stayed aboard mailed one letter to Susie Gause by way St. James. Wind nnw. All well can look down on St. James Pointarossia and other little places around. w. wind 10 knots, fished all the way from home to the great pointarossia Bay without getting a bite. 2 steamers passes us Pt. Rossia Bay. Saw 2 ladies walking the beautifull beach & then all night there. We sailed to Marco Robt got sick got to Marco on 26th its night Cushing & wife gone ashore bed time went to sleep under the sound of the 2 Georges voices singing down in the fore peak, wether calm as a thought no insects to bother us we turn over and pass away silently and hapy.

27th got up in morning went to work in the mamoth cove got the some ivory some bone & 2 pots one scull and a little connio [canoe?] Venison for supper gone to bed all is well and lonely. (Gause 1896)

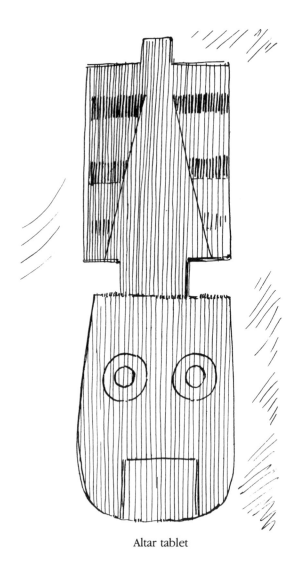

Altar tablet

Cushing's version of the day, in a letter to Pepper, repeated the enthusiasm: "I have begun work. It is now noon; but already we have found wooden articles, superb shell specimens and some of the most beautiful carved ivory hair pins I ever saw! Our entire collection will be unique and almost priceless if we keep on this way!" (Cushing 1897g). Gause continued:

Next morning venison steak for breakfoust went to work Mr. Sawyer sick all the rest well
Saturday morning went to work cove full of water & suggested making a gutter which was done. Gelousness followed by Mr. B— after that we got water out and found several boles and pessels I found a net only one ever

got Diner venison soup dined hearty. . . . to-night boys all gone fishing Mr & Mrs Cushing gone sailing myselfe and Mr Sawyer stays on board he develops his pictures I am not feeling well from last night's rain got cold, saw several girls along with other spectators amongst theme was the hardest looking case I ever Saw come Up in daylight well Mr Cushing is back on board alls well now 9 o'clock Sat night going to bed under the sound of coffee mill preparing coffee for breakfast, so tie out the sea pigon and retire.

Sunday morning got breakfast & went to Little Marco myselfe Robt and Hutson got 4 ducks saw John Weeks come home Cushing well pleased with the delightfull sports we had night supper bell time. All have a good card game and went to bed. (Gause 1896)

Apparently Pepper had still not received Cushing's letters detailing the reasons for needing extra funds and describing the quality of the artifacts. He had received the requests for funds, however, and telegraphed Cushing refusing further funds and, in language that upset Cushing, demanding to know what was going on. In a letter marked "Confidential" that Cushing wrote to Pepper on March 1, 1896, he said, "The discoveries I am now daily making are not only unique but are unparalleled in the annals of American archaeology! They are in this country what the discoveries of the Swiss Lake Dwellings were to Europe. In the old muck filled courts of these sea villages I am finding all the arts of the original inhabitants represented with a completeness never before surpassed even in such finds as those of the cliff dwellers." He goes on to say that if the Archaeology Department of the University of Pennsylvania cannot provide more funds, he can easily get them elsewhere for another season's work "as I have in hand and actually in sight at the excavations a whole section of a museum of ancient remains entirely new to our archaeology." He explained that the main difficulties were due to the delay of the *Silver Spray*'s return to Tarpon Springs, necessitating extension of his time, and continued, "I have to state that I cannot report to you more fully 'instantly' for I have ab-

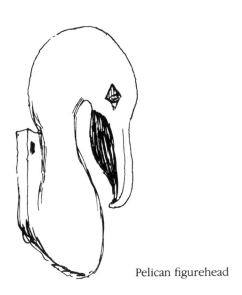

Pelican figurehead

solutely as much to do *day and night* [Cushing's emphasis], as I can do." He concluded, "And I fear I must ask that any further communication of the nature of your telegram, involving as that did my personal repute, be sent by sealed letter" (Cushing 1896h). On March 3, he wrote again, "My finds in the north were magnificent. Here they have been and continue to be unparalleled as yet in any field" (Cushing 1896i).

Cushing did not receive an immediate reply, but he tried again for funds after his pique diminished. He said that he had been loath to ask for further funding because he knew that the funds at the disposal of the Archaeology Department were already overtaxed by the many explorations progressing under department auspices in other parts of the world. However, he felt the Key Marco site to be sufficiently significant to warrant the request.

Gause continued to relate each day's events:

Monday morn got to work found some very nice spicments such as pots bowls knives spears needles and carved wood along with a conno [canoe?] spar 14 ft long which was very interesting to Mr C to supper next venison steak for super and all well after which we had a good game of cards and retired

Tuesday morning all well but Alfred Hutson gone to work found everything lovely found some very fine speciments night a game of cards Then comes Mr Barnes a deff and dumm man Frank's father but Frank could talk to him all OK got 2 opossums for 25 cts went to bed

Wednesday morning breakfast all well Mr. C had a bad headache but is better all goes to work the happies day ever gleaned on Marco Mr Burgman found 3 mask faces Robt 1 mall Alfred 5 bowls George Gause found 100 needles and 1 ball of wax then went with Mr C to examin some other places Home to supper Mrs. C over joyed with the curioes of the day Mr Sawyer says he can't talk when he saw them beauties we have found Mr Clark found a shell matted over nicely besides other thing too teedious to mention On board the Spray we talk and laugh about the days doing and in joy Mr C smiles. now for a game of cards before bed time nice it was now to bed good night hello there comes the pretties little naptha launch has caught 2 tarpon trowling alls well so we retire Wednesday night 9 oclock.

March 5 Thursday morning Mr Sawyer has finished servaying the Indian city at Marco, Mr Cushing gives Gause full controll of the men to excavate the cove and mounds to the best of his ability and have his own way with the work generaly all dine hearty on the good things poot before us while eating George Gaus points out to the crew a great storm in westerly direction—traveling slowly toworge the NE at about 3 degrees upwardly 4 pt under N storm then we have a good game of cards 7 tarpon caught today by yachtsman no letters from home as yet Mr Clark is now wrighting a letter home. good days work and all well good night. (Gause 1896)

On March 5 we have the first entry in Mrs. Margaret McIlvane Collier's diary: "Mr. Cushing and party are digging for curios. His artist Mr. Sawyer has caught the tarpon fever, so with Mr. Parker's old reel he is fishing" (Collier 1896).

March 6 was a day worth noting by both Mrs. Collier and George Gause in their diaries:

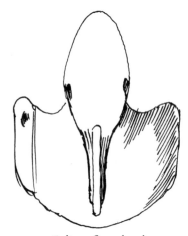

Pelican figurehead

March 6—Mr. Cushing dug up a pair of sun shells about four inches long, one side was painted in black on the inside, a man with fancy head and arm rig [pl. 9], & dug a turtle's head carved of wood, with a snout 2 inches long, it is hollow, & is painted in black and white, these are dug from below the muck which is two feet deep, are bedded in marl, and must have been put there by people before Columbus's time [pl. 19]. When they find anything nice they all give a yell and Mr. Cushing shakes hands with the one who made the find. They are making a very thorough investigation, are wheeling the muck out on the shell hills where it will be convenient for us to get it for the field. This expedition is sent out by the University of PA. and must cost a lot although the gentlemen of the party are volunteers. (Collier 1896)

Thursday doings went work early got some very interesting speciments 1 lyons image 1 womans image 1 turtle head all of good hard wood 6 bowls 2 pessels some carved boards 1 ball wax 2 little cannos 1 plummett rapped with thread and waxed found by Robt Day went off nice bowls found by Alfred bowls and pessell by George Turtle George Lyon and woman found by Mr Cushing Mrs Cushing seems well delighted then supper wild turkey baked and a stew of the same. (Gause 1896)

The next day Gause's enthusiasm grew: "Friday the 6 went to work early soon found the most purfect painting ever found by an exciber a pair of shells with Indian painted inside the I found a turtles head purfect then an Indian adz & 2 bowls 3 mallets 2 plumets 1 beautifull gorge found by Alfred Mr Clark found some nice thing such as pessell plummets and a head dress so we come in all well find 2 pleasure sch anchored near had got 2 tarpons 2 sawfish 1 15 ft long 1 14 ft long then we play cards" (Gause 1896). (The shell with an Indian painted inside was the shell that caused so much trouble for Cushing later when he was accused of fabricating it by a fellow employee of the BAE who had nothing to do with the expedition.)

March 7 was another exciting day as Mrs. Collier recorded it: "The diggers got a thin board with a strange bird painted on it in black and white. Pappa and I went down with Mr. Cushing on Capt. Cuthbert's wharf today, to see this, & the three masks they had previously dug, very curious these masks are made of wood with eyes of shell, the mouth puckered up and some paint visible. Mr. Sawyer was photographing them. Mr. Sawyer is 'an interesting specimen of sweet humanity'" (Collier 1896).

Gause says, "Saturday morning we go to work George Gause finds another adzs on the handle purfect some malls were found by Alfred and Robt George also found a great tray carved on [here he includes a small sketch] Mr C found a bird painted on a board nicely 2-1/2 ft in the muck the weeks finds are tremendous good night super bell time all have a good card game and went to bed" (Gause 1896).

Cushing was again enthusiastic when he wrote to Dr. Pepper on March 7:

As I wrote you, all the arts of the life led by these old sea dwellers are represented in my collections as completely as in the case of the Swiss Lake collections. I have not only implements, household utensils and weapons in great variety, but also idols, masks, ornaments and carvings of these wonderful ancient people. My discoveries have been literally star-

tling! For example three days ago I found under four feet of peat a closed shell in which was a *painting* of a dancer in all his paraphernalia. I found at the same time nearby a statuette of hard wood of the Mountain Lion God, equal to any from Egypt or Assyria. Painted masks fragmentary appliances and timbers of houses were found everywhere. Yesterday I made the crowning find—an altar tablet of cypress wood about 15 inches long bearing a distinct though faded painting of the King-Fisher-God carrying his double paddle as insignia, with word signs issuing from his mouth—precisely as in the paintings of the Central American and higher Mexican codices. So, I have not only discovered as I expected to, *American Pile Dwellers* but also the remains of a new culture comparable in most products to that of Mexico itself and *superior* to that of the mound builders of the further north. I *must* finish this work—go as far as possible with it now, and follow it up in the future. You cannot do better for the University Department than to join me heartily in this. I want the work to be *monographic*, its material results—except duplicates—to be concentrated. I will aid you in the effort to raise the requisite means for it and to push it, before the field is invaded as it is sure to be if left alone. There are other *urgent* reasons why I should remain here as long as possible now, notwithstanding the fact that I have to work harder than I have ever worked in my life; for occasionally the finds are so beautiful that I cannot trust *anyone* to uncover them unless under my eye. Thus I have to remain constantly in the

muck-beds. You must not blame me, if, hereafter, my notes are very brief—for I shall continue excavating until I hear from you in reply to this letter. The Collier place at least must be finished now if at all. The others only the most trusted one of my men, Mr. Sawyer and I know of. (Cushing 1896j)

The Gause chronicle continued:

Sunday morning comes we goe after oysters safford Alfred and Myselfe to Little Marco we had a lovely time the day went off fine we were in company with 3 or 4 ladies returned home with a bbl and a gal of oysters and 1 bird shot by Alfred Hutson

Monday Mr Cushing says George you must find a tager [?] in the mound which I did then 3 trays and a bunch of arrows 4 ft long no of them 24 several other fine speciments wore found such as bowls malls and adzs spears & points Day went off fine all well wind SE Blowing 6 knots at least

Tuesday morning comes after a good night's rest on fish and oysters all well we go to work early I found 3 trays and a dice 2 inches long round bone with a hole through it with holes drilled in as dice nos 84 holes several speciments found some scrapers with cords roped around theme Alfred found a ball of wax some plumets roped with waxed twine mad from palmato fibrie or scisliy hemp. . . . Mr Cushing finds his share of the speciments all well after supper we weight up the dinae and go to bed all in good cherr Capt Colyer whin around the muck pile just the same." (Gause 1896)

Mrs. Collier continued her diary: "March 10, Mr. Cushing continues to find lots of things, several large wood trays, a bundle of arrows tied together. They have moved their things into the parlor, where they can be dried and photographed" (Clarke private papers). One can imagine the inconvenience of having her parlor filled with muddy specimens that probably had just been removed from the "foul-smelling muck"

Cushing complained of, and in a house with eight children, the oldest sixteen, and with paying dinner and overnight guests.

She showed no sign of irritation, and her interest continued: "March 12—Mr. Cushing found another mask. I have not seen it yet. Julia [one of the children] told me Mr. C. dug out a little gourd made out of a pumpkin. She did not know that gourds are always gourds. Pappa is greatly pleased with the muck Mr. Cushing's men are throwing out, thinks it will be very valuable to our field. All have bad colds" (Collier 1896).

Gause told of the next day: "Wednesday comes we go to work and Mr Gause finds a bear head carved of wood some trays 1 spear point and several other beautifull thing and a storm comes down and we get a nice old wetting go home and have a good supper and a drink of good whisky and a good rest" (Gause 1896).

Wells Sawyer wrote a letter home that same day, March 12:

The winter is passing and soon it will be spring—here it is ever spring—yet after all the north has charms—great charms. Here we are miles from the railroad, the mails come irregularly and many a letter sent from these regions never reaches its destination while as to those sent here if they look attractive I fear they would be opened. Packages sent by post or Express are stolen and the world of today is whirling on while this spot of yesterday or the day before largely drones in the sun shine, disturbed only by the buzz of mosquitoes or the "squack" of the night heron. Great flocks of ducks swim about us hardly disturbed and the tarpon spring from the waters showing their silver scales in the sunshine.

The glorious color of the sunset lasts for only a few moments then rapidly fades and the star light comes out upon us. In the waters are phospherescent anamalcule which glow as a flame beneath the paddle or shoot a tongue of fluorescent light where the swimming fish speeds away.

Lazily we swing at our anchor chain here in this beautiful harbour. Yonder they dig from the Lagooon wonders more rare than are the trees or the birds for here man reached a perfection of life which was almost civilisation more than 1000 years ago. Here are the mysteries of the old men of America revealed, here the true speaking story of the ancients.

What we have found is most wonderful. No other place has been so wonderful. America, North America, the United States had once within its borders people who were the superiors in some ways of the ancient Egyptians who rivaled the first wood carvers of the world and whose works come forth from the salt sea pickle as fresh as they were when they dropped here ages ago—

The wonder of the world. I am glad to be here. (Sawyer 1896b)

Gause was not always entirely sure of the day or date, but his entries were in sequence so it is not difficult to determine them when the whole document is viewed. He continued: "Tuesday comes fair wind NE cool we go to work Mr Cushing finds a quoil of rattan mad into a tray and Mr Clark found the head of a woolf in beautiful carving of wood [pl. 21] 2 balls of wax with spear points together with a carved stone 1 selce handle beautifully carved and one pellican head carved of wood besides other things we saw on our way home to the Spray 3 girls all standing on a cuplew [cupola?] the beautifules sight of the day we bring home the finds of the day and Mr and Mrs Cushing is caried away they greet us heartily Mrs Cushing extends her thank to Mr Gause for some berrys we then have supper dine hearty on spear ribs and other good thing such as cake wine coffee tea butter potatoes bread buiscuit and Beans milk and &c" (Gause 1896).

Mrs. Collier's perspective on the days:

March 13—Mr. Cushing called this evening. He thinks these ancient people were from Central Amer. and were here about 1100 years ago. Some of the things were carefully buried. He is so well informed on the subject that we like to have him talk. a newspaperman is here and is going to write it up.

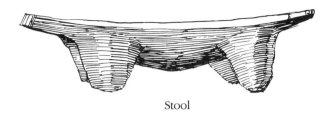

Stool

March 14—call from Mr. Chapin and his friend. They order dinner for themselves and the Cushings for tomorrow at 6.

Another lovely day. Mr. Chapin came in in a Naptha and got Pappa to go pilot his new yacht in. He says the Tampa bridge is about complete. Also that none of the Florida hotels are full, so we need not feel badly about having so few guests. . . . Mr. Chapin got his yacht in. She cost $12,000 and is a beauty, built by W. Sweat of Tampa. Her name is *Polly* for his younger daughter.

[March 15] The folks on the *Polly* and the *Silver Spray* came to dinner and said they spent a very enjoyable evening, and we certainly enjoyed their coming. Mr. Chapin and Mr. Rumrill are very plain. I was much amused to see them come each bringing a bag of laundry which my chambermaid was going to do for them. Mr. Rumrill took from his bag two bottles of cider which he had brought for dinner. We also enjoyed Mr. Cushing telling us of his experience among the Soux Indians. He was six years with them. (Collier 1986)

(Of course it was actually the Zuñis with whom Cushing had spent the six years.) Gause continued in his diary:

Saturday comes and finds all well weather pleasant wind low NE—grows cooler wind goes round to SE we go to work soon the cries go up shout after shout the head of a hornd owl with 2 gorgetts [small sketches of them] fine to look at from the coast of [illegible] Central America Indian throughout—2 boxes painted found by Alfred Gorgetts found by Gause Mr Cushing finds his shear of fine thing Alfred find ivory and pearl bead

& knives to dress the head of some squaw. Perhaps well Mr Cushing is all smiles again Mr. Clark found a ceremonial stool with a canew on top of it then an atatatal with spike in it all the shells you would looke from This is fine all cherfull and well

wether cool morning of 14 & 15 Sunday morning comes Alfred and George goes to the beach for shells, returns with 2 girls Sunday but he makes his appearance in the blacksmith shop till 4 oclock then went off with the girls till 1/2 pm. (Gause 1896)

Cushing reported at length to Dr. Pepper on March 14:

Awaiting your letter, I have continued excavations in the old water court here, foot by foot, until a little more than one third of it is worked over and a collection such as never yet seen was gathered, at least here in America, has been secured. Up to the last, however, the finds have continued increasingly rich, and each hour contained something new, for although many duplicates occur, there seems to be no end to the variety of types, especially of objects illustrating the arts and ceremonology of the ancient pile dwellers and shell builders of this region. When we arrived here I found the muck-bed under water, and work was very difficult; but by digging a viaduct through the banks and constructing a series of troughs and gutters, I was speedily able to lower the level of the water by bailing, and since a little bailing each morning has almost drained the whole area. In consequence our digging can be carried on now systematically and with the utmost care and yet much more rapidly than at first. [crossed out]: But another consequence is worrying me. The draining of the basin of the water court has caused the peat and marl containing the specimens to sink somewhat over a foot in the middle of the basin, and the carrying off of so much water or rather brine will at last, after all these centuries expose the specimens more or less to the air and lead to their rapid decay if left thus for any length of time [end of crossing out]. Thus during the past four or five days I have taken out several masks and figure heads carved and painted to represent mythic or demonic characters, as well as the deer, bear, raccoon, wolf, owl, eagle, turtle, crocodile and other creatures of the water etc. There are exquisite little carvings of ornamental and fetishistic character, and most extraordinary of all these water finds are the *paintings* and *painted* work we occasionally discover. Of course it is dim, but the designs are, when fresh, perfectly clear, and the style of art in this as in the carved work is equal to any in olden America, North or South. The culture represented by it was nothing short of a barbaric civilization. It was at once superior to and older than that of the mainland. It was related not only to the Antillean and the Maya, on the south, but to the Mound Builders of the North. It explains when interpreted, some of the most puzzling riddles in American anthropology—especially if studied in connection with my Northern finds of a less remote prehistoric period. Above all, however, we have here what I believed from the first we should find, the remains of veritable sea and lake dwellers, who built of shell with great regularity and on an enormous scale the centers or cores of their settlements who constructed around the margins of these and within them canoe ways and water or lake courts above and over which they dwelt in buildings reared on piles. Now not only do I find the remains of their daily life and arts in the places over which their buildings stood, but I also find as if by a special providence of history, that they made sacrifices in the waters of their lake courts, bundles of the choicest possessions of their dead, and deposited them in the mud beneath their places of abode. Such bundles contain from five or six to twenty or thirty objects all wonderfully perfect when first exposed, but very difficult of removal and still more difficult of preservation. The beauty of our finds is such that even the crude natives here are interested. *They* are moved to exca-

vate for themselves as soon as I shall have gone; but fortunately I made a written contract with Captain Collier that for the privilege of working undisturbed to the end I would save for him all the surface muck removed. I have reason to think even he is now beginning to regret the exclusive right he gave me. And I fear that what we now leave unexcavated will not be preserved for another season, because my draining of the place has made work excavating easier for these people. (Cushing 1896k)

Cushing continued that for this reason he wanted to finish the one court he had "opened," the actual excavation of which would require approximately another three and a half weeks at the present rate. Taking care of the specimens would require another additional two weeks. He assured Dr. Pepper, "I can positively affirm that if I can do this the collection made will be equal to any single collection of equally ancient things and in many respects the first and only collection of its kind in the world.... I feel that nothing should check the original plan that this collection or at best its first and main series should be the possession of the new University Museum, be kept together and monographic. I tell you again that it represents a new *undreamed of* primitive culture" (Cushing 1896k).

Gause continued to record his enthusiasm:

Mar 15—then aboard Monday morning comes all well we go to work the finds of the day mask of deer heads of wood bone worked beads shells wood carving &c diner time then to work rain comenced rain till night Mr Sayford saw a mare maid near the schoner *Silver Spray* we have a game & all pass the time off all OK alls well

Tuesday 17th we go to work George finds a wood carving a hawks head then a [illegible] that has very mutch interested Mr Cushing then comes the most important thing of all a [sketch] 5 ft paddle and a tablett painting some other nice finds made by Mr Clark & Alfred, Georg finds 3 plumits of great finish, the day pass of night comes super over Mr

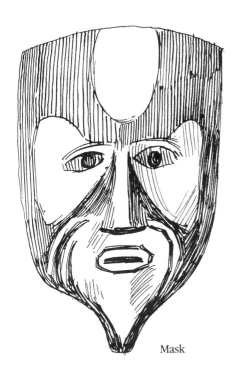

Mask

Cush goes off to the hotel & Georg takes up his time wrighting home, all well and the Spray still waves her pleasant brow to the NE wind light and cool alls well,

Wednesday morning Geo finds 3 masks made of wood all painted a board of beautiful painting some plumets and a cos x [sketch] mad of mahogania mettled bear jaws [sketch]. (Gause 1896)

On March 18, 1896, aboard the *Silver Spray* at Marco, Cushing again wrote to Pepper asking for $500: "The progress of the work since then has so amply vindicated my confidence, that I now also know you would have strenuously objected to its discontinuance even had greater expenditures been involved. The discoveries I am now daily making are not only unique but are unparalleled in the annals of American Archaeology! They are to this country what the discoveries of the Swiss Lake Dwellings were to Europe. In the old muck filled water courts of these sea villages I am finding all the arts of the original inhabitants represented with a completeness never before surpassed . . . all the difficulty arose from delay of the vessel and from the total lack of candor to-

ward both Mr. Disston and myself on the part of those who had her in charge" (Cushing 1896l). Gause continued:

Thursday comes Geo finds a grains several peaces of farafanaluar[paraphernalia?] with other thing a girl with my mud boots on lots of funn and then a talk with Mr Cushing and home on board the Spray a good super at the table of a talk we dry off from being wet with a coald rain we go to bed alfred has toothache all the rest are well wind blowing 6 or 8 from NW, good night, this is the 19th George delighted in reading letters from home also Mr Clark rejoyces in one too

Friday comes all well and lively—went to work in good spirit Mr Cushing says we can go to Palm Hammock Sunday & stay till Monday night we do good work excavating (Gause 1896)

Sawyer told of their excursion to Palm Hammock in a letter to his mother:

Your letter came to me today on my return from a long journey into the interior or, across to the mainland. It would not be a long journey anywhere else, but here in Florida it is a *very* long ways. Seven of our men and I took our sharpie and went up the channel to Goodland Bay then we went through Hell Gate into the Palm River and up to the end. The banks were covered with the mangrove, indeed all the thousand islands are. It is a very curious tree and is responsible for most of the land in this end of the state—on a sand bar or oyster bar the seed of a mangrove, floating on the tide, catches and takes root; it soon grows to be somewhat of a tree and sheds seeds as well as putting out roots which hold the soil that is held in the water. The tree does not reach the ground but its roots support it above the tide, from its branches depend tap roots to which the oysters attach themselves and soon form a solid wall of oyster bar above the tide line, into here the seeds again fall so it grows and presently an island or key is born.

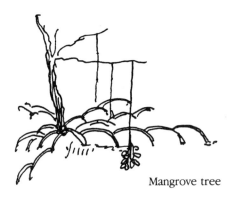

Mangrove tree

Now nature provides the seeds with a very curious spike which dart like is thrust into the ground—this catches into the little spaces between the oyster shells and presently grows.

I have gathered a sequence of the man grove but have not kept it. The little stem holds it above the tide.

Threading its way sometimes through channels only wide enough for the passage of the small skiff boat which we got further up the river, we found the Palm River—filled with fish and sometimes quite deep. The lit tle stream will soon be a thing of the past or maybe not for the tide is so strong that it clears the bed of most vegetable growth in these small channels, which by the way have been caused by the growth of the mangrove swamps toward one another. Along the shores were many deer and otter tracks and we had venison for meat, however we killed no game.

At the end of the river we found the tide so low that we all took our trousers off and shoved the boat three quarters of a mile in the shallow water.

There we reached the prairie on the main land. A broad and to the South a boundless plain. In front of us many whooping cranes were feeding but we failed to kill any. Be yond them was "palm hammock" where the Royal Palms grow and now I would better stop—for I cannot tell of the beauty—nor the density of the jungle nor of the many air plants, nor of the ferns and all that—It looked like this [sketch] half a mile away. The trees more than a hundred feet high are the only ones in the United States and our long trip and tiresome push through the mud was rewarded by a sight which I shall never for get. It *was* the tropics—jungle—and all.

When we returned I received your letter and had the mail not gone so soon I would have had this off today. I must now wait until Thursday.

As to my official status, it is the same as ever. As to the studio there is much to be said about that, however I shall probably *have* to give it up in case I should stay in Washington, an extremity which I hope to avoid. I like the city and the people but my work there is most unpleasant and brings me no advancement worth noting. I expect to have the pleasure of going to Philadelphia— at the University Museum—I say I expect, hardly for I am never so sure—but I may have the opportunity of doing so—if I can then I will and give up my job and Washing ton but a bird in the hand is worth two in the bush.

On the whole this venture if unsuccessful is a serious one if successful it is a fortunate one for I will have opportunities of study and for work in the field which can come to me *in no other way*. And further if I am success ful there is no small possibility of my going to Europe—Africa—Asia anywhere. For as art ist to a museum which looks forward to a fu ture there are many things I could do.

The museum is ambitious and I am anx ious to aid its efforts in the lines which are possible for me to follow. Think of Nineveh, Babylon, Egypt, etc.

As to letters I have written brief notes to you from the *Spray* because we are up at sunrise and working until dark because there is no writing room aboard and because I have so much work to do that I can hardly get into writing trim under the circum stances. Not at all because I do not want to write. (Sawyer 1896c)

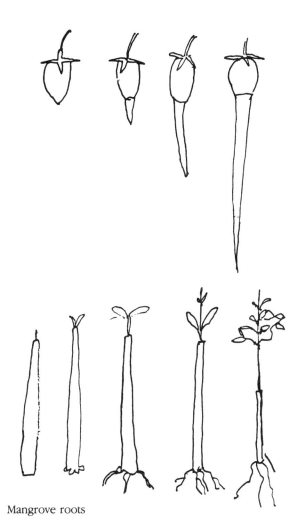

Mangrove roots

Sawyer was not the only one impressed with the beauty of the Royal Palms. Gause, too, told about the trip:

Sat comes we record our speciments to Mr C & went to work lively and willing We just at 4:30 to get a board with masks trays plumits carls shells pottery boats atatels carvings of all kinds night and all lively & in good cheer

Sunday Mr B takes us to his father where we stay all night on our way we shot duck saw a L turtle we got to Mr Barnes howse a log cab with the cracks stoped with mud and his son had kill a deer etc. which we hurd of on our way when we were met by old man B & wife deeff and dumb at the house was a woman claimed to be aunt of F next we start

supper we get potatoes & venison we sleep in a shock of stock and shucks O fear of snakes was offull but luckely we escaped being biten then morning come we get breakfast and start to Palm Hamock up the cruckededest stream on earth I know we had to take our boat by hand and head her up 4 miles to a place where they land to go to the hamock we walked out of the swamp and climbed up trees to see our way Mr Sawyer Mr Burgman Mr Sayford Mr Clark Mr Hudson Mr Barnes and myselfe Geo Gause We finaly come to a hault by a sig given by Mr Barnes the guide cranes hooping crow we grab winchesters and shoot guns and quickly march to the place where we see them as they walked around on a larger parie George fired several shots with a winchester at a dis tance of 500 yards but only got one bird we then saw glympses of the royal palms which taken away every thought that could ever aproach the mind O it was the most eligant sight ever beheld we soon were looking up over our heads to see the blooms and leaves flutter in the wind Geo takes his winchester and cuts down some blooms from the tall palms then we hurry to our boat soon we are in the creek with duds off pulling the boat in the direction of the Spray which is 12 miles away and it 1 oclock we find our way all OK get to Mr Barnes hous whose sweet bye & bye was sung with great ecos [echoes] by the misketoes then we start home to Marco to the *Silver Spray* get home at 9 ooc and all are well Monday night 9 oclock

Thursday morning we go to work and fine a fine lot of plumetts atlatels 1 fine mask painted more Mr Cushing call to George & says that girl seems stuck on some one I sopose George understands it as he likes to show the speciments to the spectatores, &c all pass on lovely. (Gause 1896)

Dr. Pepper must have finally received some of Cushing's reports because in a letter of March 22 Cushing wrote acknowledging receipt of Pepper's "very gratifying letters of March 9 and 13"

(Pepper 1896a). These must have been Pepper's letters bringing word that Mrs. Phebe Hearst had agreed to finance the expedition for as long as it took to complete excavation and preserve the specimens. Cushing continued:

The finds continue as extraordinary as ever, although the middle of the lagoon which we are now going through is naturally not as full of remains as were the borders. Nevertheless every cubic foot contains something and I wish I could merely chronicle to you the finds of even this section—masks distinc tively Maya in both form and decoration as are two nearly perfect atlatls, shell weights and two most remarkable stone anchors etc. etc.; but I must answer your question. The work has progressed more rapidly within the past few days than hitherto yet I cannot possi bly say how soon I can prudently stop it, for the remaining borders will be as productive as were those of the first side we attacked and will require corresponding patience and time.

I shall, however, pack, and leave for the north, as soon as possible, and shall make every effort to reach Philadelphia in late April so as to take advantage of the possibility you have so very kindly arranged for—of my making a preliminary announcement of our discoveries here, in the stated meeting of the American Philosophical Society on the eve ning of the first of May.

The whole difficulty is in the preparation of the specimens for shipment. This is a seri ous task. Merely to dry them sufficiently for packing requires days for they have lain in the brine-soaked peat and marl for centuries, and if dried in the open air of even a room, rapidly warp and check. I therefore have to pack them in dry sand for a time, size them, place them under clothes on shelves and thus proceed very slowly and cautiously.

This in a measure answers your question about the duplicates for the Novgorod Expo sition. I greatly fear they cannot be made ready for safe transportation in time, yet I promise to do my best to make up a box.

The project is a *very* important one. I think I can appreciate that as fully as you do and can enter as fully into an effort for its consumation. If we fail there will be one ele ment of satisfaction; the specimens will count for ten times their present worth after the strange story of their recovery and of *their marvellous meaning* is published. (Pepper 1896a).

Things were exciting for the Colliers too, aside from exotic finds of the expedition crew. On March 23, Mrs. Collier recorded that one of the younger children, Tommy, "came near burning the house by lighting some stuff that was under the east wing. Pappa was coming in to dinner when he saw it, and ran under and put it out." (This is one of the sons later drowned in the storm of March 3, 1898.) She said on March 26 that "Pappa is very proud of the muck Mr. Cush ing has thrown out for us, thinks it worth $500" (Collier 1896).

Sawyer again wrote home from aboard the *Sil ver Spray* in the Marco ship channel on Sunday, March 29, 1896:

The spring has come, hot weather, sunshine, mosquitoes and all. Tho it is not too hot, now there are too many insects now it is summer here—It's like a day in later May in the north, not a cool day but a pretty sugges tive one of the oncoming summer. The green waters lash against our boats and the greener moss trails from our hull for the Spray pull ing at her anchor chains has become moss grown and the fish beneath nibble it from her hull.

[Here there are sketches of the *Silver Spray*, sharpie, dinghy and skiff; see pl. 16.]

This is our fleet tho the sharpie, dingy boat and skiff are too large in proportion to the *Spray* which is a 2187 ton schooner carrying six sails. We have aside from the party, Mr. and Mrs. C., Bergman, Sayford and I—a crew of a "sailing master," Capt. Gomez, a Spaniard—a "mate" Brady—"a cook" and an assistant who are Blacks [pl. 8]. The cooking is done in the galley in front of the main mast, three or rather four "able seamen" and several men who work at the excavations—all souls, 14. I do not know that I have writ ten about the crew before. In fact I guess I have not done so.

You see from this that it is not a very small work which is being done, and naturally I am anxious to see it through.

Mr. Cushing has written asking an exten sion of my leave until the first of May—this will probably be granted tho I am very sorry that it is necessary. The disappointment which Kathleen will feel will surely be very keen. I hope you will drop her a letter being vague about the date of my return but telling her of the regret that I had expressed. The wind is blowing and I am writing on the quarterdeck so the paper gets blown about considerably however if you can read it you will forgive its roughness I hope.

The finds continue of import and my work is doubled. Today I am taking a splendid rest enjoying the spring under the awning which protects the cabin and quarter decks. We sit at the side of the cabin and eat off the roof it being about the height of a table above the deck.

I am very well and if Capt. Collier's scales don't lie I weigh 137 lbs—tho I question that somewhat. (Sawyer 1896d)

Gause's interest and enthusiasm continued:

Mr. Cushing shows us some painting he had found on some little boards from today a crockodile in paint on the sides of a box about 5 × 8 inches on the others were [sketch] beautifully painted in black the day has been the greatest ever experienced in America, god speed the good work says all the crue alls well and happy Friday night all OK

Tuesday morning we are all well and again march out to work together we find some good speciments

Wednesday comes the same was the case we find 1 pr [sketch] a canew 1 mask one bunch arrows one bowl 2 malletts 2 pessell 1 tray 1 jaw of a large giant [sketch] was it night

when the girls came and bade us stop work we went home with them and had a lively time got some good whisky punch and sup per and went to bed. all right Tuesday we forgoten to say rained & Mr. Clark reads his letter from home & smiles. We go to bed all well Morning comes Friday we go to work find seveal wonderfull speciments night again supper and good sailing Mr Cushing and wife gone then we have a big hoop and bid good night Sat rains we stay in till 7 ock. (Gause 1896)

On April 2, from aboard the *Silver Spray* an chored off Marco, Cushing wrote again to Pepper, apologizing for his financial difficulties and ask ing again that the additional amount he requested be sent. He said he expected "to close up here in a few days. This stay is *amply* rewarded. Once through the middle of the water court the men began to find rarer objects again. Not to speak of many little odds and ends, we have since my last writing added six other masks on three of which the painting is still well preserved. This series of masks stands alone. It is prehistoric uncontami nated. As a consequence it is the first collection ever gathered which in itself can *show* precisely the place the *mask* held in primitive religion the world over. In conjunction with the magnificent little figure heads it tells the story of the primitive sacred drama and the mythic concepts underly ing it with such vividness that a small volume of hitherto partly mysterious characteristics in bar baric civilization are also cleared up—the rela tion, for instance, of these appliances of the drama to the decoration of ewers, utensils and weapons. One day this week when a harsh wind quelled for a few hours the mosquitos I pene trated the mangrove swamps south of this ancient city of shell. My exploration was but cursory and secret. Yet I have discovered traces of sites which put this one to shame so far as extent is con cerned. I have left neither stone, shell, nor turf unturned in the latter [site]. (I am glad you so de cidedly agree we cannot leave any of it to destruc tion) yet I have but *touched* this new world in Archaeology. We must publish the matter (pre liminarily at least) early and widely in order that having shown people how to set the egg on end we may at least have the name of having shown them! For these masks will set archaeologists agog. In view of this possibility of illustrations for speedy publication I am retaining Sawyer beyond the expiration of his leave for an extension of which I have had to make a great effort and will have to pay him, but his salary is less than a hundred dollars per month and his work (color sketching of the more perishable articles particularly) simply invaluable" (Cushing 1896m).

George Gause continued to record daily activities:

Sunday comes we go to the beach George comes back Mrs Cushing invites George to catch her a shark or a tarpon but he failed to do so Monday comes we go to the cove and George was ordered to cross the wire line he did then he begins to fail to find his finds

Tuesday we go early to the cove and finish the greatest job of excavating ever done in Fla now boys go round to rest your selves up we are done George reports a finish to Mr Cushing and thanks of kindness from Mrs Cushing for the eneumerous number of nice things presented her while excavation was being caryed on. The week passes off fine we made several visits to difrent parts of the thousand islands till

Sat comes then we go to good land Point there Mr Clark Mr Cushing and George finds the pretties place of Indian works and among the beauties was 2 off the pretties girls of the cracker race O how our hearts go out in sympathy to meet theme in these disolate is lands we return to the Silver Spray and re port the notes of the day we have supper and ashore for an out late hour

Sunday comes we go over to the hotel as usul while we are there trying to spend an hour in laughter a mad dog bit a little girl of Mr Rosses then the excitement begins the dog was shot 4 times before he gave up to die then we quietly bade the ladies good eve and on board the Spray we land for supper after we do our laughing we go fishing sail ing and George goes off ashore for a few

hours but returns all OK well all is well Sun day, April 12, 1896. (Gause 1896)

The last days of excavating and a surprise visit are well chronicled: Gause told it this way:

Monday comes we get up to breakfast we are ateing the word comes to go to Bear Point to prospect we go Mr Cushing Mr Clark Mr Hudson and my selfe Cpt Toney takes some fir wood and water on ariving home we saw the great loger head turtle as they flot away down the beautifull Marco stream. Then to supper and to bed at 10

Tuesday comes we get out soon to ate our breakfast when we see a row boat coming in the direction of the Spray O the mail schooner is in thers a pasenger who is he the head of the burury mager powell, he comes on board the Spray after receiving the warm est reception we go to bear point he sees the beauties of the Forest we return after which we have diner then the same good whisky supper an ashore a good time

then comes Tuesday we take the mager to Pine Key there mager powell sees the beautifull Indian works and becoming satisfyed we return home to super we have a good drink and ashore goes George and Mr. Hudson to pay the butterflys a visit then com ing home a beautifull scenery a fine sail on the beautifull waters of Marco as they spar kled like the stary hevens

Wednesday comes the mager bids Mr Cushing stop his work, after tell all the boys by by he takes his flyt to pointgorda by via of the mail boat. (Gause 1896)

Powell's surprise visit to Marco surely made Cushing happy. Powell would now verify his reports and see the importance of what he was doing. Mrs. Collier's diary for April 8 noted, "Mr. Sawyer came in tonight and had a waltz with Emma [the daughter born aboard the schooner *Emma White* while it was anchored in the Caloosahatchee River]. He is so pleasant. Mr. Powel, Mr. Cushing's boss is here, and is well pleased with their work. They have finished their digging and are packing the specimens" (Collier 1896).

Cushing had been constantly disturbed that so many of the unique specimens he was uncovering could be neither removed nor preserved. He tried everything at hand to retain the specimens in good condition, but his results were disappointing. He wrote seeking other possible preservatives and asked advice of everyone. He commented to Dr. Pepper:

Fluid glass does not work, glue but indifferently; and I have to send away for other preservatives.

The objects found by us in these deposits were in various conditions of preservation, from such as looked fresh and almost new, to such as could scarcely be traced through or distinguished from the briny peat mire in which they were imbedded. They consisted of wood, cordage and like perishable materials associated with implements and ornaments of more enduring substances, such as shell, bone and horn—for only a few shaped of stone were encountered during the entire search.

Articles of wood far outnumbered all others. I was astounded to soon find that many of these had been painted in black, white, blue-gray, and brownish-red pigments and that while the wood itself was so decayed and soft that in many cases it was difficult to distinguish the fibre of even large objects of it, either by sight or by touch, from the muck and peat in which they were unequally distributed, but now more or less integrated; yet when discoverable in time to be cautiously uncovered and washed off by the splashing or trickling of water over them from a sponge, their forms appeared not only almost perfect, but also deceptively well preserved, so that I at first thought we might, with sufficient care, recover nearly all of them uninjured. This was especially true of such as had been decorated with the pigments; for owing to the presence in these pigments of a gum-like and comparatively insoluble sizing, the coatings of color were often relatively better

preserved than the woody substance they covered, and enabled us the more readily to distinguish the outlines of these painted objects—when else some had been partially destroyed or altogether missed—and also enabled us to take them up on broad, flat shovels, and to more deliberately divest them of the muck and peat that so closely clung to them.

Some of the things thus recovered could be preserved by very slow drying, but it soon became evident that by far the greater number of them could not be kept intact. No matter how perfect they were at first, they warped, shrunk, split, and even checked across the grain, like old charcoal, or else were utterly disintegrated on being exposed to the light and air if for only a few hours. Thus, despite the fact that after removing the surface muck from the sections, we dug only with little hand-trowels and flexible-pronged garden claws—and, as I have said before, with our fingers—yet fully twenty-five per cent of these ancient articles in wood and other vegetal material were destroyed in the search; and again, of those found and removed, not more than one-half retained their original forms unaltered for more than a few days.

Unique to archaeology as these things were, it was distressing to feel that even by merely exposing and inspecting them, we were dooming so many of them to destruction, and to think that of such as we could temporarily recover only the half could be preserved as permanent examples of primitive art. (Cushing 1896m)

He sought by every means at his disposal to remedy these difficulties but found that the time required and the additional cost of preservatives, if they could be found, would increase the cost of the operations considerably beyond the original estimates upon which appropriations had been based. He had already tried glue, shellac, and silicate of soda, all of which proved to be comparatively inefficient.

He appealed to Major Powell for suggestions

on methods of preserving the artifacts, and, instead of answering his letter, Powell made his surprise visit to Key Marco. Powell was apparently pleasantly surprised when he saw the quality and uniqueness of the specimens, for Cushing wrote to Dr. Pepper, "He [Maj. Powell] agrees with my conclusions in regard not only to the Pile Dwelling's phase of the remains found and the artificial nature of the keys, but also, with reference to my theory which he considers well supported by the facts as observed as to the derivation of the original settlers from the Venezuelan Pile Dwellers or from other pile dwelling Caribbean peoples of the South" (Cushing 1896n).

However, because the "season of rain and excessive heat" had already begun, limiting the time it would be possible to work in the flooded, mosquito-ridden mangroves, Powell urged Cushing to confine his operations to excavation of the small area he called the Court of the Pile Dwellers and to close the season with that effort. They believed it possible to extend such excavation and discoveries indefinitely, and Cushing hoped to return another season for further exploration and excavation in the area.

Stratigraphy, a most useful tool to archaeologists in establishing dates for occupation of specific sites, was impossible to establish in this case, even though Cushing said that artifacts were found at varying depths in the muck. Many articles were separated from companion pieces, such as mortars and pestles found some distance apart. Some objects were found wrapped together in bundles bound together with reed matting, but most were scattered as though they had fallen into the muck when the structure in which they were housed collapsed.

By April 10, Cushing wrote to Pepper that he had practically completed the excavations at Marco and had the main force of his workmen engaged in packing the collections. He expected to leave in two weeks. He continued, "The eastern border of the water court proved, as we both anticipated, rich in rare remains. Not only were small carved objects found, but also, the series of masks was added to by three or four of the finest examples we have yet secured. They alone would

have amply rewarded our persistence!" (Cushing 1896o).

He agreed to contribute to "Mrs. Hearst's Journal" as Pepper suggested, then added: "Unexpectedly Major Powell visited us Tuesday and Wednesday, and he pronounces the finds unique, and the discovery that of a 'new culture.' He has examined the evidence thoroughly and stands by my conclusions notwithstanding their unlooked for nature. He pronounces my discovery of the ancient Sea Dwellers or Bayou People that of a New Empire Ethnologically, and says I have a chance to make a great contribution to the Science of Anthropology not of America only but of the world, and he said that through you he hoped the University would see the importance of publishing at once and adequately the results as soon as I am able to work the collections up, for it would be a contribution to science relative to a huge phase of culture hitherto unknown. [crossed out: He said he would communicate with you personally regarding all this, and I will therefore not write more, save that you may trust Major Powell as single hearted in his devotion to science no matter what his detractors may say.] He has made me very happy by his generous relinquishment of my time for this work. I would not have missed the opportunity of showing him my field evidences, for I saw by his surprise at their extent that my simple story of it all would have been difficult of credence without such authoritative substantiation" (Cushing 1896o).

Gause wrote of their departure:

Friday comes brings rain and rest to the boys
Sat comes in and we go to goodland point where the Indian town use to stand after going over the Island we come home
Sunday comes we work one like funn to get ready to sail when a long come a vessell bound for Cedar Keys Mr Brady Mr Sayford and Mr Clark takes their departure for there homes tarpon Ft Hudson Homosasia then we get ready to sail we go ashore and bade Capt Collier and family farwell and amongst them Miss Floos the Bell of Marco we sail to Cacsimbus Pass till south for a short stay one

night we got a ground and left on the next tide for point arossia & st James, we arrived at Jerusalum whare we saw the man who call himselfe Christ or Lord we then arived at St. James in due time. (Gause 1896)

Mrs. Collier's diary of April 19 also recorded the departures: "The Gypsy came in this morning. Three of Mr. Cushing's men left today Mr. Sayford among them. They went with Bud Wilson on the Gertrude" (Collier 1896).

It must have been with a great sigh of relief that Cushing wrote on April 20 to Pepper, "As promised in my last hurried letter, I am writing to let you know that the work at Collier's is completed, the specimens packed safely on board, and we are now under way for the north via St. James City." He said that there were further fields to the north and south of Marco and, "I shall take Mr. Sawyer and a small party of men up into Charlotte Harbor on the way to clear, photograph and plan the remarkable and instructive conch faced terrace and sea wall on DeMorey's Key and the gigantic mounds at Beattie's" (Cushing 1896p).

Gause recorded the return voyage from Marco to Tarpon Springs:

Wednesday Apr 22, 96 about 1 P.M. all well good for us all OK In the afternoon we excavate a mound at St James find a ketchin in wich we found a No of relax [relics] of all kinds home to supper afte which George makes a turable break smoking in presence of Mrs C—then he takes his seat forwards like a man untill he is done

the 23 Thursday comes went to south Key until 1 P.M. then to fishermans key by the sharpey to excavate a mound Alfred, Calhone Capt Toney Mr Cushing Mr Sawyer Mr Burgman & George W Gause all well de lighted weather wind NW light

Friday morning we go to St James for Mail water tobacco fish tackel to go to Demerrys Key 10 miles NE we go to 3 other names we name Demerrys Key Josalyn Key Smith Key and Gauses Key named by Mr Cushing we saw the great wall made by prehistoric Indi

ans the mounds are not by the thousands Thes mounds very high one 163 ft on which Gause is placed under 3 live oaks to measure the mound and a photograph taken of him on the mound Gausie near the key we stayed ther till 10 at night on account of the tide then we camp again. (Gause 1896)

Cushing wrote Pepper from aboard the *Silver Spray* in Caloosa Bay saying that he had already partly finished reconnaissance there, needed one more day to finish mapping, and expected to leave on the twenty-seventh. He acknowledged another deposit of Pepper's totaling $3,000. He still needed $500 more to pay off his crew, maybe $200 or $300 more to cover Sawyer's salary, freight deposits, and homeward trip (if he failed to get passes). He proposed to borrow from Mr. Safford at the Bank of Tarpon Springs, for later repayment by Dr. Pepper. (This loan was repaid by the treasurer of the Archaeology Department of the University of Pennsylvania on May 22, 1896.) Cushing also mentioned that shipping rates for sending the collections to Philadelphia were suddenly raised but that he successfully had insisted that the shipper live by the original rate agreement (Cushing 1896q).

Gause continued, "Sunday comes we look at St James with wishfull eyes but to Fishermans Key to get the beads and corpse [?] gun and other thing we can we sail down in the Spray nearby Sunday morning 26 went to get the corps we find 18 bullett 2 qts bealls 2 knives some sulphur 3 pipes we come home in a heavy blow to supper Mr Cushing lost his watch in Charlota's Harbour, all well at bedtime Apr 26" (Gause 1896). He reported that it stormed again the next day:

Monday comes the 27th we stay on board and pk up the speciment until 4 oclock when a fearefull storm come up and takes up the Silver Sprays anchor and lets her drift off swiftly untill the Hustlers gets down the Horacin anchor which brings her up we stop so suden that Mr Sawyer gets the pole over his neck and complains of near braking his neck we have supper and orders comes to

get ready to sail at day break Tuesday morn
ing glad is the crew for the fruit is all ripen
ing verry fast and the whole excitation is get
ting tired wants to see home in good health
onc more

Tuesday comes the 28th at daylight we
hoist and set sail from Charlotte Harbour to
Capt Teavy Pass [Captivy Pass] where we are
to spend a night Turn turtle and get shells all
are well and in good cheer except Mr Sawyer
who had rather be at Washington where he
expects to meet his intended all OK we have
a splendid breakfast of the best then to the
beach and a photo of a shell wall at Cap
Teavy Pass and then a bath and set sail for
Bogousage Light and egmount and for
Anclote we sail all night Tuesday night and it
is rough you bet, we come to Anclote
Wednesday morning we work packing up our
speciments and blankets to take our depar
ture from Spray for home at Tarpon Springs
where we are again shall in joy our familys
presence We will right and haft all the excita
tions are and return to our friends who are
absence have ben and then in contentment
with hearts that are fine wind up the excita
tion in a rejoicing spree

Geo W Gause (Gause 1896)

In a letter to his mother on April 24 from Charlotte Harbor, Sawyer projected the end of the expedition:

I have left Marco for Washington. Our stops
enroute will be very short I think and less
than ten days should put me in the Capitol
City. I was surprised that you had no word
from me—the service from here must be
pretty bad. . . .

I am very well and am very happy for I
have seen wonderful things. Oh! this is a
marvelous country and the sparceness of
population makes it one of especial interest.
Then as you sail about midst the *thousands*
of islands here and there stretches of dis
tance and only the low lying trees along and
covering the keys!!—Its beautiful. New York

Harbor is beautiful its *very* splendid but this
is sublime. Tonight the little waves are play
ing against our bow and the moon is shining
so brightly overhead and the air is so perfect,
one is not of this world.

Then the romance of it all, the old old
mounds from the top of which way off in the
distance the green gulf sends its irridescent
color up to the deep sky.

No use—I can't tell about it—the seeing of
it is all there is.

I hope that I may come again. And that's a
good deal for me to say. This land of flowers
can not be seen from the cars. One must be
willing to drift into unknown passes into a
labyrinth of islands, into a maze of verdure
where the hurrying tide sends you on and on
forever.

Some have never returned for there are
such a vast number of these islands that the
man who goes unguided takes his life in his
hands. All of them are alike, all a ghostly,
wierd swamp of mangrove save only where
man, that artificer has wrought upon nature
the changes which link by link we are unrav
eling.

I hope you are all well and that you are all
as happy as I am this moonlight night at an
chor on the thrice salty water of the gulf.
(Sawyer 1896e)

By May 10, Cushing was able to write from Tarpon Springs that he had shipped from there
eleven barrels and thirty boxes of specimens recovered in Tarpon Springs and eleven barrels
and fifty-nine boxes of Key Marco specimens. He
wrote that he expected to arrive in Washington
on May 13 and "sincerely hope you will be able
to run down to Washington for the conference,
on the following day, until which time it is my
proposition to keep out of the way of everyone,
for the leading correspondents have been writing
me and are on the lookout for me, but until the
moment of my departure from here I shall leave
their letters unanswered" (Cushing 1896r).

From Washington at 3 P.M. on May 13, 1896, he
wrote to Pepper that he was hiding from the

press to guard against premature release of information on his finds. One article had already appeared in the *Washington Post* on May 3, having been released without his authorization by someone unknown to him. He added that he had not seen the article. He knew of course that such an article "scooped" official releases by both sponsoring institutions, not to mention the newspaper owned by the husband of the biggest financial backer of the expedition, Mrs. Hearst (Cushing 1896s).

9

AFTER

THE

GLORY

FOR THE REST of his life Cushing was plagued by illness, financial problems, and controversy. He was, at the same time, under pressure to finish his work amid growing feelings of uneasiness on the part of the two sponsoring institutions and his own disinclination toward the necessary paperwork. He repeatedly stated his strong preference for field investigation over the written analysis and reporting yet realized the necessity of publication, so he was constantly torn between the fieldwork he loved and the paperwork he hated.

Two days after his return to Washington he wrote to Culin in Pennsylvania that he was sick most of the time. It is a familiar refrain throughout his correspondence, and sometimes he detailed his complaints. He was not a hypochondriac. He was sickly all of his life, so much so that one wonders how he ever managed to accomplish so much in forty-two years.

Finances were another constant problem. Not only did he have a tendency to run over his budget and to be somewhat neglectful in reporting his expenditures to his financial sponsors; he also had problems with double living expenses caused by the necessity of working in places other than Washington, the site of his permanent residence.

Another repeated problem was the threat of premature publication of unauthorized reports on his finds. His concerns were twofold: that the reports might be inaccurate and that his sponsoring institutions and financial sponsors were being scooped. Mrs. Hearst was, after all, not only his financial benefactor but also the wife of the publisher of the *New York Journal*.

The problem that concerned him most, probably even more than the constant decline in his health, was the repeated threats to his professional reputation and integrity. After the Marco expedition, charges of fraud were brought against him by an individual who also resurrected a similar accusation regarding a specimen from the Hemenway expedition and who recruited every person he could find who had any sort of grudge against Cushing, real or imagined. It became the scientific scandal of the day, involving those most prestigious in his profession as well as individuals in high places in government. For the nearly four years between the close of the Marco expedition and Cushing's death, he was under constant assault from several directions. A most remarkable aspect of his character is manifest in his reactions to those who so vigorously maligned him. He never seemed to hold a grudge against any of them. They hurt him deeply, but he bent over backward to see that they were treated fairly.

A great deal of interest in the expedition and the collections had been generated by an article by C. D. Durnford in the *American Naturalist* in November 1895. It was followed by premature articles in the *Washington Post* and the *Jacksonville Citizen* in February 1896 before major work at Marco had even begun (Anonymous 1896a, b). The next one, released by an unknown party, appeared in the *Washington Post* on May 3, 1896, before Cushing had returned to Washington (Anonymous 1896c). He was determined to prevent further premature releases, correctly feeling that they were unfair to Mrs. Hearst.

He had originally been scheduled to report to the American Philosophical Society on May 1 but did not return from Marco in time to meet that date, so it was postponed until November. In the meantime, in deference to Mrs. Hearst and the *New York Journal*, Cushing prepared a full-page article with illustrations which appeared in that newspaper and the *Philadelphia Times* on Sunday, June 21, 1896 (Cushing 1896t).

The next article was a short one-page article by Henry Mercer which appeared in the *American Naturalist* of August 1, 1896 (Mercer 1896). Cushing's report to the Philosophical Society was presented on November 6 before an audience of thirty-four members and printed in their *Proceedings* of December of that year (Cushing 1897a). On October 16 he had been presented as a new member of the American Philosophical Society to the thirty members present at that meeting, Pepper having been instrumental in getting him elected.

Cushing had repeatedly said that they must publish early and widely to get the credit for what they had discovered, but he seemed to have had a great deal of trouble accomplishing much of it. He never finished the full report he intended to write. A large part of the problem was his failing health, but he was also a procrastinator. He loved the fieldwork, but, in spite of his fertile imagination, interpretive genius, and skill with words, he seemed to have had difficulty disciplining himself to write reports.

He cited numerous reasons why he could not do these tasks quickly, and he did have real problems. There was no space at the Bureau of American Ethnology where the collections could be spread out so Cushing could work on them. To remedy that, Pepper offered space in the University Museum in Philadelphia and the collections were shipped there, Pepper acknowledging their arrival on May 24, 1896 (Pepper 1896b). Cushing wrote on that date that he would "come over to Philadelphia on Wednesday and at once set about having a representative series of both Tarpon Springs and the Thousand Islands collections ready for your friends and associates for Saturday. Mrs. Hearst's secretary is helping me to get the box catalogue copied clearly in type which will make just such a selection as we wish simple and comparatively easy." He wrote a note on the side margin of the letter, "Mrs. Hearst is absolutely grand. She is the greatest friend you have." He also noted that he was preparing a lecture on the Florida collections for a course at the National Museum (Cushing 1896u).

Cushing promised also to prepare a preliminary report of operations and expenses of the expedition for the proposed meeting of the University Museum Board as requested by Pepper and Mrs. Hearst and proposed to publish a report on the Pepper-Hearst Expedition in the BAE series. The latter never appeared.

Money and health continued to be problems after he returned from Florida. The University of Pennsylvania discontinued his salary; he complained in October 1896 that he had not been paid by them since the previous May and said that he thought Pennsylvania owed it to him to continue his salary since he had been in the field when others at the Smithsonian had received raises and he had not. In June, Mrs. Hearst contributed $100 for his salary. His residence was in Washington, so the time he spent in Philadelphia created additional expense for him and apparently strained his finances. Meanwhile, his health deteriorated, and he sought greater solitude and a friendlier climate in hope of improvement.

He was pushed and prodded by both institutions to finish his work with the collections so that the reports might be published and the collections divided between the two institutions. But he lacked the interest to push the reports to completion. On September 7, 1896, having apparently been prodded once again by Pepper to get on with his writing, he responded, "But exploration is the breath of my life. It, far more than study work, is the line of all my tendencies, and has been, ever since the runaway days of my boyhood" (Cushing 1896v). Perhaps, too, he anticipated the problems that would arise in dividing the artifacts.

On September 9, 1896, he wrote to Charles P. Daly, a judge and president of the Geological Society, that his "health is so far mended that I am able to do a little work daily on my old manuscripts. I am most delightfully situated here at Manchester-by-the-Sea, in one of the pleasant homes of my friend, Mrs. Augustus Hemenway of Boston" (Cushing 1896w).

Stewart Culin, curator of the museum in Philadelphia, must have taken his turn prodding, encouraged to do so perhaps by Henry Mercer, for Cushing responded on September 17 that he had broken his glasses a couple of weeks earlier and shortly after that he had severely injured his writing hand. He returned part of the burden to the museum when he said, "Yet I judged from his letter the questions he asked in it regarding the disposition of the remaining Marco and even Tarpon Springs Collections that nothing in the way of the preparation of these latter for installation (let alone their actual installation) has been done." He went on to blame part of his decline in health to trying to do too much without glasses (Cushing 1896x).

On September 20, from Maine, he again wrote to Pepper that the work on his report was held up by his illness. "Almost in vain I long ago cut down my tobacco to a straw and my coffee to a single cup at breakfast . . . I do not know precisely what their cause may be. But food of course has much to do with it—tough meat, my principal diet. My bowels are regular in their action and my stomach rebellious only in these moderate ways. . . . I have been more or less constantly troubled with a roaring in my head the right side, and lameness in my left shoulder at times serious. Worse than all, however, have been the fits of wakefulness and despondency that have oppressed me every morning at between 3 and 4 o'clock" (Cushing 1896y). In another letter he complains, "I have been suffering from one of my attacks the first for weeks and my eyes are almost useless" (Cushing 1896z).

But he assured Pepper that he did want to return to Florida the following winter and that he *was* working: "I have dictated considerably more than a thousand closely typewritten pages—more than half of what will become a large book. But the work of revision, of detailing the collections and especially of preparation, by others of the numerous illustrations will necessarily be very tedious. . . . I am gratified to learn that Professor Putnam [director of the Museum of Archaeology and Ethnology of Cambridge, Massachusetts, and the Anthropological Department of the Museum of Natural History] has consented to join in discussing my proposed paper before the Philosophical Society on the evening of the first Friday in November. I will be driven to prepare this paper, but I will be on hand there with as good a general presentation of the subject as I can bring together after leaving here and in the course of the first revising of what I have written out in detail during the summer" (Cushing 1896z).

Pepper must have made further inquiry about how long it would take for Cushing to complete his work on the collections because on September 24 he replied from Maine, "I cannot tell just how much work will have to be done by me on those [Tarpon Springs] and Marco collections before they are in condition to be illustrated and described to best advantage. This has worried me. But now I am not sorry I have them to work up personally. What you say is very right and wise. All I want you to understand is, that I am cordially ready, always, to do as far as I can what Mrs. Hearst and you wish me to do. For the present I am anxious to push work on the Florida report because I stand engaged to all of you, to do so. I believe with you that it will constitute the source of value to the collection—if only as their full record. Moreover, I feel that I will not have discharged my obligation to our office, until I shall have turned the manuscript and full data and memoranda relative to the illustrations of the book, over to my Director. Engagements of this kind do not stimulate me. But they do not let me rest until fulfilled and until I am again free to do that which of all things I love most to do for its own sake and for my health's sake—explore and discover" (Pepper 1896c).

Meanwhile, there was another serious problem developing that was to cause Cushing, and many others, grief. An employee of the Bureau of American Ethnology, William Dinwiddie, had a real or imagined unknown grievance against Cushing that he sought to redress through an attack on Cushing's integrity. He accused Cushing of fabricating the shell with the costumed dancer painted inside and of fraudulently claiming it to be genuine (fig. 8). He offered as proof the fact that a barnacle that had grown inside the shell had not grown over the line of paint, as it first appeared, but rather that the paint stopped on each side of the barnacle. He also claimed that a smudge caused by acid applied to prove age of the shell was instead proof that the pigment used in the drawing was India ink.

He presented his evidence to all those he knew to have any real or imagined grievance against Cushing and to members of the press. He renewed the attacks on Cushing's integrity regarding the Hemenway expedition and attempted to align with him the men involved in the earlier controversy and to involve them in his current accusations regarding the painted shell from Marco.

The noted anthropologist Franz Boas is probably correct in his assessment of the situation. He wrote to Professor McGee on January 1, 1897, "I have always considered him [Cushing] one of the frankest, most generous, open hearted and honorable men whom it was my good fortune to meet. His greatest enemy is, I take it, his genius" (Boas 1897a).

Cushing's old nemesis, Mathilda Coxe Stevenson, joined the accusers. A note she attached to a photograph of the shell reads, "It was claimed by a member of the Bureau of Ethnology [Cushing] that the barnacle had grown on the shell after the figure had been painted on it. He brought it from Florida with other material he claimed to have collected there. Mr. Dinwiddie who was photographer at the time in the Bureau of Ethnology had reasons to suspect the shell was not genuine and tested it under a glass. The enlargement of the barnacle shows plainly that the paint was put on the shell after the appearance of the barnacle. Mr. Dinwiddie was instructed by the Bureau of Ethnology not to mention the matter and because he protested against such unscientific process he was dismissed from the Bureau, and the Bureau allowed the University of Pennsylvania to illustrate the shell in one of its publications knowing that it was not genuine—M.C.S." (Stevenson n.d.).

So, joined by Mrs. Stevenson and others (two identified as Mooney and McGuire, who must be James Mooney, well-known bureau ethnologist, and J. D. McGuire, also associated with the bureau), Dinwiddie did the accusing in person in an effort to discredit Cushing with his professional colleagues and publicly through the press.

Some time between June 20 and June 30, 1896, when the shells were left at the Smithsonian to be photographed, they mysteriously disappeared. "On Mr. Dinwiddie's return, the lost shells at once came to light. The shells include that containing the painting of the hand and that containing the full-length figure, with head-dress and wrist and ankle bands, each accompanied by an unpainted valve" (McGee 1896). Dinwiddie had removed them from the laboratory, wrapped in cotton, to show to a reporter for the *New York Herald*, telling him that they were frauds. A week later, a Mr. Williams who represented himself as a reporter for the *Herald* sent by Mr. Rowzer, editor of the *Herald*, called on Dr. Gates at the Smithsonian and told him he had a great big story about Cushing that would be discreditable to

Cushing and his collections alike, that the *Herald* would publish it when investigations were completed, and that it would create a stir.

Two weeks after that a tall, good-looking blonde who called herself Miss Renner, came to the laboratory. She had with her about twenty pages of manuscript and said she came for an interview regarding Cushing and his frauds. She produced her manuscript, which began with charges of immoral conduct and frauds during his Zuñi work, a sensational account that she claimed she could document.

Dr. Gates, to whom she presented all of this, told her she was utterly mistaken. He showed her around the lab. He asked that she not publish the articles, speaking of the stature of those, such as Major Powell, who supported Cushing, making such frauds most unlikely. The reporter said she was to get $50 for her article, syndicated to all leading papers. Dr. Gates promised her three articles worth $60 not to publish it. He said it would hurt him as well as Cushing and others. He finally asked that she come back the next day when he would buy the article with his own check for $50 on condition that she would promise no publication. Nothing more was heard from her until four days later, when she called to ask for one of the promised articles and said she would give her *real* name under certain conditions (Gates 1896).

That was not to be the end. Dinwiddie kept repeating his charges of fraud. Cushing asked for an investigation of the matter to clear his name, but his superiors at the Smithsonian thought such a move would be unwise and would call too much attention to the matter and perhaps give it some credence. The matter was dropped for a time.

Dinwiddie would not let the matter rest until he had convinced men of good repute and high stature that his charges were true. There were at least two others in the Bureau of American Ethnology who joined Dinwiddie in his accusations: Dr. J. Walter Fewkes, an eminent anthropologist, who had recommended reorganization or dissolution of the New Mexico expedition, and F. W. Hodge, Cushing's secretary during the Hemenway expedition who was, by this time, married to Cushing's wife's sister, Margaret Magill.

Accusations were renewed. Cushing wrote to Pepper, "I am urged to immediately return to Philadelphia to confer with you and to select a few specimens for use here, as evidence of what I accomplished in Florida last winter and spring. Unfortunately what Dr. Gates tried to write of . . . was only too true in foundation. There has been a conspiracy here, which has ended by creating the worst scientific scandal we have ever known. My integrity has been distinctly questioned by men who professed friendship until the last. A meeting of scientists here is therefore absolutely imperative. The Bureau itself, its chiefs, Major Powell and Professor McGee, are jeopardized. There is no shadow of doubt of my ability to meet all my detractors and to conquer them. They are summoned, on penalty of dismissal from the Bureau to appear before me—such of them, that is, as belong to the Bureau (mainly three). The whole matter has originated in jealousy. But it is serious, very serious, and has to be met at once. I shall see you within a few hours. I beg of you not to be concerned about this. I at least have an opportunity to reckon with men who have for five years severely worked for my harm in every possible secret way. I don't mind them, but to have my *friends* turn away is heartrending. Yet I am glad the time has come" (Cushing 1896aa).

Apparently the inspection and evaluation of the specimens by a group of eminent scientists was carried out as planned, for Cushing wrote to Dr. Pepper that, the scientists having seen them, "they are as anxious on all hands *not* to have a formal investigation as (with the exception of Major Powell) they all were to have one less than four days ago!" He said that "the collections have been examined by a number of specialists and they are uniformly satisfied—and amazed at the absolutely unique character of the discoveries. Secretary Langley and Maj. Powell have just seen them and the poor fellow who stirred up all this trouble was discharged. I interceded in his behalf [crossed out: a second time today] but fear nothing can be done for him [crossed out: that is too bad for he is not in my judgment any more to blame as those who insinuated to him that I might be the questionable source of some of my specimens, and slily supported his assertions. I bear ill will to none of them]. But it is too bad that such men can rob me of precious time. That is all I regret. I have positively not had a free hour since the day after my return from your house" (Cushing 1896bb).

On November 9, 1896, Cushing made a statement to Mr. Rowzer of the *New York Herald* saying that the collections were the property of Dr. Pepper and Mrs. Hearst and were to become the property of the Museum of the University of Pennsylvania, with duplicate series to be installed in the United States National Museum. The collections had been examined by Secretary Langley and by Major Powell:

and as a result of this and other examinations at the Bureau I regret to say that Mr. William Dinwiddie has been dismissed from his position as Photographer in the Bureau on account of insubordination in connection with his unjustifiable conduct and utterances in regard to these collections.

On November 6, the collections were exhibited before the American Philosophical Society and were made the subject of prolonged discussion between Professor F. W. Putnam, Director of the Peabody Museum of Archaeology and Ethnology, Cambridge, Mass., and of the Anthropological Department of the Museum of Natural History of New York, and of Professor Daniel G. Brinton, of the University of Pennsylvania, late President of the American Association for the Advancement of Science. I beg to refer you to these gentlemen.

I have no objection whatever to your making any publication you choose. But I warn you that I have prepared to take immediate legal action, under the best advice to be had in New York and Washington. (Cushing 1896cc)

That apparently was not the end of the matter; on November 21, 1896, Cushing wrote to Professor Putnam:

You know somewhat of the trouble they have been trying to make here over the col-

lections you so kindly discussed recently in Philadelphia at the recent meeting of the Philosophical Society. It was with reference to this that I wrote you. Messrs Dinwiddie, Hodge, and Dr. Fewkes were reported as conspiring and speaking evil reports. The matter increased in seriousness after my return to Washington. So much so that I had to take legal measures with some newspapermen, and engaged to visit various of these scandal-mongers with my attorney, no more general "investigation" being granted me.

The appearance yesterday of Doctor Fewkes' article on shell objects from the Arizona ruins in which article appeared a paragraph pointedly ignoring as a genuine antique the shell toad I had found and he had some years previously questioned the authenticity of, and of which he was reported as continuing to express distinct doubts gave color to this report in regard to his connection with these slanders. Therefore with my attorney I sought him out last night, and requested an understanding.

I am satisfied with his explanation. From first to last he has been deceived by my former secretary Mr. Hodge—who told him among other like falsehoods that to his personal knowledge I had made the relic in question. This explains much though not all of Doctor Fewkes' well known attitude toward me and my work heretofore. I am satisfied from what he said last night in presence of my witness that he has refrained from becoming involved in the present scandal, that he will indulge no more reflections on the integrity of my character, and that he will make proper reparation for his recent offense when the time comes.

Hence I wish to correct my statement founded on hearsay and what seemed to me likely. Later Doctor Fewkes had frankly acknowledged and discussed those things I felt it due him that I should do so. (Cushing 1896dd)

This did not mean, however, that Fewkes had changed his mind about the authenticity of the frog, as he wrote to Hemenway on November 30, 1896:

On my return from the West last month I found a very grave accusation had been made against Mr. Cushing by a photographer in the Bureau of Ethnology. This was a claim that there was evidence that Cushing had fabricated objective materials—painted a shell with intent to deceive. It was likewise stated by Mr. Hodge that he saw the "jeweled toad" which Morse brought back from the Southwest manufactured by Mr. Cushing. Hodge's story is a detailed one and was used by Dinwiddie, the photographer, as evidence of past fraud of Cushing. Dinwiddie reported the evidences to Maj. Powell for investigation. The outcome of which was that Dinwiddie was discharged, the official reason being given as "neglect of duty." Dinwiddie enlists the interest of the representative of the New York *Herald* with a view to publish the whole matter with a view to bring about a Congressional investigation. Mrs. Hearst who furnishes the money for Cushing, jointly with the Bureau of Ethnology retains a lawyer to sue the New York *Herald* if they publish an article of a libellous character. The *Herald* man will not take the risk unless he can get some one besides Dinwiddie to vouch for the truth of the accusations. He seeks an interview with Hodge who positively refuses to see him on the ground that as an official of the Bureau of Ethnology it would be unbecoming for him (Hodge) to make any statement to a newspaper man. Hodge says to Dinwiddie that he will state to a proper investigating committee that the jeweled frog of the Hemenway Expedition was made by Cushing and he saw him do it.

I refused to see the newspaper man; i, because I have never seen any material collected by Cushing in Florida and know nothing about the shell in question; ii, because I do not believe it proper to bring the affairs of a private person into this squabble and; iii, because I am an officer of the Smithsonian and regard it unbecoming in me to afford aid to a newspaperman in this work.

The three men, Cushing, Dinwiddie and Hodge have all called upon me. Cushing has stated that he did not make the "jeweled toad," Hodge that he saw Cushing make it, and gave the details, and Dinwiddie has shown what he regards as evidence that Cushing fabricated the Florida shell. Both Hodge and Dinwiddie have told me that they had written to you.

This whole matter of accusing Cushing of fraud originated and reached an acute state while I was in Arizona and I knew nothing of it in any way before my return to Washington. I have taken no part whatsoever in it, and have carefully avoided what has now come to be a scientific scandal in Washington. I have however my strong convictions in this matter and shall state them to the proper investigating committee if the matter is investigated. I hope the matter will be limited to the Florida shell of which I know nothing. Fortunately also I know nothing in regard to the money affairs of the Hemenway Expedition, a subject on which Cushing and Hodge are at loggerheads. I believe the jewelled frog is a fraud made to deceive your mother and if my opinion is asked by a proper committee I shall say so, and give my reasons. This scientific scandal is not of my making, and I have told all who have approached me in regard to it that I would have nothing to do with the matter. Both parties have told me their sides and both accused the others of being liars. A lady friend and guest of Mrs. Hearst called on me with Cushing a few days ago and looked over my collection asking as she left whether she could bring Mrs. Hearst to see it, and in a few days Cushing's patroness may also visit me.

I have written you about this whole matter in order that you may know what is taking place here, and if this investigation occurs, or the accusations against Cushing are published you may know where I stand in relation to them. (Fewkes 1896)

Now Pepper was concerned also for the condition of the specimens and worried about their deterioration. Cushing tried to allay those fears on December 13, 1896, when he wrote, "Mrs. Hearst told me last night that she had had a little note from you, saying that Mr. Culin had just seen you and was exercised concerning the collections. So have I been until lately. But awaiting impatiently the time when I could come over there and set to work upon them, I have been working on those portions of them which are here. I have *absolutely restored* the forms, proportions, and integrity of several of the most misshapen yet also the most important of these specimens, specimens that had come under the influence of steam heat in the room where they are kept well nigh unrecognizable. I think I told you of this happy result of the use of glycerene in the former letter, and if I am not mistaken I also referred to it in a recent note to Mr. Culin. . . . The main point in all this, is, however, that there is no cause for anxiety so long as attention to the collections over there is not too long deferred." He promised to come to Philadelphia soon and hoped to get on with the Florida report (Cushing 1896ee).

A few weeks later, after repeatedly trying without success to see Major Powell, Cushing wrote to Pepper on December 17, 1896, that he "had the misfortune to find him always away. I now learn why, and the reason is pitiable. The matter which has bothered us all so much, has been brought before a Close Committee of Congress (by the young man concerned and some of the *Herald* representatives) and poor Major Powell, rather than the Bureau, is being investigated as Director, as to exercising favoritism toward me! Of course he has to meet those concerned in the investigation face to face as I met the other crew. He has asked me to be constantly on hand, to be present at a private congressional examination of my collection. This is it which chiefly holds me here now, for we do not know when the Senator who is to conduct this examination will come down. There is much to tell you, but will have to wait until I see you; and even the little I now write is in confidence subject to later developments" (Cushing 1896ff).

Meantime, another noted anthropologist was being drawn into the conflict because of his concern for the damage it was inflicting on the science itself. Writing to Professor McGee, Franz Boas tried to help put the matter in perspective from an outsider's view:

I had hoped to be able to talk to you on your visit to New York in regard to a matter that gives me great uneasiness and I trust you will take what I desire to say not as officious meddling but as the expression of opinion of one of the most earnest friends of the Institution which you so ably represent.

I am certain the gossip and the estrangement between Cushing and Fewkes—this is the matter to which I refer—are weighing on your mind heavily and you will have decided upon the wisest course to pursue. I have not tried to obtain information in regard to the whole matter, in fact I have avoided to hear about it, until very recently when it appeared to me to assume dimensions that may become or are becoming dangerous to the welfare of the science that we have at heart. Let me say first of all that Mr. Cushing has my fullest sympathy in all the trials that he is undergoing. Although I cannot pride myself of being one of his intimate friends I have always considered him one of the frankest, most generous, open hearted and honorable men whom it was my good fortune to meet. His greatest enemy is, I take it, his genius.

But it is not the object of my letter to discuss the mentor of a personal controversy with the details of which I am not familiar and moreover do not wish to be familiar. I am convinced that only a clear view of the whole situation will enable you to cope with it adequately, and therefore I wish to make sure that you know how the matter is looked at by outsiders, so that you may be sure to see all the dangers with which it is fraught. I take it upon myself to do so, since I do not know of anyone who would volunteer to give you that information.

The principal point of view taken is this: that the matter would not be allowed by you and by Major Powell to proceed if there were not things in the past that it is necessary to conceal and which make you powerless in quelling the personal squabbles and enmities in the Bureau. I beg you to understand that I have heard this view expressed from various sides not in a sense of hostility to the Bureau, but as the gist of floating rumors and of gossip. This view begets the most morbid curiosity as to things that have been going on inside the Bureau and the work of each man is being discussed in greatest detail, particularly in how far it agrees with the law creating the Bureau, and Major Powell's deliberate slowness in publishing and thus making available accumulated material is made to tell against the Institution. . . .

You understand, of course, the situation better than I do with my imperfect knowledge of the facts. But it would seem to me from what I hear that this is an occasion for most radical action, that it is necessary to take the bull by the horns. Can you not by a dictatorial attitude to *all* concerned compel them to behave? . . .

I trust you will accept these remarks as what they are meant, as thoughts that occur to me with my imperfect knowledge of the facts, not as suggestions. I beg to assure you that my admiration of the work of the Bureau has made me one of its most sincere friends. (Boas 1897a)

Still the matter did not end. On March 3, 1897, George M. Coffin, assistant comptroller of the U.S. Treasury Department, in Washington, wrote Cushing to warn him that the *New York Herald* "intends to make a publication adversely affecting you" and perhaps the *New York Times* also. They were being urged on by "a man with a grievance" who was not named, but in all probability it was Dinwiddie whose rancor would not likely have been lessened by his having been fired from his job at the bureau over the matter. Coffin urged an investigation to clear Cushing's name because the newspapers threatened to publish the matter

by April 4 unless something happened in the meantime (Coffin 1897a). On March 6, Coffin wrote Cushing to say that he and Mrs. Hearst had talked and had agreed that Cushing should insist on an investigation by the Bureau of Ethnology (Coffin 1897b).

On March 9, Cushing wrote Coffin from the Stratford Hotel in Philadelphia that "when the matter first arose, I was eager for such an investigation." But he now thought that his superior officers were right in not doing so because "official attention of this kind would . . . have been attaching too much dignity to the principal persons concerned in an utterly unfounded series of accusations" even though there might yet need to be such an official investigation (Cushing 1897b).

Then on March 12, Cushing again requested an investigation, writing Secretary Langley:

Since my return from the exploration of the Florida Keys undertaken last winter in the joint interest of the BAE and Department of Archaeology and Paleontology of the University of Pennsylvania, accusations have been made, assailing my scientific integrity and the genuineness of certain objects in my collections. At once on learning of this I requested an official investigation; but such investigation was deemed unnecessary by my superior officers. The specimens, were, however, freely exhibited to many persons, including scientists of high authority, and have been made the basis of communications to scientific bodies in Washington and Philadelphia.

I have from the outset, been solicitous that entire satisfaction should be afforded in regard to them, lest in any way the Bureau, in which I have the honor to be an employee, should suffer.

Learning recently, that in spite of all this, the same unwarranted course of attack is continuing, I now, with due respect, have the honor to formally request the appointment by yourself of a committee to conduct in a thorough and impartial manner, an investigation of this matter, which request I venture to trust you will grant and direct at the earliest possible date. (Cushing 1897c)

He wrote at the same time to Major Powell, repeating his request for an investigation, enclosing a copy of his letter to Secretary Langley, stating that Dr. Pepper and Mrs. Hearst agreed on the advisability of such an investigation. He reminded him that Professor McGee had suggested this in the beginning but that Powell and McGee had dissuaded him. He reiterated that the papers were again threatening publication, which would hurt the bureau and upset Cushing's friends. He concluded, "It seems that the chief plea now urged in proof of my lack of integrity, is that I have avoided investigation, or at least that no investigation has been granted, presumably because it was held at the office that I could not be satisfactorily defended." For these reasons he renewed his request (Cushing 1897d).

On March 16, 1897, Cushing received a letter from Julia Coffin in which she assured him of her support, urging the necessity of dropping his present work and getting these accusations investigated to clear his name. She said she heard stories from all sides and concluded, "I suppose you know that sworn statements of accusations have been sent to each of the five members of the Committee appointed by the Chancellor of the Smithsonian. I am disgusted and shocked to hear of some of the most damaging statements being made by some of your colleagues, who afterwards introduced you with eulogy in public. What is to be expected of such men?" (J. Coffin 1897).

On March 15, Langley asked Powell for his opinion of the matter, to which Powell replied at great length on March 18, upholding the authenticity of the shell. He stated that he had visited Cushing during the excavation and had witnessed the remarkable preservation and new look of the pigments on many of the articles when they were removed from the muck; that there was profuse use of black paint; that the pigment used on this shell was the same intensely black pigment used on other artifacts; that the style of drawing was typical of the same stage of culture discovered elsewhere in North America; that Wells Sawyer, for whom he has great respect, has assured him of the authenticity of the shell; and from his own acquaintance with Cushing for twenty years and

the many brilliant discoveries he has made, he concluded that the specimen was genuine. He also stated that it was his opinion that charges so groundless, though honestly made, needed no further investigation (Langley 1897a; Powell 1897).

Enclosing a copy of Major Powell's statement to him, Langley wrote to Cushing on March 20, 1897, "I have thought it best after consideration, not to do so at present, and I am more induced to this from the recommendation contained in the communication of the Director of the BAE, under date of March 18, a copy of which is enclosed herewith" (Langley 1897b).

That apparently ended the public controversy. Interestingly enough, however, Mr. Dinwiddie surfaced a few years later, as Sunday editor of the *New York Herald*. Having occasion to write to Franz Boas at the American Museum of Natural History about another matter, he concluded his letter, "You may possibly remember me as the man who was forced out of the Bureau of Ethnology some four years ago for insisting that Frank Hamilton Cushing's Floridian collection be investigated in respect to the genuineness of his finds, and the man in regard to whom W. J. McGee wrote a most scurrilous and libelous letter to you. I would esteem it a great favor if you could see your way clear to let that letter come into my possession" (Dinwiddie 1900). It is doubtful that he ever got possession of that letter because Boas sent it along to McGee, saying that he did not know that "Mr. Dinwiddie was the same man who was with you for several years" (Boas 1897b).

And so the matter seems to have rested. Cushing's superiors seemed convinced that the shell was genuine, and today's evidence is in favor of Cushing and the authenticity of the shell. Besides Cushing's account of the actual finding of the shell, which he wrote to Pepper on March 7, 1896, from Marco (Cushing 1896j), there are statements of authentication from Sawyer (n.d.b) and Carl F. W. Bergmann (1899), present when the shell was found, as well as George Gause who actually found the shell. The letter signed by Gause and George Dorsett cited the entire excavation crew as willing to testify to the authenticity of all artifacts (Gause et al. 1904). In further support of the shell's authenticity, there are the diaries of Mrs. Collier and George Gause. Mrs. Collier's entry for March 6, 1896, read, "Mr. Cushing dug up a pair of sun shells about four inches long, one side was painted in black on the inside, a man with fancy head and arm rig, and dug a turtle's head carved of wood, with a snout 2 inches long, it is hollow, and is painted in black and white, these are dug from below the muck which is two feet deep, are bedded in marl, and must have been put there before Columbus's time. When they find anything nice they all give a yell and Mr. Cushing shakes hands with the one who made the find. They are making a very thorough investigation, are wheeling the muck out on the shell hills where it will be convenient for us to get it for the field. This expedition is sent out by the University of Pa. and must cost a lot although the gentlemen of the party are volunteers" (Collier 1896). Bergmann wrote:

In reference to those shells of the Marco (Cushing) collections which have markings on the inner side, I will state that I was present at the time the one with a human figure was found. Of this I am sure. It was found by Mr. Gause in the early part of March 1896. I remember that Mr. Cushing, who soon put in appearance at the diggings after the find was made, gave vent to some expression of displeasure, when Mrs. Collier, to whom the shell was shown, unthinkingly touched the moist pigment with her finger, leaving a mark. I remember this because very soon thereafter Mr. Cushing expressed regret that possibly his words, spoken in excitement, might have offended the lady. I was very near Gause when he, about to throw it away, opened the shell and made the discovery.

Later on my work at Marco was mostly confined to assorting, cleaning and preparing specimens in one of Mr. Collier's houses; so I was not present when many finds were made. I do not know the circumstances connected with shell with a hand design inside. But I do know, that during the whole expedition the work was conducted conscientiously; and I have no reason to believe that any ef-

fort was made to misrepresent specimens. (Bergmann 1899)

An undated memo in Cushing's handwriting, on the back of an envelope, stated that the smirch across right side of the face and foot was caused by Mrs. Collier trying to wipe roots and dirt out. He noted that the blackness on the side back and left side was caused by acid applied without authorization by Dinwiddie and Gates and that the smirch on the left hand was caused by Cushing himself by applying benzine solvent in an effort to identify the pigment.

Supporting these statements is a letter signed by five of the excavators:

"Tarpoon Springs, Fla.
Feb. 10, 1904
To extablish what I have said in regards to the finds mad by myself and others on the Cushing Exabition to Marco Fla. I hereby prduce evidence that what I have said is true these witnesses were present and found and saw me find, certain thing such as Mask Eone Drums gorgets Dear heads of wood Ivory Bill Wood Peckers! Painting and shells with paintings inside [.] these masks were placed neare each other as if they were all kept together in the camp and in the storm fell where we found them. A good many shells such as scrapes and others used I suppose for sinks and a pair of sunray shells which I found my selfe with a painting in side those ware all neare together. As I said before at least 3 feet down in the mud beneath the top layer of muck. I also said that the painted lines on these mask when first washed came out perfectly bright and so was the painted shells as well as a Board found with the picture of the Ivory Bill woodpecker. There was other things just as stunning to me. I shall not go fother as I do not think it nessary

I shall plainly prove what I have said in regards to these finds by men that were present and found and saw found all I have mentioned and a thousand other things.

truly hoping not to heare of men going round behind me disputing the truth. These are the names of men that were present and help to find those things.

any of them will testify to the above

Resp.

George W. Gause George W. Gause
          (signed)

 Frank Barns (signed)
 George Dorsett (signed)
 R. W. Clark (signed)
 J. B. Cahhone (signed)

We also have a notarized statement from George Gause, signed also by one of the excavators, George Dorsett, and dated March 8, 1905, which reads, "Regarding the finds made by myself and others on the Cushing Expedition to Marco, Fla., I wish to state that those mentioned below were present and found, and saw me find certain things, such as masks, ear drums, gorgets, deer heads of wood, ivory bill woodpecker's painting, and shells, with paintings inside. These masks were placed near each other as if they were all kept together in the camp, and in a storm fell where we found them; a good many shells, such as scrapes and others used, I suppose, for sinks; and a pair of sun ray shells, which I found myself, with a painting inside. These were all near together as I said before, at least three feet down in the mud, and beneath the top layer of muck. the painted lines of the masks when first washed out came out perfectly bright, and so was the painted shells, as well as the board found with the picture of the ivory bill woodpecker. There were other things just as stunning to me. Any one of those mentioned below were present and found or saw found all I have said and a thousand other things, and anyone would testify to the truth of the statement: Frank Barnes, George Dorsett, both of Tarpon Springs, Fla.; R. W. Clark, formerly connected with the lighthouse service, present location unknown; J. B. Calhoun, George Hudson, and Mr. Bergman of Philadelphia" (Gause and Dorsett 1905).

Logic also falls on Cushing's side. There were fourteen people living together on board a schooner anchored offshore in Marco Pass. Cushing worked on specimens aboard the schooner until he moved them into Mrs. Cushing's parlor,

and it is conceivable that he could have found an opportunity to manufacture the painted shell. But it is doubtful that he could have planted it in the site and been sure it would be found *and opened*, not just thrown away unopened as many shells were. To plant it in the site he would have had to leave the schooner after everyone else was asleep, row by himself, *without lights*, to the muddy site, plant the shell in a place where it would be sure to be found (and where would that be in so large and soggy a site?), row back to the schooner, clean the mud off, and climb back in bed without waking anyone. Besides, with the wealth of exotic artifacts he found every day, what would be the motive in fabricating one more?

The greatest logic of all, however, is that *every single member of the expedition, those who were there at the time*, testified to the genuineness of the artifact. So did Major Powell, who visited Cushing at Marco. Those who doubted it were all at least a thousand miles away and had nothing to do with the expedition.

All this controversy over the shell took place while the two institutions were pressuring Cushing to finish his study of the specimens, write his final report on them, and proceed with the final division of the artifacts so that they might be installed permanently in the new museum in Philadelphia and in the United States National Museum in Washington. He was beset simultaneously by poor health, lack of funds for living and working in both cities, and the distressing controversy over the authenticity of his specimens.

In his vigorous efforts to discredit Cushing, Dinwiddie resurrected the old scandal of the jeweled toad from the Hemenway expedition, so Cushing was not only troubled by the present but he was haunted by the past. Once things had quieted down, Professor Putnam thought the whole matter of fraud should be put to rest for all time. On March 29, 1897, Cushing reported to his superior, Major Powell, in writing: "Professor Putnam called on me yesterday for a long conference. He had the restored toad and I went into the question of its authenticity, with him, very thoroughly and quite to his satisfaction I think, for I was able to point out just what I had done to it, and also just what features in it were marks of its genuineness as an antique. . . . I write you this statement in order that you may be informed as to all that is done with regard to the Hodge and Dinwiddie allegations" (Cushing 1897e).

The statement prepared for Professor Putnam read:

> This example of incrusted shell-work was found by my workmen and myself while I was conducting excavations of the Hemenway Southwestern Archaeological Expedition in the ruins of Los Muertos, Salado Valley, Arizona, in 1887. It occurred in connection with a highly decorated water-jar and a mass of what I regarded as crude asbestos, in a room of House-Mound IV (afterward mapped H.M. XIV).
>
> Since it was the first specimen of its kind recognizable as representing the desert frog (or toad) that had then been found; since it was fragile, the inlaying more or less loosened, and since I recognized it as unique, as representing a water fetish or god, with intent to preserve it intact, I made careful study of the gum with which it was incrusted, determined it to be chiefly lac of the southern greasewood, and, with such lac freshly gathered and softened by heat, carefully restored the missing and loosened parts. (signed) Frank Hamilton Cushing (Cushing 1897e)

Dr. Pepper also wanted reassurance on the subject as well as complete satisfaction for Professor Putnam. On March 29, 1897, he wrote to Cushing, "I hope you will show me the statement and the label you prepare for Professor Putnam in regard to the toad. I think Professor Putnam is entitled to a statement over your signature, since he is the responsible curator of the collection in which the toad is to be installed. The label should of course have nothing that could suggest suspicion of any dispute ever having existed. If it is true that it is the first specimen of the kind ever found it is of course important that it should be stated" (Pepper 1897a).

Cushing wrote to Charles Garlick on November 20, 1897, for reassurance that yet another old friend had not deserted him:

> I suppose you learned last winter that Mr. Hodge and two or three others who have been, ever since the days when they broke up our dear old Hemenway Expedition, at enmity toward me and you, had circulated the vilest kind of lies, and brought formal and more or less public accusations against me in regard to the collections we all gathered in the Salado, and especially in regard to the inlaid shell frog which was found in Ruin 14 of Los Muertos.
>
> It was Mr. Hodge's distinct claim, not that I had restored that frog, but that I had made it in clean cloth, and that no such thing as it had ever been found by us. But what astonished me equally was the claim that you, when the time came, could be referred to as one of the chief witnesses against me. I disbelieved this, and I still disbelieve it. I cannot think that with all the openness which attended our repairing and restoration of specimens of all kinds, of which I made no secret at the time, and in which, indeed, Mr. Hodge and Mrs. Hodge, you, and several of the others, frequently assisted me, you could have ever for a moment supposed that fraud was intended. And I know very well that until Mr. Hodge was offended by my deposition of himself for failing to send in accounts, and my placing of yourself in charge, such ideas never entered his mind, foolish and resentful as it has ever since been.
>
> A full investigation of these and similar injurious allegations was held last winter and again last spring, and those who had preferred them were thus silenced; and although I had the most eminent legal advice that this country affords placed at my disposal, I did not consider it necessary, unless they raised the question again, to proceed against those who, directly or indirectly, created and circulated these slanders.
>
> I believed that the time would come when further researches in that region would re-

veal, not one, but probably several similar pieces of work, and when the general character of my finds there, as well as in Florida, would thus be demonstrated. I am happy to say that two such finds have already been made, that another toad was found last year by Dr. Fewkes which in almost every detail corresponded to the one I discovered, and that a very large collection of inlaid objects, far superior to any others yet discovered, was unearthed in a burial place in northern New Mexico during the early part of the present season.

As I said above, I do not believe that you have joined in those accusations . . . the peculiar circumstances which surrounded the disorganization of the Hemenway expedition. I have ever since been deprived of the opportunity of studying our magnificent and unique collections there, and presenting our results to the world—as we all so much hoped might be done. (Cushing 1897f)

In a letter to Mrs. Hearst dated May 18, 1897, Cushing seemed to be reconsidering a second report on his Florida finds. He said that it is now so comprehensive and full "it will now form a small book of itself of nearly or quite 75 pages closely printed, and quite well illustrated. Now Dr. Pepper is inclined to think, and I to agree with him, that perhaps in view of the fair completeness of my present publication of the subject already in proof and in view also of the delays I have mentioned—it may not be essential or even best for me to *fully* finish my part—without, as you will remember Major Powell suggested last June, both verifying the results and augmenting the collections, especially the photographs, by another visit to the Florida field and neighboring or related fields, possibly next autumn or winter." But, he promised, he would continue with the body of the work (Cushing 1897g).

Pepper must have prodded him some more, for he responded:

When a man talks to me as you did today and with such eminent justice I feel that I am

a culprit or a liar and a coward, all the while knowing that I am *not* any of those things in the larger sense—only a man with a bee in his bonnet a very busy bee; a man who sees a vision so beautiful that he lets the solid world go by, forgetting for the moment even the promises he loves best of all privileges of friendship.

Well, this is to say that you have killed the bee for once. I will have that collection classified and catalogued within two weeks if I cough my throat raw and you will not see me until I am very sick or there is necessity. (Cushing n.d.c)

On December 1, 1897 he wrote again to Pepper:

To facilitate my progress toward completing by close of the spring of 1898, my report on the explorations and collections of the Pepper-Hearst Expedition to Florida, the Director of the Bureau of Ethnology, Major J. W. Powell, has proposed the following.

That I prepare during the present month the collections referred to for temporary removal to my office and rooms in Washington.

That I there with expert assistance to be furnished by the Bureau, continue the restoration and classification of these collections.

That I there with expert stenographic assistance also to be furnished by the Bureau catalogue those collections and at the same time arrange them for illustration by the Bureau artists. That I thereafter prepare the original series and all extra for return to and illustration in the museum here, and a representative duplicate series for installation in the Bureau collections of the U.S. National Museum according to existing convention between the two institutions concerned.

In order that this may be accomplished within the time assigned it will be necessary for me to have during the present month the constant assistance of the Department expert Mr. Carl F. W. Bergmann and I have the honor to request that, if you approve, he be assigned to this duty. It will thus I hope become possible for me to make an approximate division of the collections in question for your approval previously to their removal. (Cushing 1897h)

By December 18 the work had not been done, and the Bureau of American Ethnology again prodded him to get on with it. On February 25, 1898, he was still working on it. He wrote to Culin of his efforts "for the better installation of the series as a whole next autumn or winter in the new museum. Dr. Pepper having asked me to have everything ready for that by October or November next. I do not think there are more than two specimens in this lot belonging to the lettered series, the a's of which are to form the National Museum series. These two I shall expect to retain here as by oral agreement with Dr. Pepper and yourself, for the series in question unless further study demonstrates that they are unique or illustrative of some special point in the original series, in which case they will be given their appropriate full Free Museum numbers, placed in the original series, and therewith returned to you, for in *no* case shall I consent to the breaking of the original series by so much as a single removal, since that series and not the duplicate series, is to stand as representing my Florida work. Therefore, in order that no question shall arise as to this in case let us say of my illness or death, I have submitted the matter to Major Powell and secured his entire approval as well as that of Ethnologist in charge, Professor McGee" (Cushing 1898a).

By May 15 Cushing reported to Culin that he was again sick most of the time (Cushing 1898b). Yet more blows were to fall upon him, the worst of which was the death of his physician, friend, and staunch supporter, Dr. Pepper. On October 14, 1898, apparently in reply to heckling by Mrs. Mathilda Coxe Stevenson, now secretary in the Department of Archaeology at the University of Pennsylvania, Cushing wrote her from Mt. Gretna, Lebanon County, Pennsylvania, explaining that he had been ill all summer but that he expected to return to Washington in November. He said it "would not be possible in any case to have the collections you call for returned to the Depart-

ment of Archaeology until considerably after I reach that city. I was most profitably working on these collections and on the final preparation for publication at the beginning of this fiscal year of my contribution relative to them for the first Pepper-Hearst Memorial Volume of the Bureau and the Department jointly, when I broke down and had to go to Atlantic City." He wrote that lack of funds for living expenses in Philadelphia, and for preservation, preparation and making of casts, "and, indeed, even his salary had been withheld since May," had necessitated transfer of the collections to Washington where Major Powell arranged to support his work. He continued that unless the department could find funds to pay his costs of continuing this work in Philadelphia, he would not advise returning the collections until after he had finished work on them. Meantime, he said that the Marco division of collections was systematically arranged, labeled, and stored in glass-sealed trays awaiting further work when he was able to take it up again.

Until all of the more fragile of the specimens are mounted their transference again would either greatly injure or utterly destroy them. Moreover, according to the terms of the agreement between the two institutions sanctioned by letters exchanged at the outset between Major Powell, Director of the Bureau of American Ethnology and Dr. Pepper, President of the Archaeological Department, these and the Anclote collections not thus far transferred were to be as is usually the custom in such circumstances—subject to me as their discoverer for such time as was requisite for study and illustration. In this sense then, the rules of your institution are not infringed for only in the obligation to return the collections as specifically directed by Dr. Pepper was their transference in the nature of a loan. Meanwhile the collections are represented in the Department by the running catalogue made by me last spring, one copy of which is held by the Director of the Archaeological Museum, Mr. Stewart Culin; the other (now in my hands for elaboration) subject to the Director of the Bureau of Ethnology.

I beg you to assure the Board of Managers that these collections are held in safety expressly subject to return when my work on them shall have been completed or previously if the expense of their installation, available by me personally as was proposed by Dr. Pepper in the new museum can be undertaken by the Department, and that in case of my death in the meantime the BAE has engaged to become responsible for their safe and prompt return intact save for the moiety of duplicates already designated for retention.

The publication you ask about has been halted that I may be able to personally revise its progress for I desire to make a fitting tribute to my two great friends in the work, Dr. Pepper and Mrs. Hearst. It will be issued in two parts, publication of the first part, which is already illustrated, to be resumed on my return to office and pushed to completion, I trust, during the coming winter. The second part cannot, I fear be printed until a year later; for although the manuscript itself is practically completed and very voluminous, the artist of the Bureau, Mr. DeLancy Gill, states such length of time as absolutely requisite for the making of the illustrations alone as they will number several hundred in addition to numerous plates both photographic and colored.

The loss of both of my parents and a brother this season together with them the loss of my friend, Dr. Pepper, has quite unsettled me. Under these circumstances you will pardon me for writing you unrevisedly and be kindly patient until I can address you in better moments and more officially as representing the two departments in this matter. Or, better still, I shall endeavor to use every effort to see you on passing through Philadelphia some time next month. (Cushing 1898c)

Both institutions were becoming increasingly anxious to have the work finished and the specimens divided and delivered to the proper places. It seemed, too, that they were becoming concerned that something might happen to alter ful-

fillment of the terms of the agreement, or, perhaps, deprive them of what they considered their fair share of the specimens. Pepper had repeatedly urged return of the collections to Philadelphia, and, on December 12, 1898, Powell wrote Cushing a formal letter to remind him of the "conditions of his Florida work for the University Museum." He quoted part of his "commission" of October 19, 1895, regarding division of the collection. He reminded him that although the division first meant to be made at the United States National Museum was to be made in Philadelphia because more space was available, there had been no surrender of public ownership, and the collections remained public property until Cushing made the final division. He reminded him also that the late Dr. Pepper had accepted these conditions and urged Cushing to complete his researches, make the division, and send Philadelphia's moiety to them, at the earliest practicable date, in order that all questions concerning the ultimate division of the collection may be set at rest (Pepper 1898).

Mrs. Stevenson insisted that the collections be returned immediately regardless of circumstances, for on February 7, 1899, Cushing replied that he could not return the Florida collections by the date the "Board requested through Mrs. Stevenson." He was still working on them and did not know when "it would be possible for me to return the major division of these collections that has been numerically and descriptively designated as belonging to the University Museum in the catalog I prepared last spring." He reminded her that according to original and all subsequent conversations between the BAE and the Department of Archaeology, all collections were subject to his control "pending necessary research upon them and subject to just division by myself between the two departments concerned, when such research was completed." He stated that the arrangements were made on the basis of mutual trust during Pepper's life, and he did not now need to "appeal to the formal documents," assuring her that he would see to the best interests of the department. He reminded her that the department had not paid his salary since May 1898 and that it was owed to him because he spent some money to work on the collections in Philadelphia and because, as he was involved in this joint work, he did not get a raise when others in the Smithsonian Institution had over a year before (Cushing 1899). And so the matter dragged on. Cushing got no further with either the division of the collections or with their analysis or publication.

His archaeological activity had not ended, however. During his summers in Maine he managed to become involved in exploration and excavation there. According to an article in the *Philadelphia Inquirer* dated October 15, 1899, he made at least one more attention-getting discovery:

A prehistoric race inhabiting the shores of Maine, a race antedating the Algonquin Indians many years, is the important announcement that Frank Hamilton Cushing, the eminent ethnologist of the Smithsonian Institution makes as the result of his exploration during the past summer on a small island on the eastern coast.

A few weeks ago the public appetite for that which smacks of the unusual or the romantic was whetted by news of the finding on one of the Maine islands of a skeleton in armor buried with all the evidences of rank accorded by Indians to their dead chiefs. The discovery directed public attention to a work which has been carried on quietly for the past three summers on the coast of Maine by well-known ethnologists connected with the Smithsonian Institution, Washington.

In the minds of these experts the discovery of the skeleton in armor is of much more importance to the ethnological world than other discoveries made within the past few weeks in the same vicinity which not only throw new light on the habits and customs of the Indians of the eastern coast of New England, but go back to a time still more remote, and indicate that a far earlier and very different people, perhaps the progenitors of the Eskimos of the present, lived here....

The work of investigating the ethnological researches of the coast of Maine was inaugurated by Major J. W. Powell, chief of the Bu-

reau of Ethnology of the Smithsonian Institution who has given it much of his personal attention. It is now under the direct supervision of Frank Hamilton Cushing, for twenty years connected with the Bureau of Ethnology whose study of Indian life has earned him a widespread reputation. (Anonymous 1899)

On April 10, 1900, Cushing died at his home in Washington, D.C., not yet forty-three years old. His obituary in the *Washington Post* of April 11 says he died after an illness of only a few days: "While Mr. Cushing had been in delicate health for a considerable time, he was able to pursue his duties until one day last week, when he was seized with a number of hemorrhages, which resulted in his death" (Anonymous 1900). Other accounts say he choked on a fishbone and died (Brandes 1965).

Sawyer wrote an *In Memoriam*. When or where it was presented is unknown, although others were given and printed by several individuals:

When Frank Cushing died, the workers in Anthropology lost a leader whose enthusiasm, patience in the face of difficulties, ready intuitions and faith in the final outcome of his labors may not easily be equaled. In December, 1895, it was my good fortune to accompany Mr. Cushing to Florida on the expedition undertaken under the auspices of the University of Pennsylvania to explore the pile dwellings at the mouth of the Anclote River.

I do not know how it has been in other expeditions, but it is certain that in this Cushing was the dominating spirit. He was the investigator, the leader, the captain. He was in fact a captain, for before the *Silver Spray* weighed anchor in the Anclote he had secured captain's papers and when the little schooner sailed to Caxsimbas' Pass it was under the command of Captain Cushing.

I wish I could give you some idea of his power to repeople the scenes around him with the spirits of their former inhabitants. He was not the seer and prophet of the future, but the historian and interpreter of the relics of the past. He had the artistic eye and the poetic imagination to seize upon and engulf himself in his surroundings. One night we rowed out of the harbor and far down the river to hear the voice of the echo. As we glided almost noiselessly through the troubled waters which gushed forth from the famous spring, Cushing stood in the bow of the boat and raised his voice in song to the mystic people of the myth-world; to those who furnish motives for poem, tale and song.

There was no moon. A faint suggestion of phosphoresence wound warmer lines of gold thread amid the paddle swirls, and the great starry lamps of the heavens dropped from ripple to ripple in long bands of light. The pine-clad hillside was but a sombre form against the sky.

In the harbor were fortunately situated masses of land and trees, and echo repeated the words of the stranger as he spoke to the night. As we rowed back, he who was of the present stood in the bow and sang the songs of a people of the past, in a baritone voice strong, clear, resonant, almost barbaric, that sent the echoes vibrating over the waters. It was the touch of an artist, and peopled for us the seas with the Pile-dwellers of the coast, with the dusky warriors and the boys splashing in the water.

We had already wrested from the roots of the pine-trees the bones and handiwork of this people and the echoing songs brought to our fancies visions of a life of which *he* felt himself to be an actual part.

The detention in Tarpon Springs resulted in discoveries of great importance to the expedition. Cushing made use of the delay to open two mounds; one at Tarpon Springs, under his own personal supervision, and one at Camp Hope, where he placed me in charge. Both were productive, and the results formed an important part of the collection. Mr. Cushing was able to secure men who had been trained in the mounds at Tarpon Springs for the work further down the coast and by his representations, explanations and

enthusiasm to keep in the best of spirits everyone who was actively employed in the work.

To be permitted to enjoy such experiences, to be on hand when splendid finds are made, when unique pottery is brought to light, when new designs, suggesting one or the other influence, are discovered, was more than a pleasure, but to have been with Cushing at such a time was also a great privilege, for he wove about all a web of enchantment, and brought forth from rude fragments stories of splendor. His genius supplied the details which assembled and unified the fragments. Generally accurate in judgment, for he could supply causes for nearly all things.

Impatient to possess the information which could be gained from the finds merely for the sake of knowledge, his ardor and enthusiasm, limitless and all-pervading, dominated his life in the field.

I shall never forget the first impressions of the muck hole in Marco, which, under the same magic touch, became the famous Court of the Pile Dwellers; the little shoots of mangrove coming up here and there, many curious weeds growing not more than twelve or sixteen inches high, all underlaid by foul-smelling black muck, into which a few trenches had been dug. These were filled with water, and indeed, the whole place was like a thick sponge saturated with water holding a great quantity of salt and a large variety of smells.

We had brought a crew of workmen from up the coast, but almost to a man they looked with absolute revolt upon the unpromising hole. Each face showed the feelings of its owner, and in the group of faces only one was lighted by enthusiasm as we stood on the edge of the Court of the Pile Dwellers.

Captain Cushing waded into the mud, moved boards about and in a short time the men, who reluctantly began work, were following him and working with an enthusiasm and will which hardly flagged through the weeks of wading in mud and slime and of working under a semi-tropical sun in the muck-covered swamp, where the mosquitoes were plentiful and the sand-fleas almost like the sands of the sea, the annoyance of the insects alternating with the smoke of the smudge supposed to bring relief. Squatting on their knees in the slime, with hands and arms covered with mud, these men worked day after day, bringing forth treasures which, if seen now as we then saw them, would command the attention of every student of American archaeology.

Mr. Cushing in the midst of it, down in the diggings, was often the fortunate one to unearth a find.

All those who worked were kept keyed up to concert pitch by the enthusiasm of the leader, and when something of special interest was found all would eagerly crowd to hear its import.

Often it seemed that the work was progressing too rapidly. The diggings were so productive that we were fairly bewildered with the results.

When evening came and George, the cook, had prepared the evening meal, across the shell heaps came the defile of the returning workmen, bearing on their heads, or in their arms, the trays containing the choicest prizes which their hard day's work had won.

After dinner these were washed on the rail of the schooner, and when free from mud, we saw them, perfect in form and in many cases brilliant in color and fairly solid, all eloquent commentaries on the life of the vanished people. As night fell, Mr. Cushing and I would sit on the stern of the *Silver Spray*, Cushing rolling his cigarette and passing matches or tobacco while far into the evening he talked of what we had seen.

Day after day, for over five months, the party labored to produce results.

Photographs and drawings were made of hundreds of articles; surveys and sketch maps of many shell settlements, and copious notes were taken. It is to be sincerely hoped that the data are in such shape that they can be published and that others will have an opportunity of studying the results of the labors of this true anthropologist. Even if incomplete, the notes would be of great value. They certainly cannot be so incomplete as the fragments left by Paschal.

In anthropology there must be great value in the suggestive, sketchy notes of a man of genius. Time alone can establish the ultimate value of the deductions; but there is much, I am sure, that will last for ages in the rough field notes from the hand of Frank Hamilton Cushing.

Battling against ill health, disappointment, temporary reverses and delays, Cushing brought together on this expedition a collection of vast interest, regarding the integrity of which I now, as heretofore, am pleased to attest.

The prime characteristic of our lost friend was his intimate sympathy with alien peoples that enabled him to recognize the ethnic forces that are the causes of their special peculiarities. We may well apply to him those noble words of Virgil:

Felix gin potrist verum cognoscere causas,
Atque metus omnes, et inexorabile fatum
Subjecit pedibus, strepitumque Acherontis
Axari.

Happy is he who has been able to seek out the causes of things, for he has put under his feet all fears, even relentless fate and the noise of the greedy gulf of death. (Sawyer n.d.d)

10

THE

FINAL

HASSLE

CUSHING HAD NOT written his final report on either Key Marco or Tarpon Springs before he died. Unfortunately, his death did not end the controversy over the authenticity of the artifacts, nor did it solve the other remaining problem: the division of the specimens between the two sponsoring institutions. The written agreement and the understanding of the Bureau of American Ethnology were that all artifacts were to be divided into two moieties, to be as identical as possible. That portion assigned to the United States National Museum would bear consecutive numbers followed by the letter "a."

From today's perspective this arrangement seemed agreeable to all concerned, and when it was made there was little doubt on the part of either institution that it could be met. Yet, for an unknown reason, Cushing seems to have made an oral commitment to Dr. Pepper before leaving on the expedition that the University Museum would have all unique specimens and the most full and complete series of specimens. He reiterates this expectation again and again to Pepper from the

field as he discovers more and more unique specimens, and he repeats it in correspondence after his return to Washington.

The sad fact is that there were few duplicates of any kind, and the Bureau of American Ethnology seems to have been unaware of Cushing's promise to the University Museum. At least there is no written record or correspondence to indicate that they had any knowledge of it.

Whether Cushing put himself in this bind, knowingly or unknowingly, or whether surviving records are incomplete, is not known. But the discrepancies in the understanding of the two institutions, both of which thought that Cushing would meet their expectations according to their understanding of the agreement while he was representing the interests of both institutions, caused great difficulties for both sides.

It is a tribute to the generosity and fair-minded understanding of the men of both institutions and the government officials who became involved that the ultimate division was effected as it was, according to the statements made to Pepper by

Cushing. Secretary Langley of the Smithsonian Institution stands especially tall. We must bear in mind that the problem was coming into focus before the accusations of fraud against Cushing were laid to rest, and the atmosphere of suspicion and distrust was still very real.

Cushing was prodded repeatedly by both institutions to finish his writing and get about the business of dividing and delivering the specimens so that they might be installed in the respective museums. He did not accomplish this before he died, so the problem had to be solved by others without benefit of his arbitration. His death, of course, saved him from having to confront two institutions with divergent expectations, the source of which could only have been Cushing.

It was decided that a representative from each sponsoring institution would make the final division, Stewart Culin for the University of Pennsylvania and W. H. Holmes for the Bureau of American Ethnology. Holmes was not happy when he reported to McGee after their first meeting:

In accordance with an arrangement recently made with you and Mr. Rathbun, I notified Dr. Stewart Culin, of the Free Museum of Science and Art of Philadelphia, that I was ready to join him in dividing the collections made by Mr. Cushing in Florida. The instructions received by me through Mr. Rathbun contain the following paragraph relating to the proposed division of The Cushing Collection of archaeologic material from West Florida: "It should perhaps be explained that in the original arrangement with the University of Pennsylvania it was mutually agreed that the collection resulting from explorations should be equally divided between the U.S. National Museum (on behalf of the Bureau) and the Free Museum of Science (on behalf of the University of Pennsylvania), and that Mr. Cushing should act as the agent of both institutions in making the division of material. The action now under consideration is made necessary through Mr. Cushing's death; and early movement in the matter is, I understand, made desirable by reason of conditions in the

U.S. National Museum, where a considerable part of the collection is now placed for study purposes."

On Mr. Culin's arrival in Washington the collections in the possession of the Museum were spread out and separated into two parts, as arranged for by Mr. Cushing in a tentative division made by him. To one series he had given numbers beginning with 1, and to another series certain of the same numbers distinguished by the addition of letters (a, b, c, d, & e). According to my recollection, Mr. Cushing once told me that the specimens indicated by the plain numbers were intended for the Philadelphia Museum, and that those designated by letters were intended for the National Museum. I thought it best to have the separation made on this basis; but I beg leave to report that the division does not conform strictly with your instructions. Of the 1047 numbers of the catalogue, 591 are by this means assigned to the Philadelphia Museum and 524 to the National Museum. As indicated by these numbers the division seems approximately just, but it is to be noted that specimens of the first order of excellence are in all or nearly all cases given to the former institution, and those of the second, third or fourth order to the latter institution. The relative scientific and museum values of the lots as they stand are perhaps two, three or four to one in favor of Philadelphia. It thus becomes a question, considering your instructions, whether this division shall be considered satisfactory.

When your instructions were received I was under the impression that the entire collection was in Washington, but I have learned that there are other Cushing collections from West Florida in Philadelphia. I am not certain that my instructions to participate in a division refer to the latter materials.

I have learned also that a third party (Mrs. Hearst) has an important claim on these collections. The problem of separation is thus rendered more complex than I had any reason to anticipate, and I am therefore constrained to ask that you will excuse me from further participation in the matter. I beg leave, however, to make the suggestion that the entire collection be assembled in Philadelphia, and that Mr. Culin be asked to make the separation according to his understanding of the claims of the three parties to the contract, and that some disinterested person be then designated to pass upon the fairness of the division. (Holmes 1900)

Holmes wrote Culin, enclosing a copy of his letter to McGee. On August 15, 1900, Culin responded to Holmes: "I received your note in reference to the Cushing collections, Dr. McGee having sent me a copy of his letter to you in reply to the one of which you sent me a copy. You will recall that Mr. Cushing divided the Marco collection before it left Philadelphia in accordance with the original arrangement. I do not see any reason that the division made by him should not stand. I believe it was done in full accordance with the spirit of the original arrangement. I have written in similar terms to Dr. McGee" (Culin 1900).

On August 24, McGee answered Culin's letter: "While I know nothing about the details of the labeling, it may be worth mentioning that I repeatedly enjoined Mr. Cushing to use original and consecutive numbers in designating the Government's moiety of the collection; this for his own protection and that of the Bureau in case of public inquiry" (McGee 1900).

At the same time Culin turned to Bergmann for his recollections about the matter. On August 27, Bergmann replied: "In reference to the collections from Marco, Fla. I was detailed to aid Mr. Cushing in cataloging it, at the time Mr. Cushing made the division for the University and the National Museum. The lettered specimens were designated by him for the National Museum" (Bergmann 1900).

In an effort to review the whole situation and to understand it better, with an ultimate satisfactory settlement in mind, Smithsonian Secretary S. P. Langley asked Major Powell for pertinent correspondence prior to the official letter of October 19, 1895. Powell regretfully reported that there was none (Powell n.d.).

Culin apparently decided that he and W. H.

Holmes would never achieve a meeting of minds, so he objected to McGee about having to work with Holmes and asked that he be replaced. McGee refused to replace him because "the same considerations still exist, and it would naturally raise a question in the minds of future inquirers as to the integrity of the division were he replaced by any other representative of the government interests." Again he suggested an arbiter if they could not agree (McGee n.d.).

When his suggestion was not taken, Culin decided to appeal to government authorities for help and support of his claim. On January 25, 1901, he wrote to Congressman H. H. Bingham, representative from Philadelphia:

The matter concerning which I requested a personal consultation with you is a question that has arisen between the BAE at Washington and the Department of Archaeology of the University of Pennsylvania over the division of a collection of archaeological material made by Mr. Cushing in Florida. In accordance with an agreement between Dr. Pepper and Mr. Cushing this institution was to receive as a result of the expedition, we defraying all the expenses, all unique specimens, the division to be made by Mr. Cushing. We expended some $8,000, and Mr. Cushing's death occurring with the collection in his hands in Washington, we requested its return on the basis of the division made by Mr. Cushing before his death.

Greatly to our surprise, the Bureau of Ethnology proposed a new division, half and half, and declined to accede to our request for a settlement upon the basis of the original agreement.

This department and University, having expended a large sum in good faith in carrying out an important scientific work in which it took the initiative, feels that not only is it deprived of the results due it, but that the proposed re-division of the collection would be contrary to the interests of science.

Other means failing, it was suggested that I appeal to your good offices on behalf of the University. I have the honor to enclose copies of the following documents bearing upon the case:

A — A statement signed by Mr. Cushing in reference to undertaking the work.

B — Mr. Cushing's letter of instruction from the BAE

C — Dr. Pepper's letter of acceptance

D — Mr. Bergmann's letter in reference to the division. (Culin 1901)

Bingham apparently referred the matter to Senator Boise Penrose, who said he knew nothing about the "question that has arisen between the BAE and the University of Pennsylvania," but from his acquaintance with the officers of the University of Pennsylvania he is satisfied that the position they have taken appears to them to be justified. He hopes for satisfactory adjustment. He may give letters of introduction to Pennsylvania officers who will call to discuss the situation" (Penrose 1901).

On February 9, 1901, Powell made a written statement to Langley outlining the bureau's involvement and understanding of the situation:

The plan of work thus agreed upon was put into execution; and I directed the operations partly from the office, partly in the field, where I personally supervised the researches and the making of collections. The work resulted in important additions to scientific knowledge concerning the archaeology of western Florida, and also in a considerable collection of relics. When the field work was completed, Mr. Cushing arranged to ship the collection by freight, and then came to Washington to make provision for temporarily placing the entire collection in the United States National Museum for purposes of study, classification and labeling, and for effecting the division of the relics between the two institutions concerned; but finding that there was no available space in the museum at the time, he proposed to forward the collection to Philadelphia and to unpack and label it in the museum attached to the University of Pennsylvania; this plan I approved, solely by reason of lack of available space in

the National Museum. The collection was duly delivered in Philadelphia, and after a preliminary classification and labeling a considerable portion of it was reshipped to Washington and placed in the United States National Museum for the purpose of study by Mr. Cushing, and for the purpose of completing the division contemplated in Mr. Cushing's original work commission.

Throughout the Florida work, the operations were conducted in accordance with Mr. Cushing's commission, it was never annulled, set aside, or (so far as the collections were concerned) modified in any manner whatsoever; and it constantly received the acquiescence of both Dr. Pepper and Mr. Cushing in all subsequent conferences and correspondence.

Some time after the death of Dr. Pepper, and soon after the death of Mr. Cushing it was deemed necessary to effect a final division of the collection; and for this purpose Professor W. H. Holmes, of the United States National Museum, was designated to act on behalf of the Bureau and the National Museum, while Professor Culin was designated to act on behalf of the University of Pennsylvania. When these gentlemen met, Professor Holmes suggested a division of the portion of the collections now in the National Museum into moities, in accordance with the terms of the commission under which the work was executed; while Professor Culin urged a division which would give the University of Pennsylvania more than three-fourths of the relics and at least nine-tenths of the value of the collection.

As the basis of this claim Professor Culin produced a paper purporting to be a copy of a memorandum of agreement between Mr. Cushing and Dr. Pepper, so framed as to subvert or directly contravene the provisions of Mr. Cushing's commission from this Bureau. This alleged agreement, ostensibly entered into for the purpose of evading and circumventing Mr. Cushing's commission as a public officer, was never authorized by me, was never brought to the knowledge of this office in any manner until after Mr. Cushing's death, was never mentioned by either Dr. Pepper or Mr. Cushing in any of the many conferences with them; I repudiate it utterly.

I am informed by Professor Holmes that when he and Professor Culin failed to agree as to the mode of division of the collection, the former proposed that they two should select a third party to arbitrate any and all points at issue between them: but Professor Culin rejected the proposal. There the matter rested for several months.

I have assumed that the Secretary may perhaps wish to give special attention to the matter now that it has been brought to the notice of a representative of the Legislative branch of the government. (Powell 1901a)

Langley must have agreed that it was time to do something to settle the matter finally. On February 11, 1901, he wrote to the Honorable Robert Adams, Jr., congressman from Philadelphia, regent of the Smithsonian, a graduate of the University of Pennsylvania, and an acquaintance of Provost Harrison and the late Dr. Pepper; with a foot in both camps, he, if anyone, should surely be impartial.

The department of Archaeology of the University of Pennsylvania has brought a complaint of unfairness on the part of the Bureau of American Ethnology, to the attention of Senator Penrose. it arises over the question of division of collections part of which are now at Philadelphia and another and very considerable part in the Museum building at the present time.

As you are both a Regent of the Institution and a graduate of the University of Pennsylvania, and could do justice, I am sure, to both interests, I am going to ask you if you will not be good enough to come here where the collections can be seen and help me in forming a conclusion.

I think the briefest inspection will serve, and I will ask you if you can name an hour when you will call tomorrow, and if you think well of it, to ask Senator Penrose himself to take a look at them. (Langley 1901a)

On the same day he replied to Senator Penrose: "Your letter of the 6th instant, enclosing some correspondence relative to a question that has arisen between the Bureau of American Ethnology and the Department of Archaeology of the University of Pennsylvania, reached me on the 8th, and I am now taking steps to get at the exact facts in relation to it. You may have noticed that the letter which you have transmitted and which is written upon paper bearing the heading of the University of Pennsylvania, is unsigned. While in any event I should have the matter, which has never before been brought to my attention, examined into, it seems to me but natural to expect that the person who is bringing before you a virtual charge against the fairness of the Bureau, should be willing to take the responsibility of appending his name to the document" (Langley 1901b). One wonders if perhaps Mrs. Stevenson had again managed to intrude herself into the situation. On February 15, Langley again wrote to Adams:

In Dr. Pepper's letter of November 9, 1895, to Mr. Cushing, there is an acceptance of the conditions stated in Major Powell's letter of October 19, 1895, supplemented by the qualification as explained by you [Mr. Cushing]. The effect of these words is seen in the memo of the same date (November 9, 1895) which purports to be signed by Mr. Cushing, though in terms which indicate that it was not dictated by him but by another. Here the explanation appears to be, not so much unwarranted by his official instructions, as a direct contradiction of them. Though this memo is dated November 9, 1895, its existence or the nature of its contents was first known to Major Powell, the Director of the Bureau, in the last month, by what purports to be a copy of said memo enclosed by Mr. Culin, in a letter of January 25, 1901, referred by General Bingham to Major Powell.

How unequal it is, you have yourself seen. . . which constitute more than five-sixths of the value of the whole San Marco collection, independently of the collections made at Tarpon Springs, which are nearly equal to the San Marco series, and which are already in Philadelphia. (Langley 1901c)

Adams was a wise choice. He made an immediate effort to find a solution acceptable to both sides. In a note to Langley dated February 17, he says, "I called on Provost Harrison last evening. He had heard nothing of the matter. I left the papers with him and he said he would consult with the executive committee of the archaeological museum of which Mr. Robert C. H. Brock is chairman. I hope for an amicable adjustment of the difficulty" (Adams 1901a).

Later, on March 28, Adams again wrote to Langley: "After several conferences with the University authorities we have concluded it is best for our Mr. Robert C. H. Brock, Chairman of the Committee, and yourself to have a talk together. He will come to Washington any day next week that you notify him of. He will take the 8:30 train arriving at 11:30 so he can return on the 3 P.M. train" (Adams 1901b). Brock in turn wrote to Langley on March 29, "I asked Mr. Adams in making the appointment to include Mr. Samuel T. Bodine of the Museum Board, who with me represents the University of Pennsylvania" (Brock 1901a).

It was apparently an amicable and fruitful meeting, according to an unsigned report, probably from Holmes, to Secretary Langley on April 1:

Messrs. Robert C. H. Brock and Samuel T. Bodine, of Philadelphia representing the University of Pennsylvania, called at the Institution to discuss the matter of the division of the archaeological material collected by Mr. Frank H. Cushing in Florida, about which there now exists a difference of opinion between the BAE and the University. At my request the discussion was attended by Maj. Powell.

The gentlemen declared, in substance, that they make no question of the right of the Institution to the "moiety" of the collection on the evidence that was submitted, and that the legal claim was inexpungable; but they represented that the Philadelphia subscribers had given their money in good faith on the representations of Mr. Cushing, an agent of the Bureau, that the University was to have, not half, but the whole, or nearly the whole, of the proceeds of the expedition. That this was done without authority, and without the knowledge and against the wishes, of the only persons who were authorized to treat on the part of the Bureau, they did not deny, but the subscribers could not know this, and had contributed upon the representations specified above; and on these grounds they asked consideration.

Mr. Brock also stated that, in his recollection, the University had a receipt from someone for these collections. I told him that no one was authorized to give such a receipt, either by myself or by Maj. Powell, and that it was to be feared that this was but another portion of the double dealing which had been carried on.

With reference to the letter from Maj. Powell stating that the Bureau had been charged with an unfair division of the collection, by an officer of the University, Mr. Brock said that he felt sure that Mr. Culin, the writer of the letter, did not intend any such implication.

I took these gentlemen to lunch and to the zoo, and the discussion was continued informally on the way.

I stated in conclusion that I should probably ask Maj. Powell to take into consideration what might be called the moral claim of the Philadelphia subscribers, as well as the indubitably legal one of the Bureau, and to recommend to me some course which might possibly be in the nature of a compromise. (Anonymous 1901)

This position must have been difficult for Holmes, and for Langley too. It would mean that all of the exotic specimens would almost certainly be consigned to Philadelphia. In spite of the personal feelings he must have had, Langley wrote to Brock:

I have consulted with the Director of the Bureau of American Ethnology, Major J. W. Powell, in regard to the collections made at Marco.

I am not desirous to insist upon what appears to be the legal rights of the Institution, in view of the facts stated by you, that the promoters of the expedition, in Philadelphia and elsewhere, understood (however incorrectly) that the material collected was going chiefly to the Philadelphia museum.

I have asked Major Powell to look over the collections again with Mr. Holmes, and taking them as a whole, to select a minimum typical collection to be retained by the Institution, sending to the University of Pennsylvania in final settlement the greater portion of the objects, both in number and in value. I cannot state numerically what this greater portion will be, but it will represent certainly more than 4/5 of the whole in number and value, and will be a complete representative collection. This will be done at once, and I hope that you and our Philadelphia friends will feel that your visit has resulted in a satisfactory arrangement, which both Major Powell and I have great pleasure in making.

A list of the objects retained here will presently follow. (Langley 1901d)

Major Powell did look the collection over, making a careful and detailed study of the artifacts and reporting back to Langley on April 8, 1901: "On the 5th and 6th instant I carefully examined tray by tray the Marco collection comparing the moiety which has been selected to go to Philadelphia with the moiety to remain in Washington. I have added to the latter the objects listed on a separate sheet. It seems to me that this makes a representative collection, though it is the smaller having fewer duplicates and generally less interesting specimens, but I desire to make the Philadelphia share the better one for reasons which you already know" (Powell 1901b).

Langley accepted Powell's choices and notified Brock, sending the list of retained specimens:

I have, after consultation with Major

Powell, retained for the Smithsonian Institution in addition to the articles already set aside by Mr. Cushing, the following objects mentioned in the enclosed list, making a small but representative collection of the Marco findings. The remaining articles in the Marco collection, very much exceeding those retained in the Institution, in numbers and in value, are ready for shipment to the University of Pennsylvania.

I believe you are prepared to send Mr. Bergmann to Washington to pack the objects, and as soon as you may conveniently arrange for him to come the collection may be shipped. Packing boxes are already in readiness here. (Langley 1901e)

One item Langley decided to keep was the little panther statuette. Pennsylvania, of course, wanted it too, so Brock made a gentle gesture to get it, dated April 13:

I have your favor of the 11th instant, with its enclosure.

I want to ask you, as a personal favor, and in order that the settlement of this matter may be such a one as I can heartily and unequivocally recommend to my Board of Managers, that you will strike out from the list of objects to be retained by the Smithsonian Institute and add to the objects to be sent to the University of Pennsylvania, the panther-headed figure. I very much hope that you will see your way clear to do this. (Brock 1901b)

One can sympathize with Langley in wanting to retain *one* of the choice pieces in the collection of the United States National Museum. His answer was gentle too, but firm:

I have your letter of April 12th. Some years ago when I looked at the collection of objects from San Marco Springs, there were three which particularly impressed me as being distinctly valuable as art objects, and which I should have wished to retain for the Institution, namely, the head of a deer, the head of a duck, and the little panther figure. I have consented to the transfer of both the deer and the duck to the University of Pennsylvania, but I am going to ask you to sympathize with my wish and purpose to retain the other.

I sincerely trust that you will feel, as I do, that in sending the vastly superior portion of the San Marco finds to Philadelphia, the decision to retain this as one of the very few objects of value in the series reserved for the Institution, does not conflict with the very liberal disposition which the Institution has already shown in this matter. (Langley 1901f)

Brock willingly acceded to Langley's wish, bringing a final and satisfactory conclusion to the matter:

I thank you for your letter received this morning, and though I must confess having some personal disappointment, yet I hope you will believe me when I tell you that it in no sense diminishes the feeling of gratitude for the fairness with which you have treated us. Both Mr. Bodine and I feel that we had no right to ask or expect kinder treatment than that which we have had at your hands.

Again thanking you, as well for your hospitality as for your kindness. (Brock 1901c)

Bergmann, packing the specimens, made a careful list of missing specimens. It included both painted shells and a gray diorite pendant. Bergmann seemed satisfied, as he reported to Culin on June 7, 1901: "So far we have found quite a number of minor things missing, mostly shells &c, out of lots. All in all, considering the handling, I think we can be satisfied with the condition of the material. Some specimens I feel satisfied will be missing at the end, for both sides; but I hope nothing of importance. . . . Among the list of newly added specimens to the National Museum share I find a pestle and cup have been separated—they taking the cup and we the pestle" (Bergmann 1901).

The University of Pennsylvania's share was shipped to Philadelphia on August 9, 1901. Somehow, in the years since final division and ship-

ment, the controversial shell with the dancer figure painted inside appeared again. It is now in the possession of the University of Pennsylvania, on exhibit in the University Museum. The other painted shell, with the hand inside, has never been found.

Long after Cushing's death, Hodge managed to have the last word on the fraud controversy involving the jeweled toad when no one was left to refute his word. In a statement to Emil Haury, dated October 5, 1931, he said:

I promised long ago to write to Mr. Willoughby [of the Peabody Museum where the Hemenway collection is housed] in regard to the turquoise frog, but have neglected to do so. These are the facts:

A shell frog, encrusted with turquoise mosaic (and I believe, some red stone or shell) was in possession of Lincoln Fowler, a one-armed real estate dealer of Phoenix. I do not recall whence it came, but there was no doubt as to its genuineness, and, besides, others have since been found in southern Arizona. I do not know what became of this frog, and I believe Mr. Fowler died long ago.

As soon as Cushing saw the frog he was overwhelmed with enthusiasm and expectancy. Several plain frog-shape shells were found at Los Muertos (they should be in the collection), but none decorated with mosaic. Some time later, Cushing was engaged in work that seemed to necessitate his retirement in a closed tent. During this time he sent out the two Zuñi Indians who were with the Expedition (Weta and Siwtitsalu) to gather gum (mesquite, I think), and he was bewailing the fact that he had no bitumen.

Some days later he appeared, holding in his clenched hand a beautiful mosaic frog. That he had intended to palm it off as a specimen found in the ruins, I have no doubt. When he opened his hand and showed the object to me, I did not exclaim, but spoke of it casually as his own handiwork, as if he was aware that I knew he had made it, whereupon he said, "But it looks too new." This, coupled with the secrecy with which the frog was manufactured, confirmed my belief that he had intended to represent it as of Indian manufacture, but on account of its newness had abandoned the idea and thought of preserving it only as a model.

Some time later, Professor Edward S. Morse visited Los Muertos (the camp was called Camp Hemenway). It was, I believe, in the evening of the day of his arrival that Cushing brought out the frog, and showed it to Morse, first holding it in his closed hand as before. As soon as Morse put eyes on it, he exclaimed, "Great Lord, Cushing, where did you find that?"

Cushing responded nonchalantly, "In a jar in Ruin III."

I was present during this performance. Not once did Cushing pretend to me or to anyone else in camp that the frog had been found in the ruins.

In his own belief, Cushing had won, for if the frog could deceive Morse, it would deceive anyone. The result was that Morse took the frog to Boston and showed it or gave it to Mrs. Hemenway, never suspecting that the object was anything but genuine. It was thus that the frog found its way into the Hemenway collections.

The question of the genuineness of the frog was discussed several times later, especially following a reference to its lack of authenticity in one of Fewkes' papers in the *American Anthropologist*. It was either on account of this or in connection with some other discussion that Cushing asked me if I had told anyone that the frog had not been found in the excavation, whereupon I informed him that I had always told the absolute truth about its origin and should continue to do so.

I remember now that the question of Cushing's probity was assailed when he was accused of altering or faking some of the Key Marco finds, at which time the genuineness of the frog was also discussed. Major J. W. Powell, aware of all this contention, informed me, after Cushing's death, that he did not regard Cushing as mentally responsible.

I have hesitated a long time to make the history of the frog a matter of record, but as the object is still displayed as a genuine thing, instead of as a model, I believe it to be in the interest of Science that the story be told.

Of course, what I have here written is not for publication, but suggest that it or a copy thereof be placed in the archives of the Peabody Museum, and I shall be glad if you will show it to Mr. Willoughby. (Hodge 1931)

Hodge's statement stands in direct contradiction to Cushing's detailed description of his handling of the frog when the specimen was found. In a draft of a report to Professor Putnam of the Peabody Museum, on June 14, 1897, Cushing stated:

The specimen of an incrusted shell toad or frog relative to which you ask me was found by my workmen and myself in House-Mound IV (north of the central Temple mound and after renumbered I believe House Mound IV) of the ruined and buried city of Los Muertos in the Salado Valley of Arizona in connection with a decorated water jar, masses of what I regarded as crude asbestos and other objects. It was perfectly recognizable in all details as a toad-figure, some of the inlaid work being still intact, and nearly all of the parts present, although more or less loosened. That the example which was unique at that time might be perfectly preserved and shown in its entirety I made a drawing of it as found, a careful study of the gum with which the shell had been coated and in which the fragments of turquoise and red stone or shell etc. had been set, determining with the expert aid of Doctor Jacob L. Wortman, Anthropological Assistant on the expedition, that it like other examples in the collection was principally of greasewood gum and that this was in turn (caused by parasites) a kind of lac, containing, however, powdered charcoal or carbonaceous shale or some other fine carbonaceous matter. I then, with some of this lac freshly gathered, and with powdered carbon I made a kind of fire-gum whereof and with it undertook to cement the loosened parts to restore the portions missing, in it, and to replace the stones etc. I used the utmost care to restore each fragment even to its place as nearly as possible by aid of my sketch and a working model. The annules that surround the eyes and the anal opening (or its representation) seemed to be beads. The latter being still in place, the former disturbed, and the right eye missing and impossible to find. In a few cases I replaced missing stones where I could be certain of their shape with other fragments gathered from the surface of the Pyral mounds, and in three or four cases from fragments given me for the purpose by two Zuñi comrades Waihusiwa and Siwahtusai who at that time accompanied me on the expedition. When I had completed these preliminary operations I endeavored to solidify the more fragile parts by gently heating the entire surface—by which the whole work coalesced in such manner that the portions were almost indistinguishable from the others. Then hoping to bring out the difference I cautiously rubbed the surface on a piece of buckskin, using as buff the very fine loam of the ruins. This did not accomplish what I wished. I frankly acknowledge it was a mistake but a conscientious mistake. I offer the statement here as accounting for the scratched surface and the fresh looking condition of the specimen. For, altho some small portion of the original surface showed both grinding and a high polish it was generally dull and in some of the more decayed spaces, brownish in color. Since this was the first recognizable specimen of its kind that had to my knowledge been found, since I used such care in its restoration, and since subsequently another specimen identical with it in general and in several specific characteristics has been found farther North in Arizona by Doctors Fewkes and Hough, you may without hesitation exhibit this example as accurate and authentic. (Cushing 1897i)

Hodge's statement to Haury stands also in some contradiction to a letter he wrote to E. DeGolyer on April 3, 1946:

Cushing's health was anything but robust when the arrangements were made for him to accompany James and Mrs. Stevenson to Zuñi in 1879. The Stevensons never forgave Cushing for blaming them for leaving him at Zuñi against his will, as mentioned in My Adventures in Zuñi. As a matter of fact, Major Powell sent Cushing to Zuñi to study its people and to remain indefinitely, and he returned to Washington not by reason of his health, but because Senator John A. Logan demanded his return under threat of killing the Bureau of Ethnology's appropriation. The cause of this trouble was Cushing's fight against certain army officers at Ft. Wingate including Major Tucker, Logan's son-in-law, who seized the Nutria Spring of the Zuñis on which they depended for a third of their water supply. In this Cushing was supported by Sylvester Baxter of the Boston *Herald* and William Elroy Curtis of the Chicago *Inter-Ocean*. The army officers referred to had established a cattle ranch in the Zuñi Mountains known as the Box S Ranch and needed the Nutria Spring water. The matter was carried to President Arthur, who proclaimed the Zuñi reservation, which included (and still includes) the three great springs—Nutria, Pescado, and Ojo Caliente.

Powell was aware of Cushing's eccentricities, for he told me so one day as we drove together from the funeral of Dr. Elliott Coues. At the same time he regarded Cushing as a genius with a remarkable insight into Zuñi modes of thought.

Concerning the inlaid frog, I presume that Dr. Haury has told you all that there is to tell. Cushing did not intend to foist it on anyone as a piece of purely aboriginal work, but when Professor Edward S. Morse visited the camp in the Salt River Valley where Cushing was excavating "El Pueblo de Los Muertos," he handed the object to Morse, who regarded it at once as the "real thing" and took it back to Boston with him. Having deceived

Morse, he let the deception rest there, instead of revealing the frog as a mere reproduction. The shell on which the inlay was applied was genuine. A number of such were found. (Hodge 1946)

Since, in this instance, we do not have notarized statements of eyewitnesses or diaries of persons there at the time these events took place to authenticate any of these statements, judgment will have to be left to the reader.

A last note on Mrs. Stevenson. Cushing was not the only person to have problems with her. In a letter from Lucy E. Peabody to Dr. McGee on January 19, 1902, Peabody wrote, "Major says to tell you his tussle with Mrs. Stevenson began in the Hoe Building, when he notified all absentees that they would be expected to do their work in the office where they would be in a fire proof building. She said she could not work where there was so much noise and confusion and appealed to the Director. When we moved into the Adams Building he again told the lady she would have to do her work in the office just the same as the others did and told her she could select her room and he would fit it up nicely for her. She again appealed to the Director and you know the result. We both wish you success in your present endeavors. The Bureau lost so much by allowing a few of its members so much latitude that we congratulate you in your desire to change matters. Mr. Henshaw tried to object but with the usual result—appeal to the Director" (Peabody 1902).

11

POSTSCRIPT

THE COLLIER SITE on Key Marco is unique. It was even more a sensation in 1895 than it is today. Organic materials are often found well preserved in dry caves or desert climates, but they do not last long in a humid, semitropical climate such as South Florida's. It is the preservative qualities of the muck in which they fell, caused by the tannic acid from the mangrove trees, that is responsible for the remarkable condition of so many artifacts of wood and fiber.

The artifacts from the Cushing expedition are some of the most exotic materials ever retrieved by archaeologists in North America. Unfortunately, the fledgling science of archaeology in 1895 did not have adequate preservative techniques for many of the fragile items, nor did it have means of restoring those in poor condition, so it is fortunate indeed that Cushing had the foresight to include a competent artist and photographer among the expedition's personnel. In the case of many of the fragile items, the detailed descriptions written by Cushing and the watercolors and photographs by Wells Sawyer are the

only evidence we have that these things ever existed. Many did not survive even long enough to be shipped from Marco.

There will always be controversy over the dating of the site. We are handicapped by the lack of stratigraphy on which to establish a time sequence based on specific diagnostic types for each era. And many items which might otherwise be indicators of fairly specific periods, such as bone projectile points and atlatls, both Archaic period weapons, are not significant for dating since they were first used thousands of years earlier and were still in use when Europeans made contact with the Calusa.

Some question the validity of the radiocarbon dates on the basis of the long period of storage of the artifacts under diverse environmental conditions before they were subjected to this process. Questioned too is the possible influence of the use of chemical pesticides used in the area where they were stored before dating. We may never have exact answers to these questions.

In recent years there has been increasing emphasis on wetlands archaeology and several significant sites have been discovered in Florida, but none has produced as great a variety of artifact types or so complete a picture of the culture as the Cushing site. New awareness of the significance of such sites, together with the increasing appreciation of the natural environment and preservation of such areas for their contribution to the existence of human and animal, is helping to make it possible for archaeologists to examine such sites when they are discovered in the course of development projects. In many cases the cost of archaeological exploration is borne by the developers.

In Southwest Florida the rapid development and fast-growing population has produced ever-increasing activity in the field of archaeology, accompanied by greatly increased awareness and interest among both archaeologists and the public.

In the Swiss Lake Dweller sites Cushing refers to (1897a), somewhat similar materials had been found though none so exotic as those from Marco. These Neolithic villages were first discovered at Meilen in 1855 in the Alpine area of Switzerland. These early villagers had protected their houses by building them on pilings driven into the mud of the lake bottom, by crib work placed in the water of rivers, or by wooden platforms in peat bogs. Many such areas covered extended time periods. In Lake Neufchâtel they had built habitations of logs supported on piles, placed in the shallow water around margins of the lake. Abundant cultural remains—bone pendants, stone beads, fish nets and baskets, and clay loom weights—were found in the mud and sand around the stumps of the piles that supported the villages. These people subsisted by agriculture and hunting. At Aichbühl on the Federsee they built long platforms of logs and rectangular megaronlike houses on the shore. Many of these villages were destroyed by floods which raised the water level of the lakes; some villagers retreated to lakes in the Italian Alps and there built similar villages (Hibben 1958:150–55).

It is easy to see why Cushing thought the Collier site was similar. He came to this conclusion on the basis of Durnford's account before he ever saw the site. In spite of finding no pilings large enough to support such large platforms and finding house timbers on the shell ridges, he never revised his opinion.

The house-building tradition in this part of Florida is that of building on shell mounds, often quite high. Evidence indicates that this pattern held at Marco. In recent years more muck sites have been investigated and many more well-preserved wooden artifacts have been recovered, most notably at Ft. Center just west of Lake Okeechobee (Sears 1982).

The Collier site was unique in other ways. Such a complete range of artifacts was found, along with the tools of their manufacture, that it is possible to reconstruct the technologies used in making them. There were tools not found so far in other sites, most notably those with shark tooth blades. These were beautifully made and highly efficient tools, responsible for the sophisticated level of art achieved at Marco.

In the past, dating of the Key Marco artifacts has been somewhat confused and controversial, made more so by a series of five radiocarbon dates run in 1975 on wooden artifacts recovered by Cushing from the muck deposit. Those dates are much earlier than a single date run in the 1960s. There are also two collections of pottery from Marco, that recovered by Cushing from the muck and a collection made by Cushing and others from the surrounding shell midden deposits. But when all of these lines of evidence are examined together, they support my contention that the site was occupied over a considerable period of time.

Generally, archaeologists can date sites using pottery decorative styles (certain motifs were used during specific periods of time), the shape of pottery vessels, stratigraphy (the relative vertical position of artifacts in the ground; older materials lie under younger ones), and radiocarbon dating (which yields a date range). The amount of decorated pottery recovered with the wooden artifacts from the Marco muck deposits, however, is very small.

John M. Goggin, Florida archaeologist, examined the Marco collections in the late 1940s or early 1950s and, on the basis of decorative motifs

(Glades Tooled and Fort Walton pottery), dated the artifacts to the Glades IIIb period (Goggin n.d.: 249–55). Today, based on the work of John Griffin, we know that the Glades IIIb period dates from A.D. 1400 to 1513 (Milanich and Fairbanks 1980:234). This range for the artifacts is close to the radiocarbon date of A.D. 1670 ± 100 derived from fibers excavated by Cushing and dated in the 1960s. Goggin also noted that the wooden bowls recovered from the muck by Cushing included one with a Surfside Incised decorative motif around the rim, a motif that is a marker for the Glades IIIa period, A.D. 1200–1400.

Five additional radiocarbon dates were run in 1975 directly on wooden artifacts from the muck (see Gilliland 1975:257 for the items dated): A.D. 55 ± 60, A.D. 670 ± 60, A.D. 700 ± 50, A.D. 775 ± 100, and A.D. 850 ± 50. There are those who argue that the dated materials had been contaminated by older hydrocarbons contained in such things as insecticides sprayed near the Marco collections, causing the dates to show as earlier than the artifacts actually are (cf. Milanich 1978). And certainly there is a real possibility of contamination of the Marco collection, stored for nearly a century prior to radiocarbon dating.

On the other hand, a larger sample of pottery taken from the Marco shell middens surrounding the muck deposit supports four of those five dates which together are clustered in the period A.D. 670–850 (the A.D. 55 date seems to be an error). Goggin (n.d.:247–49) also examined that midden collection, which contained cord-marked pottery, Surfside Incised, and Sanibel Incised, and dated it to the Glades II and III periods, A.D. 750–1513 (Milanich and Fairbanks 1980:234).

Together the radiocarbon dates and the two pottery collections suggest that the Marco sites and the artifacts recovered from the muck depos-its span a long period of time, perhaps from A.D. 750 or slightly earlier to 1513, prior to European contact.

The residents of Marco made most efficient use of their environment. They were unique in that they were not fully agricultural, yet they were a sedentary population. Like the residents of the Northwest Coast of the United States and Canada, they were sea-oriented but used land resources as well. South Florida lacks hard stone for projectile points and clay suitable for pottery, so they made tools and utensils from wood and shell, leaving us a complete range of both. The carryover of the primitive bone and fire-hardened wood projectile points is likely due to this fact also.

Another holdover was continued use of the atlatl or spearthrower. They used bows and arrows but retained the earlier weapon as well.

Archaeologists had long surmised that residents of this area certainly must have made use of the abundant mullet, but until mullet bones were found at Marco there was no proof. Mullet have to be netted, and Marco provided the first evidence of such nets. They were found intact with wood or gourd floats to keep the top of the net at the surface of the water and shell sinkers to keep its bottom down.

A great variety of netting, cordage and rope was found, all beautifully made. It ranged in thickness from today's ordinary sewing thread to rope an inch in diameter. Some was simple twist, some was cabled, all fine quality, all made from local fibers.

While other muck sites have produced other artifacts of organic materials, this site remains unique. The quality, beauty, and sophistication of the art work has never been surpassed.

REFERENCES

NMNH: National Museum of Natural History, Smithsonian Institution, Washington

BAE correspondence: Bureau of American Ethnology Correspondence, National Anthropological Archives, Smithsonian Institution, Washington

P. K. Yonge Library: P. K. Yonge Library of Florida History, University of Florida, Gainesville.

UM: University Museum, University of Pennsylvania, Philadelphia.

Hodge-Cushing Collection: Hodge-Cushing Collection, Southwest Museum, Los Angeles.

Hodge-Hemenway Collection: Hodge-Hemenway Collection, Southwest Museum, Los Angeles.

Adams, Congressman Robert, Jr.
  1901a   [Letter to S. P. Langley, February 17.] Accession file, NMNH.
  1901a   [Letter to S. P. Langley, March 28.] Accession file, NMNH.

Anonymous
  1883   [Note by J. D. McC., July 1.] BAE correspondence file, 1883.
  1896a   [Article on Marco excavations.] *Jacksonville Citizen,* February 2.
  1896b   [Article on Marco excavations.] *Washington Post,* February 3.
  1896c   [Article on Marco excavations.] *Pittsburgh Post,* February 3.
  1899   [Article on Maine archaeology.] *Philadelphia Inquirer,* October 15.
  1900   [Cushing obituary.] *Washington Post,* April 11.
  1901   [Report (probably by W. H. Holmes) to S. P. Langley, April 1.] Accession file, NMNH.

Baird, Spencer
  1882a   [Letter to J. W. Powell, April 25.] S. Baird file, BAE correspondence.
  1882b   [Letter to J. W. Powell, date unknown.] File 4677, BAE correspondence.

Baxter, Sylvester
  1881   [Letter to S. Baird, August 3.] File

4677, BAE correspondence.

Bergman, Carl W. F.
1899 [Letter to S. Culin, May 8.] Photostat, Wells Sawyer papers, P. K. Yonge Library.
1900 [Letter to W. J. McGee, August 27.] Correspondence file, UM.
1901 [Letter to S. Culin, June 7.] Accession file, NMNH.

Boas, Franz
1897a [Letter to W. J. McGee, January 1.] File 4672(3), BAE correspondence.
1897b [Letter to W. J. McGee, November.] File 4372(3), BAE correspondence.

Bourke, Lt.
1884 [Letter to F. H. Cushing, June 30.] File 59, Hodge-Cushing Collection.

Brandes, R. S.
1965 *Frank Hamilton Cushing, Pioneer Americanist.* Ph.D. dissertation, University of Arizona, Tucson. Ann Arbor: University Microfilms.

Brock, Robert C. H.
1901a [Letter to S. P. Langley, March 29.] Accession file, NMNH.
1902b [Letter to S. P. Langley, April 13.] Accession file, NMNH.
1903b [Letter to S. P. Langley, n.d.] Accession file, NMNH.

Coann, E. T.
1891 [Memorandum.] File 104, Hodge-Hemenway Collection.

Coffin, George M.
1897a [Letter to F. H. Cushing, March 3.] File 237, Hodge-Cushing Collection.
1897b [Letter to F. H. Cushing, March 6.] File 237, Hodge-Cushing Collection.

Coffin, Julia
1897 [Letter to F. H. Cushing, March 16.] File 251, Hodge-Cushing Collection.

Collier, Margaret McIlvane
1896 [Diary.] Margaret Parrish Clarke private papers.

Collier, William Thomas
n.d. [Reminiscences.] Typescript, Margaret Parrish Clarke private papers.

Culin, Stewart
1900 [Letter to W. H. Holmes, August 15.] Accession file, NMNH.
1902 [Letter to H. H. Bingham, January 25.] Accession file, NMNH.

Cushing, Frank Hamilton
1879 [Letter to S. Baird, October 29.] File 4677, BAE correspondence.
1880a [Letter to S. Baird, April 8.] File 4677, BAE correspondence.
1880b [Letter to S. Baird, May 5.] File 4677, BAE correspondence.
1880c [Letter to S. Baird, July 8.] File 4677, BAE correspondence.
1880d [Letter to S. Baird, July 18.] File 4677, BAE correspondence.
1880e [Letter to S. Baird, July 20(?).] File 4677, BAE correspondence.
1880f [Letter to S. Baird, July 22.] File 4677, BAE correspondence.
1880g [Letter to S. Baird, August 19.] File 4677, BAE correspondence.
1880h [Letter to S. Baird, August 29.] File 4677, BAE correspondence.
1881a [Letter to S. Baird, January 25.] File 4734, BAE correspondence.
1881b [Letter to J. W. Powell, June 11.] BAE correspondence file, 1879–88.
1881c [Letter to Lt. Bourke, date unknown.] File 59, Hodge-Cushing Collection.
1881d [Letter to S. Baird, September 24.] File 4677, BAE correspondence.
1881e [Letter to S. Baird, October 12.] File 4734, BAE correspondence.
1881f [Letter to S. Baird, December 4.] File 4734, BAE correspondence.
1881g [Letter to S. Baird, December 24.] File 4734, BAE correspondence.
1882a [Letter to S. Baird, January 3.] File 4677, BAE correspondence.
1882b [Letter to J. Pilling, January 24.] File 4734, BAE correspondence.
1882c [Letter to S. Baird, July 8.] File 4677, BAE correspondence.
1883a [Letter to S. Baird, date unknown.] File 4677, BAE correspondence.
1883b [Letter to J. W. Powell, February 3.] File 4734, BAE correspondence.
1883c [Letter to S. Baird, March.] File 4734, BAE correspondence.

1883d [Letter to J. W. Powell, August 20.] File ?, BAE correspondence.

1884 [Letter to J. W. Powell, January 29.] BAE correspondence, 1884.

1885 [Letter to J. W. Powell, October 31.] File 4024c, BAE correspondence.

1889 [Letter to J. Walter Fewkes, May 10.] File 106, Hodge-Cushing Collection.

1895a [Diary.] File 233, Hodge-Cushing Collection.

1895b [Letter to W. Pepper, May 26.] Cushing file, BAE correspondence.

1895c [Letter to J. M. Kreamer, November 15.] File 238, Hodge-Cushing Collection.

1895d [Letter to Jacob Disston, November 24.] File 304, Hodge-Cushing Collection.

1895e [Letter to W. Pepper, December 1.] File 304, Hodge-Cushing Collection.

1896a [Letter to Charles Garlick, November 20.] File 109, Hodge-Cushing Collection.

1896b [Article on Marco excavations.] *New York Journal,* June 21, pp. 17–19.

1896c [Letter to W. Pepper, January 13.] File 242, Hodge-Cushing Collection.

1896d [Letter to W. Pepper, February 7.] File 242, Hodge-Cushing Collection.

1896e [Letter to W. Pepper, February 21.] Correspondence file, UM.

1896f [Letter to W. Pepper, February 24.] Correspondence file, UM.

1896g [Letter to W. Pepper, February 27.] Cushing file, BAE correspondence.

1896h [Letter to W. Pepper, March 1.] File 243, Hodge-Cushing Collection.

1896i [Letter to W. Pepper, March 3.] File 249, Hodge-Cushing Collection.

1896j [Letter to W. Pepper, March 7.] File 243, Hodge-Cushing Collection.

1896k [Letter to W. Pepper, March 14.] File 244, Hodge-Cushing Collection.

1896l [Letter to W. Pepper, March 18.] File 243, Hodge-Cushing Collection.

1896m [Letter to W. Pepper, April 2.] File 244, Hodge-Cushing Collection.

1896n [Letter to W. Pepper, April 10(?).] File 242, Hodge-Cushing Collection.

1896o [Letter to W. Pepper, April 10.] File 244, Hodge-Cushing Collection.

1896p [Letter to W. Pepper, April 20.] File 245, Hodge-Cushing Collection.

1896q [Letter to W. Pepper, April 24.] Correspondence file, UM.

1896r [Letter to W. Pepper, May 10.] Correspondence file, UM.

1896s [Letter to W. Pepper, May 13.] Correspondence file, UM.

1896t [Article on Marco excavations.] *Philadelphia Times,* June 21.

1896u [Letter to W. Pepper, May 24.] File 235, Hodge-Cushing Collection.

1896v [Letter to W. Pepper, September 7.] Correspondence file, UM.

1896w [Letter to Charles P. Daly, September 9.] File 304, Hodge-Cushing Collection.

1896x [Letter to S. Culin, September 17.] File 270, Hodge-Cushing Collection.

1896y [Letter to W. Pepper, September 20.] File 245, Hodge-Cushing Collection.

1896z [Letter to W. Pepper, September 24.] File 245, Hodge-Cushing Collection.

1896aa [Letter to W. Pepper, date unknown.] File 246, Hodge-Cushing Collection.

1896bb [Letter to W. Pepper, date unknown.] File 246, Hodge-Cushing Collection.

1896cc [Memorandum to George M. Rowzer, November 9.] File 262, Hodge-Cushing Collection.

1896dd [Letter to F. W. Putnam, November 21.] File 145, Hodge-Cushing Collection.

1896ee [Letter to W. Pepper, December 13.] File 246, Hodge-Cushing Collection.

1896ff [Letter to W. Pepper, December 17.] File 246, Hodge-Cushing Collection.

1897a Exploration of Ancient Key-Dweller Remains on the Gulf Coast of Florida. *Proceedings of the American Philosophical Society* 35(153). Philadelphia.

1897b [Letter to G. Coffin, March 9.] File 237, Hodge-Cushing Collection.

1897c [Letter to S. P. Langley, March 12.] File

237, Hodge-Cushing Collection.

1897d   [Letter to J. W. Powell, March 12.] Correspondence file, UM.

1897e   [Letter to J. W. Powell, March 29.] File 146, Hodge-Cushing Collection.

1897f   [Letter to C. Garlick, November 20.] File 109, Hodge-Cushing Collection.

1897g   [Letter to Mrs. Hearst, May 18.] File 254, Hodge-Cushing Collection.

1897h   [Letter to W. Pepper, December 1.] File 246, Hodge-Cushing Collection.

1897i   [Draft of report to Prof. Putnam, June 14.] File 145, Hodge-Cushing Collection.

1898a   [Letter to S. Culin, February 25.] Correspondence file, UM.

1898b   [Letter to S. Culin, May 15.] Correspondence file, UM.

1898c   [Letter to Mrs. Stevenson, October 14.] File 260, Hodge-Cushing Collection.

1899   [Letter to Mrs. Stevenson, February 7.] File 260, Hodge-Cushing Collection.

n.d.a   [Letter to J. W. Powell], File 242, Hodge-Cushing Collection

n.d.b   [Memorandum.] Correspondence file, UM.

n.d.c   [Letter to W. Pepper.] File 246, Hodge-Cushing Collection.

Diaz, Bernal

1956   *Bernal Diaz Chronicles*. Albert Idell, translator and editor. New York: Doubleday and Company, Inc.

Dinwiddie, William

1900   [Letter to F. Boas, November 15.] File 4372(3), BAE correspondence.

Durnford, C. D.

1895   The Discovery of Aboriginal Rope and Wood Implements in the Mud in West Florida. *American Naturalist* 29:1032–1039. Philadelphia.

Fewkes, J. Walter

1896   [Letter to Augustus Hemenway, November 30.] File 4372(3), BAE correspondence.

Fontaneda, Hernando d'Escalante

1945   *Memoirs of Do. d'Escalante Fontaneda Respecting Florida. Written in Spain about the Year 1575*. Buckingham Smith, translator and notes, David O. True, editor. Coral Gables, Florida: Glade House.

Garlick, Charles

1887   [Letter to F. H. Cushing, October 27.] File 109, Hodge-Cushing Collection.

1889a   [Letter to Mr. and Mrs. F. H. Cushing, May 15.] File 109, Hodge-Cushing Collection.

1889b   [Letter to Mr. and Mrs. F. H. Cushing, summer(?).] File 109, Hodge-Cushing Collection.

Gates, [Merrill E.(?)]

1896   [Memorandum of statements recorded by F. H. Cushing, undated.] File 262, Hodge-Cushing Collection.

Gause, George W.

1896   [Diary.] Helen Sawyer Farnsworth private papers. Sarasota.

Gause, George W., Frank Barnes, George Dorsett, R. W. Clarke, and J. B. Calhoun

1904   [Statement, February 10.] Wells M. Sawyer Papers, P. K. Yonge Library.

Gause, George W., and George Dorsett

1905   [Statement, March 8.] Wells M. Sawyer Papers, P. K. Yonge Library.

Gilliland, Marion Spujt

1975   *The Material Culture of Key Marco, Florida*. Gainesville: University Presses of Florida.

Goggin, John M.

1964   The Indians and History of the Matecumbe Region. In *Indian and Spanish Selected Writings*, pp. 39–48. Coral Gables, Florida: University of Miami Press.

n.d.   The Archaeology of the Glades Area, Southern Florida. Typescript (724 pp.). P. K. Yonge Library.

Goggin, John M., and William C. Sturtevant

1964   The Calusa, A Stratified, Nonagricultural Society (with Notes on Sibling Marriage). In *Explorations in Cultural Anthropology: Essays in Honor of George Peter Murdock*, pp. 179–219, Ward H. Goodenough, editor. New York: McGraw-Hill.

Green, Jesse, editor
1979 *Zuni, Selected Writings of Frank Hamilton Cushing.* Lincoln: University of Nebraska Press.

Hawkins, John
1965 The Voyage Made by M. John Hawkins Esquire, to the Coast of Guinea, and the Indies of Nova Hispania, begun in An. Dom. 1564. In *Hakluyt's Voyages,* edited by Irwin R. Blacker, pp. 115–160. New York: Viking Press.

Hibben, Frank C.
1958 *Prehistoric Man in Europe.* Norman: University of Oklahoma Press.

Hodge, Frederick Webb
1931 [Letter to Emil Haury, October 5.] Photostat, manuscript file, Hodge-Cushing Collection.
1946 [Letter to E. DeGolyer, April 3.] Manuscript file, Hodge-Cushing Collection.

Holmes, William H.
1900 [Letter to W. J. McGee, August 7.] File 1848, BAE correspondence.

Horsford, E. H.
1883 [Letter to J. W. Powell, November 19.] File 4024c, BAE correspondence.

Kennan, George
1880 [Letter to F. H. Cushing, August 23.] File 4734, BAE correspondence.

Langley, S.P.
1897a [Letter to J. W. Powell, March 15.] File 239, Hodge-Cushing Collection.
1897b [Letter to F. H. Cushing, March 20.] File 239, Hodge-Cushing Collection.
1901a [Letter to Robert Adams, Jr., February 11.] Accession file, NMNH.
1901b [Letter to Boise Penrose, February 11.] Accession file, NMNH.
1901c [Letter to Robert Adams, Jr., February 15.] Accession file, NMNH.
1901d [Letter to R. C. H. Brock, date unknown.] Accession file, NMNH.
1901e [Letter to R. C. H. Brock, April 11.] Accession file, NMNH.
1901f [Letter to R. C. H. Brock, date unknown.] Accession file, NMNH.

Lowery, Woodbury
1959 *The Spanish Settlements within the Present Limits of the United States,* 1512– 1561. New York: Russell and Russell.

Lyon, Eugene
1976 *The Enterprise of Florida.* Gainesville: University Presses of Florida.

McGee, W. J., Professor
1896 [Letter to F. H. Cushing, date unknown.] File 240, Hodge-Cushing Collection.
1900 [Letter to S. Culin, August 24.] Correspondence file, UM.
n.d. [Note to S. Culin.] Accession file, p. 64, NMNH.

Mark, Joan
1980 *4 Anthropologists: An American Science in Its Early Years.* New York: Science History Publications.

Mercer, Henry
1896 [Article.] *American Naturalist,* August 1, p. 692.

Milanich, Jerald T.
1978 The Temporal Placement of Cushing's Key Marco Site, Florida. *American Anthropologist* 80:682.

Milanich, Jerald T., and Charles H. Fairbanks
1980 *Florida Archaeology.* New York: Academic Press.

Peabody, Lucy E.
1902 [Letter to W. J. McGee, June 19.] File 4372–16, BAE correspondence.

Penrose, Senator Boise
1901 [Letter to H. H. Bingham, February 6.] Accession file, p. 51, BAE correspondence.

Pepper, William
1895a [Letter to J. W. Powell, April 22.] Cushing file, BAE correspondence.
1895b [Letter to J. W. Powell, July 2.] File 248, Hodge-Cushing Collection.
1895c [Letter to F. H. Cushing, November 9.] Cushing file, BAE correspondence.
1895d [Memorandum, November 9.] File 248, Hodge-Cushing Collection.
1896a [Letter to F. H. Cushing, March 22.]

File 244, Hodge-Cushing Collection.

1896b [Letter to F. H. Cushing, March 24.] File 244, Hodge-Cushing Collection.

1896c [Letter to F. H. Cushing, September 24.] File 246, Hodge-Cushing Collection.

1897 [Letter to F. H. Cushing, March 29.] File 248, Hodge-Cushing Collection.

Pilling, James C.

1884 [Letter to F. H. Cushing, January 19]. File 86, Hemenway Collection.

Powell, J. W.

1895 [Letter to F. H. Cushing, October 18.] Cushing file, BAE correspondence.

1897 [Letter to S. P. Langley, March 18.] File 239, Hodge-Cushing Collection.

1898 [Letter to F. H. Cushing, December 12.] File 250, Hodge-Cushing Collection.

1901a [Letter to S. P. Langley, February 9.] Accession file, NMNH.

1901b [Report to S. P. Langley, April 8.] Accession file, pp. 45–47, NMNH.

n.d. [File notation.] Accession file, p. 64, NMNH.

Romans, Bernard

1962 *A Concise Natural History of East and West Florida.* [Facsimile reproduction of the 1775 edition.] Gainesville: University Presses of Florida.

Sawyer, Wells M.

1895 [Letter, December 13.] Wells M. Sawyer Papers, P. K. Yonge Library.

1896a [Letter, January 10.] Wells M. Sawyer Papers, P. K. Yonge Library.

1896b [Letter, March 12.] Wells M. Sawyer Papers, P. K. Yonge Library.

1896c [Letter to mother, March 24.] Wells M. Sawyer Papers, P. K. Yonge Library.

1896d [Letter, March 29.] Wells M. Sawyer Papers, P. K. Yonge Library.

1896e [Letter to mother, April 24.] Wells M. Sawyer Papers, P. K. Yonge Library.

n.d.a [Letter.] Wells M. Sawyer Papers, P. K. Yonge Library.

n.d.b [Portions of manuscripts.] Wells M. Sawyer Papers, P. K. Yonge Library.

n.b.c [Letter to folks at home, undated.] Wells M. Sawyer Papers, P. K. Yonge Library.

n.d.d [Cushing memoriam, probably 1900.] Wells M. Sawyer Papers, P. K. Yonge Library.

Sears, William H.

1982 *Fort Center, An Archaeological Site in the Lake Okeechobee Basin.* Gainesville: University Presses of Florida.

Sheridan, Philip H.

1882 [Letter to Lt. Bourke, June 8.] File 59, Hodge-Cushing Collection.

Stevenson, James

1882 [Letter to S. Baird, December 12.] File 4677, BAE correspondence.

Stevenson, Mathilda Coxe

n.d. [Notes attached to photographs.] File 4372(3), BAE correspondence.

INDEX